WORLD WAR TWO
THE
PERSONALITIES

WORLD WAR TWO
THE
PERSONALITIES

Edward Davidson and Dale Manning

ARMS AND
ARMOUR

500225953

Arms and Armour Press
An Imprint of the Cassell Group
Wellington House, 125 Strand, London WC2R 0BB

Distributed in the USA by Sterling Publishing Co. Inc., 387 Park Avenue South,
New York, NY 10016-8810.

British Library Cataloguing-in-Publication Data:
a catalogue record for this book is available from the British Library

ISBN 1-85409-396-7

Designed and edited by DAG Publications Ltd. Designed by
David Gibbons; layout by Anthony A. Evans; edited by Michael Boxall.
Printed and bound in Great Britain.

INTRODUCTION

Since Man inhabited the planet he has gone to war. That nation has fought nation, and created alliances to advance its aims, is an undeniable fact of world history; whether for land, for influence, for trade or in response to foreseen threats, national leaders have acted provocatively or protectively to suit their cause.

As Man's inability to live in peace with his neighbour has stimulated the wars, so these conflicts have produced personalities of outstanding character; political or monarchical personalities have declared the wars, military hierarchies have devised them, designers of arms and armament have provided the equipment, and the multitude of common foot soldiers have fought them. Wars have thrown up inspirational commanders, administrative giants, battlefield geniuses, logistical and strategic supremos,

intelligence gatherers, solo warriors, spies and saboteurs, and even inventors of dramatic new weaponry and tactics – and good numbers of rogues and wretches.

The World War of 1939–1945 was an awesome global conflict which created more than its fair share of military moguls; its events cannot be studied without understanding the roles, function and status of the leading players. They provide extra insights into the combatant nations and the nature and course of the war itself.

For all but the older generations the war is now examined as formal history without personal recollection and nostalgia playing a part. The characters therefore have to be freshly introduced and placed into the context of each theatre of action.

This volume allows the historian at all levels of expertise to have a single-source reference to those

whose leadership duties or dramatic performance caused them to have a significant influence on the action or theory of the war. No bias is intended in the personalities featured, no consideration is given to the favours and colours of those included; all of them, of whatever nation, played an important part in this major military confrontation in history. We cannot understand so diverse, so pervasive a war as that of 1939–1945 if we know only the victors, or acknowledge only the faults and errors of the vanquished. The soldier who follows a suspect cause or a dubious leader is no less the brave warrior. Through these people a clearer perspective of the total event can be obtained.

CAPITALS denote references to personalities who have their own entry in this volume. There are indexes for these and for places, units and events.

Otto
ABETZ
1903–1958

From the fall of France to 1944 this diplomat was the German Ambassador to Paris where, once the whole of the country was occupied, he ran the SD operations including anti-Jewish round-ups and manhunts. He supported LAVAL at the time of his recall and the two co-operated in the supply of French labour to German factories. Abetz was sentenced to 20 years' imprisonment by a French military court, but was released in 1958. His death in a car crash shortly afterwards bore the hallmarks of a revenge attack by French Resistance veterans.

Lieutenant-General Hatazo
ADACHI
1890–1947

He personified the daunting determination shown by Japanese forces of all ranks. A member of the Army General Staff just three years after graduating from War College, from the moment he assumed command of Eighteenth Army at the end of 1942 until his surrender with 13,500 men in September 1945, he showed great resilience in the face of increasingly long odds. His Rabaul HQ was in a logistically weak position, its seaborne access under constant air threat from the US forces.

His retreat towards Hollandia was stalled at Wewak in April 1944 when the Americans launched an amphibious attack on the former stimulating an attempted breakout by Adachi which General Hall's XI Corps was able to hold. The besieged Japanese tried to escape again in May 1945 but lost 9,000 men against the Australian 6th Division and formally surrendered at Cape Woon airstrip on Wewak on 13 September 1945. Hatazo Adachi received a life sentence for war crimes but committed suicide by hanging himself in his cell on Manus Island on 10 September 1947.

Rear-Admiral Walden
AINSWORTH
1886–1960

The 'Tokyo Express' runs by the Japanese Navy through the waters of the Kula Gulf brought him to prominence. Commanding a group of three cruisers and five destroyers escorting the New Guinea invasion force, he lost the destroyer *Strong* and 46 of her crew on 5 July 1943 and the cruiser *Helena* on 6 July during shelling and interception actions. It was thought that he had repulsed the reinforcement fleet but it did manage to reach New Guinea. A week later he faced another Japanese run and fell foul of the Long-Lance torpedoes of the enemy which saw the destroyer *Gwin* lost and other vessels damaged. Nevertheless the Japanese failed to get through to Vila.

Field Marshal Viscount
ALANBROOKE
(Formerly Alan Brooke)
1883–1963

His first task in the war was to command British II Corps and evacuate Dunkirk. The calm competence he

showed in this exercise was impressive and when CHURCHILL sought these qualities at the head of the General Staff he turned to Brooke, as a replacement for GENERAL DILL, in the hope that his understanding of the leader's aims and ambitions would help raise morale and performance. That many of Churchill's theoretical dreams reached reality was down to Brooke's thoroughness; his excellence in liaison with the Americans was a less obvious but equally important asset.

Albert
ALEXANDER
1885–1965

Having taken over from CHURCHILL as First Lord of the Admiralty, Alexander held that post throughout the war years. Among his more difficult negotiations was that with the Vichy French in June 1940 when he sought to persuade them to remove their fleet from the German threat. He failed, at least to the extent of securing prompt action, and the British bombardment of the vessels followed.

Field Marshal Sir Harold
ALEXANDER
1891–1969

Perhaps an early indication of this man's commitment to military achievement was a passage from a letter to his mother written when he was a junior officer: 'I'm afraid the war will end very soon now, but I suppose all good things must come to an end sooner or later, so we mustn't grumble.'

He was to become one of Britain's outstanding commanders; he enjoyed the trust and respect of CHURCHILL who gave him some of the trickiest of tasks. He commanded 1st Division of the British Expeditionary Force and was in

Field Marshal Alanbrooke with Air Vice Marshal Coningham during Churchill's tour of Royal Air Force units in the Middle East. (IWM CM3349)

Jackson, W. G. F. *Alexander of Tunis as a Military Commander*, 1971
Keegan, J. *Churchill's Generals*, 1991
Nicolson, N. *Alex*, 1973
North, J. *The Alexander Memoirs*, 1961

General Vittorio
AMBROSIO
1879–1950

A career soldier, he found himself – as many before – treading the fine line between divided loyalties to his men, his country and its rulers. He was never supportive of the alliance with Germany but his inevitable association with it sowed seeds of doubt about his aims and objectives when it came to his personal advancement under BADOGLIO.

Having succeeded CAVALLERO as Chief of Staff to MUSSOLINI at the end of January 1943, his distance from the decision-making in the North Africa campaign only fuelled his long-held belief that Italy was seen by the Germans and by her enemies as a very junior party in the Axis structure.

He accompanied MUSSOLINI on missions to HITLER at Salzburg in April and Feltre in July, but was dismayed by the former's acquiescence and naïvety in negotiations. Soon Badoglio had been appointed Prime Minister following the Grand Council's censure of Mussolini, with Ambrosio doing all he could to make the transition a smooth one, even to the extent of sending the dictator's élite bodyguard on manoeuvres at the time.

Still walking his tightrope – trying to convince the Germans of his disillusionment at the change while actively supporting it – he was sent to take charge of negotiations with the Allies; the discussions, which he did little to advance, went on until the end of September before the surrender was signed. This delay

charge of the last corps to leave the beaches of Dunkirk. Sent to Burma with I Corps in January 1942, later that year he was appointed Commander-in-Chief, Middle East where he managed the triumphs of Eighth Army over ROMMEL. Thereafter he worked under EISENHOWER in Tunisia before becoming Supreme Allied Commander in the Mediterranean. His work in Italy was hindered by the concentration on the landings in France and he never held back in his criticism of

lack of materiel. His partnership with MONTGOMERY met with great success, but he was his own man with fixed views on discipline and man-management.

A career soldier, who had served on the Western Front in World War One and received the German surrender at the end of World War Two, Alexander had few detractors; his apparent lack of authoritative behaviour belied a tough, determined and resourceful individual.

enabled the Germans to occupy Rome and strengthen their position in northern Italy, which caused the Allies to frown upon what they saw as Ambrosio's duplicity.

General Korechika
ANAMI
1887–1945

This dynamic military student was EMPEROR HIROHITO's aide-de-camp, a position he first occupied in 1929. Ten years later he was Vice Minister of War and then held commands in China and Manchuria before transferring to direct the action in New Guinea at the end of 1943. Even after Hiroshima and the Russian invasion of Manchuria, Anami rejected the Potsdam terms and would have fought on. Once the surrender was signed he was urged to join an army officer-led coup to prevent its announcement. He was not persuaded, however, and committed traditional suicide within a matter of hours of the signature.

Lieutenant-General Wladyslaw
ANDERS
1892–1970

For a man who had felt the full force of the Blitzkrieg as it swept aside his own country's forces – he was commanding the Nowogrodek Cavalry Brigade in the south of the country at the time – Anders showed great resilience in returning with his countrymen to serve the Allied cause so well in the Italian theatre. The respect he earned from his fellow Poles saw him represent their community abroad after the war, especially in England where he made his home.

When the Germans invaded Poland, Anders was captured by the Russians, but was released when HITLER's troops invaded the USSR. Disinclined to join the war on the Soviet side, as he was urged to do, he gathered up all the Polish men who had been held as he had. Although STALIN was personally involved in the pleas to have Anders and his men join the Red Army, the Soviet hierarchy finally agreed that they could leave the country for Palestine – all 160,000 of them.

In their new home Anders and his men were prepared for fighting by the British and at the end of 1943 they linked up with Eighth Army in Italy. Here they fought bravely, especially at Monte Cassino, and, after seeing action at Pescara and Ancona, formed the liberating forces at Bologna. The Polish Army was disbanded at the end of the war, but few of its officers and men returned home, preferring to remain in the West.

General Sir Kenneth
ANDERSON
1891–1959

He commanded forces in the Dunkirk campaign before being given command of British First Army in 1942 when the invasion force for North Africa was put together under EISENHOWER. Failing to match the high expectations of CHURCHILL and ALEXANDER, he served the last years of the war in administrative posts in Britain and East Africa.

Sir John
ANDERSON
1882–1958

Forever associated with the domestic bomb shelters which he intro-

General Anami who committed ritual suicide six hours after the Japanese surrender. (IWM HU69904)

Lieutenant-General Anders returning from a visit to an observation post. (IWM NA13684)

General Kenneth Anderson in his armoured car. (IWM NA198)

duced in 1940, Anderson was Home Secretary in CHAMBERLAIN's cabinet and a trusted figure in CHURCHILL's administration. During the latter part of the war he was Chancellor of the Exchequer.

The Anderson shelter, designed by a Scottish engineer, William Patterson, who produced the prototype in a fortnight, was made of corrugated iron. The interior was 6 feet high in the centre and 4 feet 6 inches wide. Emplaced in a pit in the garden and covered with earth, it was simple and functional, and by September 1940 2,300,000 had been produced. Many people sheltering in them survived the worst of the bombing when buildings all around were devastated.

Marshal Ion
ANTONESCU
1882–1946

Romania had a unique war, providing support for the Axis powers before changing allegiance and fighting stoutly for the Allies. Antonescu assumed power after KING CAROL II had abdicated and appointed him prime minister. He had previously taken the leadership of the Fascist Iron Guards and clearly posed a threat to Carol whose token imprisonment of the rising star was a futile gesture ended by his own weakness.

By September 1940 Antonescu had signed up with HITLER and MUSSOLINI and his troops joined Army Group South in its invasion of the USSR, and the attack on Stalingrad. The reversal there did not rest easily with this timid man who was soon urging Mussolini to withdraw from the alliance with Hitler, along with Hungary and Romania. Although the Italian dictator feigned agreement neither man was strong enough to bring it about. In August 1944 KING MICHAEL called Antonescu to a humiliating interrogation which

ended with his being arrested and replaced. After the war he was tried for war crimes and executed.
Axworthy, M. *Third Axis, Fourth Ally*, 1995

General Aleksei
ANTONOV
1896–1962

He had commanded the Transcaucasian Front in 1941–2 before acting as MARSHAL VASILIEVSKY's representative in Moscow and then serving with the Voronezh Front. Thereafter, as Deputy Chief of the General Staff, he was often the buffer between STALIN and his commanders while also planning the tactics for Operation 'Bagration' and the final drive against Berlin. Although he did not enjoy the best of relationships with STALIN, his

advance through the ranks and his performance on the battlefield and in Moscow administrative posts led him to a seat at many of the Allied conferences towards the end of the war and, in April 1945, the appointment as Chief of the General Staff.

Duke Amadeo of
AOSTA
1898–1942

The gentlemanly Duke, as he was known, invaded British Somaliland in August 1940 with the Italian forces based in Eritrea and Ethiopia. As Commander-in-Chief, and Governor of Italian East Africa, he must have been encouraged by the early successes he achieved, though he would also have understood that the British would retaliate once they were alerted to the situation and

The Duke of Aosta inspects British troops after surrendering. (IWM E3239)

could reinforce. Only eight months later they re-occupied Addis Ababa and forced a surrender within the month. Aosta was held in Kenya until his death in 1942.

Rear-Admiral Masafumi
ARIMA
1895–1944

Commander of 26th Naval Air Flotilla, he is credited with being the first Japanese naval kamikaze pilot. He was one of 20 pilots lost in an attack by 86 aircraft on a US carrier off Formosa.

Colonel General Hans-Jurgen Theodor von
ARNIM
1889–1971

With a background of membership of the German General Staff and command in Russia, von Arnim emerged as HITLER's expedient choice to take charge of Fifth Panzer Army in North Africa in December 1942. From his initial base in Tunisia he liaised with ROMMEL in his advanced position and then, after the latter's departure, was appointed Commander of Army Group Afrika. During this post-Rommel period, however, both von Arnim and General MESSE were even more starved of supplies and their forces were driven back towards the coast. Despite calls from Berlin for a last defiant stand, von Arnim signed the surrender on 12 May; he had been given too great a task with too few resources, and could not even fight the determined rearguard action that he would have wished. He was a fine organiser and trainer of troops.

General Henry ('Hap')
ARNOLD
1886–1950

His nickname was short for 'Happy', which reflected his pleasant disposition, popularity and accessibility. A West Point graduate of 1907, he 'changed codes' to command the USAAF in all theatres during World War Two.

Having begun his career in the infantry, he soon moved to the aviation section of the Signal Corps and was one of the first US army officers to gain his 'wings'. During the inter-war years he demonstrated his proficiency in planning and organisation, and his elevation to Assistant Chief of the Air Corps in 1936 and

Field Marshal von Arnim in England after his capture in May 1943. (IWM CH9628)

'Hap' Arnold seen with Henry Ford in Detroit, endeavouring to coax a higher output from American industry. (IWM NYP46128)

the Allied cause was a significant one. He was made a full General in 1944 and was the USAAF's first 5-Star General when it separated to become an equal third force with the Army and the Navy.

Clement
ATTLEE
1883–1967

At the outbreak of war there were few British parliamentarians who were apparently as different from each other as Attlee and WINSTON CHURCHILL, and yet their backgrounds were not that dissimilar, both in education and military service – both had been to public schools and had served as infantry officers. While Churchill was charismatic and demonstrative, Attlee was unemotional and quiet, his power base in the Labour Party coming from his honest, unsung work in London's poverty areas and his intellectual dominance in debate.

The two men worked hand in glove in the running of the war, showing a common drive to achieve the industrial momentum, military belief and public support needed for victory. Attlee, with BEVIN, ensured the solidarity of the Labour Party and Trades Unions and worked diligently in his official post of Deputy Prime Minister in the coalition government formed in the spring of 1940. In the General Election of July 1945 he led his Party to a sweeping success, replacing Churchill at many of the end of war discussions including the Potsdam Conference.

Field Marshal Sir Claude
AUCHINLECK
1884–1981

'The Auk', as he was known, was a soldier's soldier. 'I don't like being

Chief of the Air Staff two years later showed that his superiors had recognised these gifts. His energy and enthusiasm secured aircraft and training facilities beyond the scope of routine funding; production increased more than 40-fold during his period in office, and Air Force personnel had expanded 90-fold by 1944.

He advocated support for Britain and for the Allied policy of strategic bombing, dismissing any proposal for American isolation or independent decision-making as short-sighted. Although convinced that air power would win the war, he found that some of his cherished theories proved impracticable in the heat of battle. But he was adaptable and prepared to work with those who held contrary views; his relationship with CHARLES PORTAL, his British counterpart, was a strong and productive one. Having evolved the correct tactics he saw to it that the Eighth Air Force carried them out and that adequate air support was offered to bolster land and sea actions.

The role he played in mobilising American aviation commitment to

Looking incongruous in his formal 'Whitehall' suit, Clement Attlee visits Polish troops in Scotland in 1942. (IWM H18882)

The 'Auk' meets India's youngest Victoria Cross winner, Kamal Ram, aged 19, in September 1944. (IWM IND3717)

separated in comparative luxury from troops who are living hard,' he was to say in 1976.

After service in the Indian Army he was recalled in 1939 to take command of IV Corps. He was Commander-in-Chief in northern Norway and of Southern Command in 1940, before returning to India early in the following year. In June he was again recalled to replace WAVELL as C-in-C Middle East.

The next year was a mix of great achievement and disappointment, and it took all of Auchinleck's drive and determination to finish on the plus side. At the time of his appointment ROMMEL had quashed Operation 'Battleaxe' but before the year was out Auchinleck had devised and set in motion the counter-attack, 'Crusader'. This successful push brought victory and the relief of Tobruk after the longest siege in British military history. but against an opponent as resourceful as Erwin ROMMEL there was no chance to consolidate; the Germans forced a withdrawal to Gazala and Bir Hacheim. May saw fresh fighting and British victory at the first of the El Alamein conflicts but this setback for the enemy did not entirely restore CHURCHILL's faith in 'the Auk' who was sent back to India as Commander-in-Chief there. ALEXANDER came in to complete the victorious desert campaign which Auchinleck had brought from imminent disaster, via wildly fluctuating fortunes, to significant success.

Auchinleck remained with the Indian Army until 1947, enjoying the affection and respect of his officers and men.

Warner P. *Auchinleck: The Lonely Soldier*, 1981

Erich von dem
BACH-ZELEWSKI
1899–1972

This SS general is best known for his leading role in suppressing the 1944 Warsaw uprising with brutality. He had previously been an SS officer and police chief of Army Group Centre on the Eastern Front where he conducted many operations against partisans.

Group Captain Sir Douglas
BADER
1910–1982

He was far more than an exceptional fighter pilot who overcame the loss of both legs in a pre-war flying accident to fly again in combat. Like Richthofen in World War One, this star achiever was a born leader, a strategic wizard and one whose code of flying and the lessons he taught continued long after his retirement. Having been invalided out of the RAF following his accident, Bader devised a route back to flying by way of the Volunteer Reserve. By June 1940 he was commanding the Canadian-manned 242 Fighter Squadron where his performance earned him command of five squadrons during the Battle of Britain.

That he was a maverick cannot be denied – it was a contributory factor to his horrific injuries – and his regular conflicts with Fighter Command Headquarters often came from his utter disregard of orders, but, like all great warriors, Bader knew what would unsettle his enemies and while his superiors dismissed his 'Big Wing' theory, the Germans found it a mighty problem.

In August 1941 a mid-air collision brought Bader down and he spent the rest of the war in POW camps.

Bader, D. *Fight for the Sky*, 1973
Brickhill, P. *Reach for the Sky*, 1954
Burns, M. *Bader: The Man and his Men*, 1990
Turner, J. F. *The Bader Wing*, 1981

Field Marshal Pietro
BADOGLIO
1871–1956

He had fought in Ethiopia in 1896, in Libya against the Turks fifteen years later and against the Austrians in World War One. The inter-war years saw him as Chief of Staff, then Governor of Libya, and commander of the forces which swept into Ethiopia in 1935 after which he was Viceroy of that country. He again took the post of Chief of Staff on Italy's entry into World War Two, but saw the failure of the invasion of Greece in December 1940 as a resigning issue.

Well outside MUSSOLINI's circle of power, he was party to the dictator's downfall in 1943 and was appointed Prime Minister by the king on 25 July, signing the Armistice with the Allies in September.

Badoglio, P. *Italy in the Second World War*, 1948

Marshal Italo
BALBO
1896–1940

He was considered by many to be the finest theorist of Italian military aviation, and he was certainly his country's principal innovator of air warfare strategies. In 1940, when Commander-in-Chief of Italian forces in Libya, he was shot down by his own anti-aircraft batteries, but his tactics lived on. Some historians credit him with formative thinking on the theory which became the 'big wing' fighter plan which the Royal Air Force adopted with success.

Lieutenant-General Hermann
BALCK
1893–1950

This fine tactician was renowned for his strong affinity with the ordinary soldier. After experience in the First World War, he began the Second leading GUDERIAN's panzers in May 1940. He spent much of his time in the front line with his troops, talking to them and trying to motivate them. Promoted to command a division on the Eastern Front, he proved to be a master of tactical advance. Within eighteen months he had been made a full general and was put in command of Army Group G in France in September 1944. Like others at the time, he was blamed by HITLER for failing to prevent the Allied invasion and advance.

Mellenthin, J. von. *German Generals of World War Two*, 1977

Doctor
BA MAW
1893–1987

A Burmese lawyer, he opposed Burma's involvement in the war and was imprisoned for this in 1940. He escaped two years later and set up a regime, under the control of the Japanese, which he used to negotiate for greater autonomy. When the British regained Burma, Ba Maw went into hiding to run clandestine operations against the Allies. He was back in prison, in Tokyo, for six months at the end of 1945 and, after his release, formed the Maha Bama Party.

Stepan
BANDERA
1909–1959

A Ukrainian who led a militant breakaway unit from the OKN and, when the Germans invaded the USSR in June 1941, he declared an independent Ukrainian state. This was done without any connivance with or support from the Germans who took Bandera and his Prime Minister, STETSKO, captive and did not release them until September 1944 when they could be used to work on resistance against the counter-attacking Red Army. Bandera was eventually assassinated by Soviet agents.

Pietro Badoglio at Italian Navy Headquarters with Lieutenant-General Sir Noel Mason-Macfarlane after the Italian surrender. (IWM NA7027)

Klaus
BARBIE
1913–1991

Head of the Gestapo in the Lyons region of France, he was responsible for the hunting down and killing of many members of the French Resistance. Despite this record, and the clear case for post-war conviction, Barbie was spirited away to South America with the overt assistance of the US Counter Intelligence Corps.

When he was eventually located and extradited to France for trial in 1983 the embarrassment of the American administration at the time was all too apparent, though there were some protestations of ignorance of the worst of his crimes. The 'Butcher of Lyons' was sentenced to life imprisonment in 1987 and died four years later.

Marshal Ettore
BASTICO
1876–1972

As Commander-in-Chief of Axis forces in Libya in the summer of 1941, he was theoretically in charge of ROMMEL and his forces, but the younger, more adventurous and offensive-minded German often ignored the Italian's orders and set his own policy. Once Rommel was made a field marshal the situation grew worse, and although fresh instructions clearly stated that Bastico was in charge, MUSSOLINI found his man's weakness unacceptable, and recalled him.

General Fritz
BAYERLEIN
1899–1970

A German general with truly diverse, multi-theatre experience.

He served with GUDERIAN in France in 1940 and commanded a combat group of XXXIX Corps in the advance on Moscow in 1941. After serving in North Africa as Chief of Staff of the Afrika Korps, he commanded the Panzer Lehr Division in the Ardennes offensive. He described the desert war with the words: 'Here everything is in flux; there are no obstructions, no lines, no water or woods for cover; everything is open and incalculable.'

Elyesa 'Cicero'
BAZNA
1905–1970

From his pre-war position as valet to the German Ambassador in Turkey, Bazna crossed to a similar posting with the British Ambassador during the war. This clearly sowed the seeds of intrigue in the

Accompanied by Lieutenant-General Macready and Air Chief Marshal Sir Charles Portal, Max Beaverbrook is seen here en route to the USA. (IWM H16493)

Albanian's mind and by October 1943 he was offering Moyzisch, the German Intelligence Attaché, secret British documents for £20,000. In time he passed across minutes of the Teheran and Cairo Conferences and the Allied plans for the invasion of France. His earnings were now well into six figures, but he began to be suspected by the British and 'Cicero', as he was named by the Germans, disappeared. Remarkably, the Germans never wholly trusted the information they received from this source they appeared to be paying so well; for example, it never reached the eyes of HITLER and was acted upon only in the most cursory fashion. In the late 1940s Bazna was found in South America trying to pass the forged money which, it turned out, the Germans had used to pay him. Bazna, E. *I Was Cicero*, 1962

Lord Maxwell Aitken
BEAVERBROOK
1879–1964

If it be accepted that civilian personnel can contribute significantly to a war effort, it must be said that Beaverbrook did so in World War Two. This Canadian press baron had run the government's information services in the First World War and when his friend WINSTON CHURCHILL took the premiership in 1940 he was destined for power again. This time he was put in charge of aircraft production where his natural energy, business brain and ruthless commitment to a target invigorated the industry and produced results.

His 'battering ram' techniques appealed to Churchill whose own tendency to get things done without concern for etiquette was mirrored in the Canadian. Beaverbrook later served as Minister of Supply and Lord Privy Seal as well as organising the valuable Lend-Lease plan with the US in 1942.

Colonel Josef
BECK
1894–1944

During his time as Poland's foreign minister in the years before the war, Beck opposed close ties with either of the perils represented by HITLER and STALIN, adjudging them both to be of equal menace. His desire to ally Poland with the western European nations drove him into a treaty with the British after finally rejecting any settlement of Hitler's territorial claims. The guarantee given in this treaty proved illusory when it spurred Hitler to start the war, but in turn it brought Britain into the conflict. Beck fled to Romania when the Germans invaded.

General Ludwig
BECK
1880–1944

This excellent officer, proven in World War One and Chief of the Army Staff for three years from 1935, became a central figure in the opposition to HITLER. He disagreed with the decision to invade Czechoslovakia, but failing to find sufficient high-ranking support he resigned in August 1938.

From then on his overt work with those resisting Hitler marked Beck as a potential replacement had the dictator been deposed. After the disappointment of the July plot in 1944, he was arrested by Friedrich FROMM who induced him to commit suicide.

General Walter
BEDELL-SMITH
1895–1961

A consummate soldier-diplomat of the type required by all war leaders, he was also an administrative factotum who saw that policies were implemented and that the rough edges of alliance were smoothed.

At the start of the war he was Secretary of the US Joint Chiefs of Staff and much involved in the US

Alongside Montgomery and with Alexander and Patton looking on, General Bedell-Smith is seen in discussion on a Sicilian airstrip in May 1943. (IWM NA5016)

side of the Anglo–American Chiefs group. After coming to England in 1942 as Chief of Staff to EISEN-HOWER he had the opportunity to exercise his negotiating skills with the Italian and German surrenders in 1943 and 1945. Kim Philby, intelligence officer and later spy, is quoted as saying that Bedell Smith had 'a precision tool brain'.

Patrick
BEESLY
1913–

The importance of the ULTRA cryptanalysis to Allied success in the war was immense, especially with regard to the intercepted communications between U-Boat Command and the vessels in the Atlantic. Patrick Beesly was a senior analyst in the Operational Intelligence Centre with special responsibility for the ULTRA work and one of those who promoted close liaison with the American agencies working in the same field.

Menachem
BEGIN
1913–1992

In September 1940 he was arrested by the Russians in Poland and imprisoned in Russia. When the Germans invaded in June 1941 he was released and promptly joined ANDERS' II Polish Corps, but while it was based in Palestine in December 1943 he left to join the Irgun Jewish military group. He quickly assumed the leadership and directed attacks on British military premises and personnel. He was Israel's Prime Minister from 1977 to 1983.

President Eduard
BENES
1884–1948

He left Czechoslovakia when the Munich Agreement required it to give up the Sudetenland to the Germans. When his country was over-run in 1939 he formed a Czech Nationalist Party in Paris and, later, London. He worked to get the Munich Agreement revised and demonstrated his support for the Allies by encouraging fellow refugee countrymen to serve in the British forces.

He organised the assassination of REINHARD HEYDRICH by Jan Kubis in May 1942, and his growing support among the Allies brought a recognition by Britain of his government and a repudiation of the Munich Agreement.

At the end of the war he facilitated the transfer of many Czech Germans back to their homeland but the stability this brought to the country under its returning President did not secure his tenure. He resigned when the Communists won power in 1948 and died shortly afterwards.

Air Vice Marshal Donald
BENNETT
1910–1986

In the summer of 1942, when daylight bombing was seen to be too risky and night raids too inaccurate and indiscriminate, the Royal Air Force turned to an Australian civil

President Benes poses with Czech troops on their return from the Middle East Theatre in 1943. (IWM H31998)

'Pathfinder' Bennett introduces his staff to Her Majesty the Queen during a royal visit. (IWM CH9955)

airman, Don Bennett, to command a newly created force of élite pilots and navigators – the Pathfinders. The young Bennett enthused his equally youthful crews to lay their flares and markers with an accuracy which transformed the effectiveness of the Allied night bombing offensive.

Maynard, J. *Bennett and the Pathfinders*, 1996

Lavrenty
BERIA
1899–1954
As head of Soviet Intelligence, Beria worked closely with STALIN,

particularly in the supply of battle-field reports. He controlled clandestine activity behind the German lines and was brutal in securing the 'loyalty' of the population to work against the German forces; his hand was also behind the assassination of Leon Trotsky in Mexico in 1940. He directed the management of the prisoner-of-war camps and was undoubtedly one of Stalin's most significant lieutenants, a fact shown by his being entrusted with the Soviet atom bomb project. His reputation as a lecher was well founded; he is

said to have 'married' one of his own rape victims.

Count Folke
BERNADOTTE
1895–1948
A close friend of King Gustav V's, while heading the Swedish Red Cross he organised the exchange of injured prisoners in October 1943 and September 1944. While working to repatriate Danish and Norwegian prisoners in early 1945 he was visited at the Swedish embassy in Lübeck by a disenchanted HEINRICH HIMMLER with an offer to

19

surrender Germany to the Western Allies. The letter was passed to EISENHOWER but was rejected. HITLER was so furious that he ordered his arrest.

Bernadotte, F. *The Curtain Falls*

Brigadier-General Gustave
BERTRAND
1896–1976

He had headed the French Army's code-breaking unit during the pre-war years and controlled a network of agents, one of whom – Hans Schmidt – furnished him with some provisional data on the ENIGMA codes which Bertrand developed during the early years of the war.

Captain Payne
BEST
1885–1976

Between 1938 and the end of 1939, Best, under instruction from MI6, met various German emissaries in Holland with the aim of advancing and supporting opposition to HITLER. Among these contacts was a double agent who set up a further clandestine meeting on the border at Venlo at which Best and an associate were ambushed by German officers and taken for investigation. At the liberation he was found in a small camp in Bavaria.

Werner
BEST
1903–1995

Before the war this German lawyer and early convert to the Nazi cause worked closely with HEYDRICH and was employed by HITLER to explain away the deaths occurring in German prisons. After a term as head of the German military administration in occupied France, he was appointed Reichs Commisioner for Denmark. There he adopted a rare degree of humanity towards the Danes, especially the Jewish frater-nity which he at least alerted to the dangers ahead even if he did not help them to escape. Despite his connivance with the Danes it was they who sentenced him to death in 1948, although the punishment was commuted to a short prison term.

Sir William
BEVERIDGE
1879–1963

Beveridge was an economist who produced a Report on Social Insurance and Allied Services when in CHURCHILL's administration as

William Beveridge, the British social welfare economist. (IWM AP71598)

Ernest Bevin in a lunchtime queue with women war production workers. (IWM P1944)

Under Secretary of Labour. It was widely acclaimed as the foundation for a future social welfare system, providing benefits for health, marriage, maternity, unemployment, widowhood, old age and death. Churchill and his cabinet chose not to implement the whole report and introduced only portions of it. Although Beveridge distanced himself from party politics, he did become a Liberal MP for a short time at the end of the war.

Ernest
BEVIN
1881–1951

As Minister of Labour and National Service in CHURCHILL's war cabinet, it was Bevin who was charged with mobilising manpower to support the war effort. His dra-

conian measures ensured that many of the nation's aims had been met by 1943. After the war he became ATTLEE's Foreign Secretary and attended the Potsdam and United Nations Conferences. He had a strong anti-Colonial bias, and stated that the nation must 'leave behind for ever the idea of one country dominating another'.

Georges
BIDAULT
1899–1975

For the threat he posed as leader of the French Catholic faction, Bidault was imprisoned by the Germans when they overran his country. He was released in 1941 but promptly ran the risk of re-arrest by the Gestapo when he resumed his resistance work. After

MOULIN's capture and execution in the summer of 1943 he became head of the National Council for Resistance and later served in DE GAULLE's cabinet as Foreign Minister.

Francis
BIDDLE
1886–1968

As Solicitor General and Attorney General in America's wartime administrations, he employed a reasoned and tolerant approach to the regulation of foreign nationals in that country. At a time when much vitriolic anger was being hurled at American citizens of Japanese, German and Italian background, Biddle sought a just treatment and insisted on having the final sanction on prosecutions and deportations. He showed similar moderation as a member of the International Military Tribunal at Nuremberg.

General Gaston Herve Gustave
BILLOTTE
1875–1940

He was commanding the British Expeditionary Force and the French First and Seventh Armies, and his death in a road accident was a blow to the Allies who were seeking to counter-attack the advancing German forces. While he might have had no greater success than his successors, it will never be known just how effective he might have been in his use of 1st Army Group. Although he had undertaken withdrawals to the Escaut and the Dendre, these were well-considered moves prior to mounting further attacks.

Sir Thomas Blamey with Lieutenant-General Eichelberger outside a Japanese pillbox in New Guinea. (IWM AUS1489)

General S. S.
BIRYUSOV
1904–1964

On STALIN's death, Biryusov became Chief of the General Staff, having previously commanded 48th Army and fought at Stalingrad as Chief of Staff 2nd Guards Army. He also commanded 37th Army in Romania.

Major General Clayton L.
BISSELL
1896–1972

He advanced the cause of professional military intelligence in the US Army during the war. After serving with STILWELL in China and, from August 1942, as Commander of Tenth Air Force in the China/Burma theatre, he returned to Washington to become Assistant Chief and then Chief of Intelligence for the Army Air Force where, under his management, the Army Security Agency was formed.

General Sir Thomas
BLAMEY
1884–1951

This Australian veteran of World War One was called from his career in the police to take command of the Anzac forces in Greece in 1941. He controlled the evacuation from Crete and Rhodes before transferring to Egypt to become Deputy Commander-in-Chief, Middle East. On his return to Australia in March 1942, he came under GENERAL MACARTHUR as Commander-in-Chief, Allied Land Forces, and was the target of American criticism of the Australian forces' capability. Rather than refute these charges, he adopted a system of closer control as a protective measure, and led his troops to the recapture of Buna before tackling the Japanese at Wewak and in the Solomons, finally moving on to retake Borneo.

Field Marshal von Blaskowitz. Were former members of the SS involved in his death? (IWM PL83971)

Field Marshal Johannes von
BLASKOWITZ
1883–1948

In March 1939 he led German Third Army into Bohemia as Czechoslovakia was overrun, and at the outbreak of war was the seventh ranked general in the Wehrmacht. In September he took Eighth Army to Poznan to hold the Polish forces there, and by October, despite criticism from HITLER for a temporary retreat, he had been put in command of the occupying army.

He retained an independence of mind and spirit and prepared memos protesting against SS brutality and treatment of the Jews, though these were 'lost' by those who should have passed them up to the Führer. In 1944 he was given command of Army Group G in southern and western France, but was relieved of this position when the Allied landing – Operation 'Dragoon' – in the South of France was successful.

Due to be tried at Nuremberg as a war criminal, he committed suicide, but there was conjecture at the time that former SS members might have had a hand in his death.

Hugo
BLEICHER
1899–1991

This highly successful intelligence officer worked in Holland and France. A skilful clandestine operator – in France he worked under the pseudonym 'Colonel Henri' – he was instrumental in the arrest of SOE agents PETER CHURCHILL and ODETTE SANSOM. He created his own resistance network, 'Lisiana', which received information from local informers and double agents.

Field Marshal Werner von
BLOMBERG
1878–1946

In the early years of the Third Reich, having achieved the post of War Minister in HITLER's first cabinet, Blomberg quickly became an earnest disciple. He was promoted field marshal in 1936, but Hitler then used him as a scapegoat in his determined endeavour to reduce the independent-minded army to a subservient force.

The BLOMBERG–FRITSCH crisis was the culmination of the debasement of the Army. These leading generals were removed from office, with undiluted humiliation, and their antagonism towards Hitler's more extreme plans left with them. Both Hitler and GÖRING had been witnesses at Blomberg's wedding to his second wife, but this sign of apparent support was short lived. For the minor 'crime' of an injudicious marriage and subsequent scandals Blomberg lost all status when others around him were guilty

Blomberg during his time as War Minister. (IWM MH10676)

in their attempt to persuade HITLER to end the war in the winter of 1944/5. He was given command of First Parachute Army in the west during the last months of the war.

Field Marshal Fedor von
BOCK
1880–1945

With VON RUNDSTEDT and VON LEEB, von Bock was one of the top three army group commanders at the beginning of the war. He commanded the all-conquering Army Group North in Poland before moving to command Army Group B which overran Belgium and Holland and broke the line of the lower Somme in the Battle of France.

Promoted field marshal, his next appointment was to lead Army Group Centre which advanced from Poland to Moscow in the second half of 1941. Now over sixty, he was suffering from ill health and was unable to control his troops as directly as he wished; the drive on Moscow saw him make errors and utterly exhaust his men. After the Soviet counter-offensive in December von Bock, von Rundstedt and other generals were dismissed, but early the next year he was recalled to replace the stricken VON REICHENAU as commander of Army Group South. The new appointment did not last long, and another dispute with the Führer, during the drive into the Caucasus, saw him removed from office again. This determined, traditional soldier was killed in a car crash on 2 May 1945.

Niels
BOHR
1885–1962

This acclaimed physicist advanced nuclear research in the pre-war years, but his Jewish nationality made him a sought-after prize for the Germans once the war had

of greater deceit and ill judgement. He died in an American prison at Nuremberg in March 1946.

General Günther
BLUMENTRITT
1892–1967

Author of a book which gives great insight on the collapse of morale among the German military hierar-chy after the failure of the Russian campaign – his biography of VON RUNDSTEDT – this experienced officer commanded Army Group South in the early years of the war. He was Chief of Staff of Fourth Army when Russia was invaded and his experience there no doubt contributed towards his joining MODEL, VON MANTEUFFEL and DIETRICH

begun. He escaped the clutches of the Gestapo in Denmark and fled to Sweden where he persuaded the authorities to accept other Jews seeking an outlet from the Low Countries.

Moving to the USA he was able to advise those involved in the development of atomic weapons, but was constantly warning ROO-SEVELT and CHURCHILL that they should work towards universal regulation of such armaments, urging them to bring the USSR into discussions. These sentiments caused the Allies to have doubts about Bohr's personal agenda and he was kept apart from subsequent high-level planning.

Moore, P. *Niels Bohr: the Man and the Scientist*, 1967.

Major Richard
BONG
1920–1945

The USAAF's top scorer, with forty 'kills', Bong was awarded the Congressional Medal of Honor. He served in New Guinea with 5th Air Force and was later leader of the 'Flying Knights' Fighter Squadron equipped with P–38 Lightnings. He was killed in 1945 while test-flying a P–80 in California.

Ivanoe
BONOMI
1873–1951

He had been a consistent opponent of the Fascist movement in Italy and when the Italians accepted the armistice in September 1943 and found themselves invaded by the Germans, he moved under cover to lead the Rome Committee of National Liberation. When the city was freed in June 1944 his group engineered the removal of the king and prime minister BADOGLIO, forming a coalition government to replace them; later that year

Bonomi headed a new administration which lasted until June 1945.

Commander Prince Valerio
BORGHESE
1912–1974

This master of clandestine naval tactics commanded the 10th Light Flotilla on its many actions in the Mediterranean. The use of midget submarines and human torpedoes brought this unit 73,000 tons of Allied ships sunk and its leader a gold medal from MUSSOLINI. His attack on the British battleships *Valiant* and *Queen Elizabeth* in Alexandria was his most audacious; the three chariots launched from his submarine *Scire* on 18 December 1941 crippled the warships before they could react. He enjoyed less success when in charge of a destroyer group and land-based escort craft off the coast at Anzio, but was one of the stars of the Italian underwater war.

King of Bulgaria
BORIS III
1894–1943

At the outset of World War Two Bulgaria's position was complicated by the fact that the marriage of Boris to an Italian princess had caused him to side against any anti-Italian stance in the Balkans. HITLER constantly tested his indecision and desire to maintain his country's neutrality. At a meeting at Berchtesgaden in November 1940 the pressure became too great and, though he was allowed to leave without giving the commitment Hitler sought, he agreed to sign a pact with Germany shortly afterwards.

Within the year he had declared war on both Britain and the USA, though he steadfastly refused to do so against the USSR. He died on 28 August 1943 after another meeting

with Hitler; the cause was probably a heart attack, but it was inevitable that conjecture would follow such coincidence.

General Tadeusz
BOR-KOMOROWSKI
1895–1966

Count Komorowski led the partisan movement in the Warsaw uprising of 1944. His somewhat haughty aristocratic style gave authority to his leadership but he probably lacked the inspirational qualities which would have been ideal. 'Bor', to use his code-name, had stayed in Poland after the German invasion and took control of resistance in the south of the country. When Rowecki, the AK leader, was arrested in the summer of 1943, Bor took over and immediately implemented his three-prong anti-German strategy which was to see intelligence gathering and sabotage followed by subversion and guerrilla tactics and, ultimately, a general insurrection. This final stage was scheduled for August 1944, but the requisite equipment and resources were never available and although his men got early control of much of Warsaw city, German reinforcements were called in to undertake a prolonged and bloody recapture street by street; air drops by the USSR came too late.

By the time Bor and his remaining forces surrendered in early October, nearly 200,000 Poles had died and the remainder were evicted. Komorowski was imprisoned in Colditz; he had shown great resolve but perhaps not the tenacity required to inspire the partisans.

Martin
BORMANN
1900–1945

He showed his colours early. He was a member of the same Freikorps

Martin Bormann. Dead or alive after the war? In Germany or South America? (IWM NYP77063)

is certain that some of Hitler's most extreme actions were stimulated by this cruelly severe loyalist.

In his last days Bormann was Hitler's sole mouthpiece and enforcer. He witnessed the wedding of the Führer and EVA BRAUN and watched the death of the leader with whom he had worked so closely. When it became clear that the Allies would not negotiate with him Bormann vanished. Whether he was killed outside the bunker or was spirited away to South America we shall probably never know. The remains found in Berlin and claimed to be those of Bormann are as inconclusive as the sightings in Argentina. The West German government declared him dead in 1973.

Stevenson, W. *The Bormann Brotherhood*, 1973
Whiting, C. *The Hunt for Martin Bormann*, 1973

Subhas Chandra BOSE
1897–1945

As a nationalist Bose sought every opportunity to hasten Britain's departure from India, and the war was just such a chance. He travelled to Berlin in 1940 to organise Indian volunteers in opposition to the Allies and, later, to Tokyo to establish a puppet government and a Nationalist Army. Some of his troops fought at Kohima and Imphal alongside the Japanese forces attacking these Burmese cities. His career ended with the Japanese defeat and he died in an air crash at the end of the war.

Colonel Gregory BOYINGTON
1912–1988

This charismatic US Marine squadron commander led by example and was credited with 28 Japanese aircraft 'kills', a performance which

as HESS and GÖRING and, in his early twenties, after release from a year in a Leipzig prison for collaborating in the murder of his former elementary schoolteacher, was an eager recruit to the new Nazi Party.

When Hess flew to Britain in May 1941 Bormann succeeded him as Head of Chancery and two years later became secretary to HITLER, in which role he became doorkeeper/bodyguard/confidant to the Führer, acting as the wholly supportive assistant while running his own campaigns against Christianity, prisoners of war and minorities. Even other members of the hierarchy found themselves unable to get to their leader except with Bormann's approval and, usually, attendance. It

Minister of Information Brendan Bracken (centre) with Churchill and Harry Hopkins, Assistant to Roosevelt, at a conference of Allied Forces in Canada. (IWM NY1070)

earned him a reputation as a supreme combat pilot. He commanded the 214th Marine Fighter (Black Sheep' Squadron in the Solomons campaign until he was shot down and captured in January 1944.

Brendan
BRACKEN
1901–1958

In the opening years of the war this British politician was CHURCHILL's trusted Parliamentary Private Secretary and a general factotum greatly admired for his 'oiling of the wheels' as the nation cranked up for war under Churchill's driving leadership. He was appointed Minister of Information in July 1941 and was one of three parliamentarian members of the Political Warfare Executive.

General Omar
BRADLEY
1893–1981

He enjoyed the patronage of EISEN-HOWER, a classmate at West Point. He was appointed Commandant of the Infantry School by MARSHALL in 1941, but was first noticed when he took command of II Corps from PATTON in North Africa. Here he showed great determination when in May 1943 his troops stormed Bizerta and took 40,000 prisoners, before moving on to the Sicilian operations.

Eisenhower then chose Bradley to command the US forces in Operation 'Overlord', the D-Day landings. Having got the US First Army ashore, Bradley relinquished command to PATTON but took a supe-

rior position as Commander of 12th Army Group from which he masterminded Operation 'Cobra', the breakout from the Cotentin Peninsula which led First Army and Patton's Third Army into Brittany and on across France.

From this point until VE-Day Bradley had overall command of 1.3 million troops and, though he had served under Patton and had surely learnt from him, the new order seemed acceptable to both men. During the Ardennes offensive, when his forces were taken by surprise, it was Bradley's calm decisiveness which prevented a full breakthrough by the Germans. After severing the Siegfried Line, his men crossed into Germany at Remagen in March 1945 and,

Omar Bradley meets Montgomery when the latter decorated American soldiers with British awards for their part in the Normandy campaign. (IWM PL29464)

weeks later, met the Soviet forces.

This reserved man undoubtedly inspired great loyalty among the officers whom he drove so hard. He recognised the damage to morale that could be caused by showing a lack of confidence: 'Anxiety can spread like cancer down through command.' It was this understanding and his astute tactical judgement which led Eisenhower to adjudge Bradley as 'the ablest field general the US ever had'.

Bradley, O. *A Soldier's Story*, 1951
Weigley, R. *Eisenhower's Lieutenants*, 1981
Whiting, C. *Bradley*, 1970

Field Marshal Walter von BRAUCHITSCH
1881–1948

Although not in accord with the concept or chances of success of HITLER's aggressive policies, von Brauchitsch accepted seniority from, and showed loyalty to, his superiors; he was urged to join BECK's plot for the arrest of the Führer if Czechoslovakia were invaded but declined. He was appointed Commander-in-Chief of the Army on the sacking of FRITSCH and won general admiration among his officers. Although he led the operations against Poland, he and HALDER had not been in favour of the moves westwards and had even considered a coup in the spring of 1939 before cancellation of the plan removed the need.

Von Brauchitsch – with others – began to be omitted from his leader's decision-making and was often taken out of the command structure during the advances in France and the strategic planning for the invasion of Russia. During 'Barbarossa' he suffered a heart attack, was too incapacitated to organise a response to ZHUKOV's counter-attack on the outskirts of Moscow, and quickly offered his resignation. Out of power, von Brauchitsch was never used by Hitler again and, in fact, found himself publicly berated for his failures. He died in Hamburg in October 1948.

Eva BRAUN
1912–1945

This peculiar woman was Hitler's mistress for almost thirteen years. They met when she was working for Hoffmann, HITLER's staff photographer, and she was soon living secretly with the Führer. She was attractive, with a slim figure honed by sports and dancing, and seemed content to stay in the background,

Field Marshal von Brauchitsch (right) in discussion with Erich Raeder. (IWM GER1273)

taking no interest in the war and ready loyally to serve and comfort Hitler at his behest.

She was known to be jealous of those who shared their days with the dictator and joined him on his trips to other countries. Fearing that there might be other women in his life, she attempted suicide in November 1932 and again in May 1935; later, his pre-occupation with the war should have convinced her that she had little to fear on that score.

Sent to Munich in the spring of 1945, she refused to stay and rejoined Hitler in Berlin to be 'rewarded' for such devotion when he married her on 29 April. He was impressed by her desire to share the appalling siege conditions with him; they are believed to have discussed a joint sui-cide on several occasions and finally agreed to this act one day into their marriage, although the timing, nature and circumstances of their deaths have been disputed from that day on. She may not have been the 'great woman' who is said to be behind every great man, but Eva Braun was undoubtedly an important character in the life of Adolf Hitler.

Gun, N. E. *Eva Braun: Hitler's Mistress*, 1969

Wernher von BRAUN
1912–1977

Technical Director of the Rocket Research Centre in the Baltic town of Peenemünde at the age of 25, his staff had devised long-range self-propelled explosive rockets well before the Third Reich had declared war. Although their work was ham-pered by lack of funds, his team worked quickly once they were given the go-ahead to produce the V–1 'flying-bomb' in 1943. By June 1944 this dramatic new weapon of war was being targeted on Britain and 10,492 were launched; it was followed by the launching of 1,403 V–2 rockets from September 1944 to March 1945. The damage caused was colossal and 33,442 British civilians were killed or injured. Von Braun surrendered with his 450 staff at Oberammergau in 1945 and his expertise set the Americans on course for space exploration.

Major General Lewis Hyde
BRERETON
1890–1967

Appointed Commander of the US Far East Air Force when Japan seemed set on war, he was afforded only a limited number of B–17s in the Philippines and these were promptly destroyed on the ground by the Japanese. He then became Commander of the new US Middle East Air Force, based in Italy, where his primary task was the training of fledgling pilots. By October 1942 he was Commander of the US Ninth Air Force in support of the Tunisian campaign and a year later he transferred to England to accelerate the development of the Ninth into the supreme tactical force it needed to be to undertake the attacking of the German transport network prior to 'Overlord', destroying communication lines further inland and damaging the bridges over the main rivers of France. As the first Commander of the First Allied Airborne Army he took part in the planning of the Operation 'Market Garden' air-drops at Nijmegen, Eindhoven and Arnhem.

Air Chief Marshal Sir Robert
BROOKE-POPHAM
1878–1953

Governor of Kenya, he was recalled to command the British forces in the Far East. He urged implementation of the plan to invade Siam – the agreed means of delaying the Japanese – but the order came too late. He was replaced by Lieutenant-General Pownall when the Japanese were preparing to attack Malaya in December 1941.

Lieutenant-General Frederick ('Boy')
BROWNING
1896–1966

Of the more enlightened Army officers who quickly saw the potential of the airborne deployment of ground troops, Browning was the trail-blazer who urged and then managed the use of the strategy in the Bruneval raid in February 1942 and then in the North Africa and Sicily campaigns.

In January 1944 he commanded I Airborne Corps which was used in the Normandy landings and then was Deputy Commander of First Allied Airborne Army which saw Operation 'Market Garden' into action on the Rhine at Arnhem. It was at this time, ahead of the event, that he advised MONTGOMERY that the plan might be taking the Allies 'a bridge too far'. From November 1944 he was MOUNTBATTEN's Chief of Staff in South-East Asia Command.
Ryan, C. *A Bridge Too Far*, 1964

Colonel Maurice
BUCKMASTER
1902–1992

This tall, tough, positive intelligence officer had worked with the British Expeditionary Force in France before being recruited to head F Section of the Special Operations Executive. He was a fine choice for a complex task; by his encouragement and enthusiasm, about 500 agents were trained in Britain for work in France and their subsequent actions – running resistance groups, passing information back to England, and undertaking sabotage, subversion and rescue missions – caused havoc among the occupying German forces.

F Section lost nearly a quarter of these agents and constantly saw their cause damaged by Gestapo action or double agents, but Buckmaster's driving management kept up the flow of agents into the field.
Foot, M. R. D. *The SOE in France*, 1984

General Simon Bolivar
BUCKNER
1886–1945

Born into a military family, he commanded the US forces in the Aleutians for much of the war. He led

Lieutenant-General Browning with Brigadier Hicks and Brigadier-General Urquhart after an address to Arnhem veterans in London. (IWM HU63317)

Tenth Army in the assault on Okinawa, the last act before the charge
for the Japanese home islands themselves, and here established a reputation as a daring and resourceful
leader although his persistence with
frontal assaults was criticised in the
American press as being unimagina-
tive. He was killed in action on 18
June 1945, just before the end of the
battle, when a shell exploded near a
forward observation post he was
visiting; the highest ranking American army commander to die in battle during the war.

Foster, S. *Okinawa 1945*, 1994

Marshal Semion
BUDENNY
1883–1973

Having probably survived the
Purges of 1937–8 because of his
friendship with STALIN dating back
to the Civil War, he found himself
commanding the Soviet armies in
the Ukraine and Bessarabia before
the German invasion in June 1941.
He was then given command of the
combined South and South West
Fronts, but was unable to repel the
rapid German attacks despite
sundry rather lightweight attempts
and was removed from his post on
13 September. He was never
returned to front line work though
he held command of various Cau-
casian Fronts and was made Commander of the Cavalry of the Soviet
Army early in 1943. But for his
backing from Stalin, this cavalier
but ineffective commander would
surely not have achieved marshal's
rank.

Field Marshal Ernst
BUSCH
1885–1945

It can be said of him that the status
he achieved was in direct relation to
the subservience he showed to
HITLER. He was to have com-

Field Marshal Ernst Busch, whose disillusionment with the war deepened with
the increasing loss of German troops. (IWM MH6031)

manded Sixteenth Army had the invasion of Britain taken place, but was instead sent to the Eastern Front to command Army Group Centre. His duties there lasted from October 1943 to June 1944 and in that time he was greatly affected by the loss of so many men. Much depressed by his perceived failure personally to prevent this, he accepted his replacement by MODEL just before the destruction of that Group in what was Hitler's greatest reversal. He was moved to Norway where he remained until he surrendered his troops in April 1945; he died in July, a prisoner of the British.

Vannevar
BUSH
1890–1974

He was Director of the newly created Office of Scientific Research whose aim was to utilise US scientific resources in support of the war effort. It was this agency which co-ordinated research into the atomic bomb.

James
BYRNES
1879–1972

A Supreme Court judge, he was used by the US administration as a trouble-shooter, much as BEAVERBROOK was used in Britain. His forte was the implementation of schemes and agreements and he directed the Selective Service and Lend-Lease acts through Congress. As Director of War Mobilisation he activated many plans at home to support the war abroad. He accompanied ROOSEVELT to Yalta and served TRUMAN as Secretary of State, assisting in the drafting of the Potsdam Declaration. In this position he was first to reject Japan's conditional surrender in August 1945, a fact which demonstrated his tough, legalistic approach to politics and war.

Major-General John
CAMPBELL
1894 -1942

'Jock' Campbell won a Victoria Cross for his daring and initiative in commanding the Support Group of 7th Armoured Division against the Italian/German force at Sidi Rezegh in November 1941. At the outbreak of the war with Italy he had been in command of 4th Regiment, Royal Horse Artillery in the Western Desert where he organised many harassing raids and moves during the retreat. He was killed in a car accident shortly after assuming command of 7th Armoured Division, the 'Desert Rats'.

Admiral Wilhelm
CANARIS
1888–1945

A U-boat commander in World War One, by the outbreak of the Second World War he was head of the Abwehr, the Intelligence Division of the German Forces. It is certain that this organisation leaked information to Germany's enemies and was involved in plots against HITLER, and it is known that Canaris assisted BECK in rallying those who resisted the Führer's policies. He was not prepared to back an assassination attempt but was well placed – and well suited – to conduct a clandestine programme of disruption without prejudicing

his official role. The strain of 'playing for both sides' did finally tell, however, and he was dismissed prior to the July plot which brought his arrest. He was executed at Flossenburg concentration camp on 9 April 1945, just weeks before it was liberated.

Brissaud, A. *Canaris*, 1974
Hohne, H. *Canaris: Hitler's Master Spy*, 1979
Paine, L. *The Abwehr*, 1984

Major-General Giacomo
CARBONI
1889–1973

He was chief of Italian Army Intelligence during the first thirty months of the war until his continued apathy to the ever closer, and hugely subordinate, liaison with Nazi Germany caused his dismissal. He returned to play a significant part in ousting MUSSOLINI in July 1943.

Brigadier General Evans
Fordyce
CARLSON
1896–1947

Seen by many as the creator of special-purpose units within the American military, this Marine commander led the 2nd Raider Battalion for the landing on Guadalcanal where his dramatic 150-mile march embodied many of the specialised battlefield skills with which, he believed, élite units could enhance larger forces.

King of Romania
CAROL II
1893–1957

Although of German background, Carol favoured alliance with Britain and France and he secured a guarantee that his country's borders would be defended by them. In the summer of 1939 he proclaimed himself dictator, but after the fall of

Poland and the invasion of France he found himself unable to resist pressure to declare himself in favour of the Axis and was forced to sacrifice Bessarabia and northern Bukovina to the USSR in June 1940 in order to keep the Russians out of the war. Two months later he succumbed further, losing Transylvania to Hungary and, shortly thereafter, southern Dobruja to Bulgaria. The subsequent loss of support brought his abdication, on 6 September 1941, in favour of his son, MICHAEL.

Mathilde
CARRÉ
1908–1971

With the fall of France, she was recruited by the French underground and, under the code-names 'Lily' and 'Cat', she set about reporting German progress to intelligence officers in London. On 17 November 1941 she was caught by the Germans who promptly 'turned' her, on threat of a firing-squad, to work for them providing details of Resistance agents and networks.

The information she gave led to many agents and units being arrested or compromised, but when she raised suspicions in an SOE operative she was helping liaise with London, his questioning brought an admission that she was under German control. Now, with SOE acquiescence, she was 'turned' a second time to reveal many of her Abwehr contacts. In April 1942, when her position was prejudiced by the arrest of the SOE agent she had helped, she was taken into custody until the end of the war. Mathilde was a triple agent whose information had assisted and damaged the clandestine operations of Germans and the Allies alike.

General Georges
CATROUX
1877–1969

This Algerian-born Army officer was Governor-General of French Indo–China at the outbreak of war. He was utterly opposed to the Germans and, after his replacement by a Vichy regime loyalist, he sided with DE GAULLE in 1940, becoming the only Army general to do so and earning a death sentence from PÉTAIN for his pains. He commanded the Free French forces for de Gaulle in Syria and was an original member of the Committee for National Liberation. He later became Governor-General of Algeria and, at the end of the war, Ambassador to Moscow.

Marshal Ugo
CAVALLERO
1880–1943

After Italy's abortive campaign in Greece it was Cavallero who replaced BADOGLIO as his country's Chief of the General Staff. He quickly sought to modernise the Army in the style of the Germans he so admired. He achieved some success but was affected by the changing fortunes of his forces in the war, and in January 1943 the fall of Tripoli gave MUSSOLINI an excuse to sack him. When the dictator was forced from power, the Marshal optimistically made a play for power again but no faction was prepared to support him; he was found dead in his garden in September of that year. He was a man who presented a favourable and ambitious character to his superiors in order to retain his position.

Neville
CHAMBERLAIN
1869–1940

He found himself the senior politician in Great Britain when his country, unready for war, was faced with German militancy. His desire to preserve the peace, at least until he could prepare for war, brought the accusation of appeasement, accentuated by his sacrificing Czechoslovakia, which he unfortunately described as 'a far-off country of which we know little'.

In 1939 he acknowledged the need to combine with others against the expansionist signals from HITLER and he linked with France to guarantee protection to Poland, an assurance quickly tested by the German invasion in September. His quest for peace and the early defeat of the British Expeditionary Force brought constant and loud expressions of doubt as to his credentials as a war leader and he transferred the premiership to CHURCHILL on 10 May 1940.

His experience had been gained exclusively in Home Affairs and his natural diplomacy ill-prepared him for the assessment he had to make of a dictator of burgeoning ambition and disregard for formal politics. Churchill referred to him as, 'alert, businesslike, opinionated and self-confident', but also noted his almost obsessive desire to be remembered as a peacemaker. His inability to succeed in his diligent quest for peace was too great a failure to carry and he died in 1940. The nearest one can get to a compliment for Chamberlain could be to suggest that his statesmanship might have found a happier home in another, more peaceful decade.

Major General Claire Lee
CHENNAULT
1890–1958

Already retired because of a hearing disorder and based in China on advisory work, he was recalled to Washington in November 1940 to recruit pilots. The end result of his

Major General Chennault watching flight operations in China. He was known as 'old leather face'. (IWM NYF15301)

work – some 100 veteran flyers of assorted backgrounds and a similar number of ground crew – became the 'Flying Tigers'. In six months this miscellaneous group claimed nearly 300 Japanese aircraft in the Burma theatre.

In April 1942 he became leader of the US (Vol) Army Air Force in China. Having obtained a larger share of resources than other forces in the area, Chennault's airmen drove the Japanese back but, because of the imbalance of supplies, the counter-offensive could not be repulsed for ever.

A belligerent man who fought hard for his cause, he resigned in July 1945 when the decision was taken to disband the Chinese–American wing of the Chinese Air Force.

General Ivan
CHERNYAKHOVSKY
1906–1945
Among those who recognised the abilities of Ivan Chernyakhovsky was ZHUKOV and it was through his sponsorship that this youthful Jew became the youngest High Commander of the Soviet Army in World War Two. He achieved hero status when he led Sixtieth Army to the recapture of Voronezh and Kursk and then, commanding the 3rd Belorussian Front, he enjoyed success at Minsk and Vitebsk. He then took Vilna and Kaunas before returning to action for the attacks against Königsberg. He was killed in action in February 1945.

Group Captain Leonard
CHESHIRE
1917–1992
The early evidence of his leadership qualities ensured that Cheshire promptly achieved the command of 617 Pathfinder Squadron which, guided by the seasoned skill of DON BENNETT, enabled new levels of accuracy to be set by the RAF night bombers. He witnessed the atomic

Ivan Chernyakhovsky, who prospered under Zhukov's sponsorship.
(IWM PIC29260)

bomb drop on Nagasaki when, during his posting to the Far East, he was the official British observer in the camera aircraft.

After the war he set up the charitable Cheshire Homes organisation which remains a thriving testament to the enthusiasm and energy of this son of a law professor.

Cheshire, L. *Face of Victory*, 1962

Generalissimo
CHIANG KAI-SHEK
1887–1975

With his tenuous hold on power, constant threats from the Communists and limited support from the USA, Chiang Kai-shek was not ideally placed to play a major role in the Allied response to the Japanese invasion of Burma in 1942. Furthermore, his dictatorial attitude towards the highly experienced JOE STILWELL, his American Chief of Staff whom he appointed to command the armies he sent to Burma, did little to make the move as effective as it could have been. Upset by the lack of American aid, Chiang chose to back CHENNAULT and his opinion that air power would be the decisive factor. The Allies' reluctant agreement to such an offensive saw it bring some success but also, as Stilwell had always claimed it would, a Japanese counter-attack which destroyed US air bases in eastern China.

The US–Chinese rift was now greater than ever, with the future of Stilwell at the centre of the debate. The American policy saw Chiang's forces being used to keep the Japanese occupied away from the main Pacific hotspots and he was given considerable materiel to undertake this, but much of this equipment was diverted to the fight against the Communists, a confrontation which continued after the war.

Chiang Kai-shek. (IWM CHN803)

The Americans certainly viewed Chiang as potentially a leader of a great Fourth Power, but could never find a successful equation to bring this about. To CHURCHILL, Chiang was a 'calm, reserved and efficient personality', but one who was destined to play a minor role.

Frederick Lindemann, Lord
CHERWELL
1886–1957
This French-born British scientist was a friend of CHURCHILL's who recruited him first as scientific adviser then as Paymaster-General to his War Cabinet. His scientific work at the Royal Aircraft Factory at Farnborough and his Oxford lab-oratory had convinced him of various air bombing theories which he avidly promoted, including that of 'carpet-bombing'. He courted controversy because of his outspoken views and his apparent clear line to the ear of Churchill.

General Dietrich von
CHOLTITZ
1894–1966
He had been involved in the siege of Sevastopol and with Army Group South as it struggled against Russian counter-attacks. He was placed in command of German forces on the Cotentin peninsula at the time of the D-Day landings, but his troops had been brushed aside by the Allied forces by the end of July and he was relocated to control the troops defending Paris. He rejected the contrary instructions from HITLER and surrendered the capital.

Lieutenant-General Sir Peter
CHRISTISON
1893–1993
In the celebrated Admin Box battle, the first important British victory of the Burma campaign, Christison stood his ground with his XV Indian Army Corps and foiled the rampant Japanese who struggled against the small, air-supplied enclave. Eventually, support troops encircled the Japanese.
Turnbull, P. *The Battle of the Box*, 1979

Marshal Vassili
CHUIKOV
1900–1982

This World War One veteran said 'when a decision is taken belatedly its execution inevitably leads to haste' and his efforts at Stalingrad gave evidence of this attitude. After inter-war service as a military adviser to CHIANG KAI-SHEK, Chuikov served at the War Ministry in 1941–2 before being appointed commander of Sixty-Second Army in the battle for Stalingrad. His army heroically held the Russian space on the Volga and then played a major role in the defence of the city. He next led the newly titled Eighth Guards Army in the great offensive that swept the Germans from the country, and having secured Berlin he accepted the German surrender on behalf of the Soviet Union. He later wrote a fine account of his Stalingrad experiences.

Chuikov, V. *The Beginning of the Road*, 1963
Wieder, J. *Stalingrad*, 1995

Lieutenant-Colonel John (Jack)
CHURCHILL
1906–1996

'Mad Jack' as he was affectionately nicknamed, was a true war maverick, a man made for the hurly-burly of the battlefield where his charismatic, devil-may-care leadership proved inspirational.

There can have been few who used a bow and arrows in World War Two and led his troops into battle wearing a kilt and playing his bagpipes, but Jack did both – he was a crack shot with the bow and played the pipes professionally. He shot his bow against the Germans on the Maginot Line and was seriously injured during the subsequent fighting in France. He was soon back at the sharp end, the bullet still

in him, to lead Commando units in Norway and then through Sicily and the landings at Salerno. His conduct at the latter saved the Allied beachhead and won him the DSO to add to his MC. He then saw service in the Adriatic where he was wounded again and captured. This shy, sensitive man from southern England became a dramatic war hero.

Peter
CHURCHILL
1909–1972

A noted, perhaps notorious, agent of the Special Operations Executive's French Section, Churchill was used to monitor, fund and manage Resistance groups and, after three visits to France, began his celebrated liaison with ODETTE SANSOM. Because of his reluctance to operate clandestinely, he risked compromising the very networks he had been sent to improve and inspire, and his main *réseau*, 'Spindle', had to keep on the move to evade capture. The Germans infiltrated his groups and in April 1943 he parachuted into an ambush and spent the rest of the war in prison camps.

Sir Winston Leonard Spencer
CHURCHILL
1874–1965

Inspirational qualities have always been useful to the individual who leads a nation through war. Today, Churchill would have been able instantly to encourage the military and civilians by vigorous use of modern communications – as it was he was an eager broadcaster in those formative years of radio – so magnifying the charismatic flavour of his leadership. He knew how to present himself to the film newsreels, to the thronging crowds on the Home Front, and to the troops facing all manner of deprivation on foreign

soil; he was a PR man's dream, for what publicist could fail to warm to a client who could offer 'blood, toil, tears and sweat'?

Churchill's pre-war career was uneven at best, but after he surrendered First Lordship of the Admiralty to take over as Prime Minister from CHAMBERLAIN in May 1940 he had found his niche, his calling; this was *his* finest hour as well as that of the people he urged to greater efforts. His genius was a combination of oratorical authority, an insatiable appetite for detail both written and verbal, a determined work ethic, the ability to focus himself and others on a point of issue, and skill in drawing diverse and divergent views together on both the local and international stage. He said, 'I felt as if I were walking with destiny', and his people quickly came to believe it.

He had an enthusiasm for military history and an appreciation of the strategy and tactics of war; among British politicians at the time he was one of few with experience as a traditional battlefield leader. When he moved into the premiership, however, his recent practical experience was of politics but he used his knowledge of military theory to master the art of war statesmanship where a greater awareness of the broader perspective stood him in good stead. He appointed his staff with care; where toughness and bullying was called for he chose a suitable character to deliver the goods, and if administrative care were required he invariably found his man.

There is no doubt that his close friendship with PRESIDENT ROOSEVELT accelerated American participation in the war effort, even before that country's troops were involved. Their almost daily com-

A typical Churchillian gesture on a visit to the Eighth Army in North Africa. He travelled tirelessly throughout the war – across Britain, to conferences around the world anc to front-line troops. (IWM CNA846)

The cigar adds to the informality of Churchill's meeting with the crews of anti-aircraft batteries on the Home Front. (IWM H39493)

munication and readiness to travel to meet face to face gave public evidence of unity; their relationship was often able to smooth over the problems caused by the divergence in policy promoted by their advisers.

Churchill's dogmatic adherence to his own beliefs was both a benefit and a drawback. His mistrust of STALIN and readiness to listen to the advice of those beyond the political and military hierarchy caused problems with sundry allies and senior commanders; his commitment to the Mediterranean and Balkan theatres infuriated those who wanted to concentrate on Operation 'Overlord'; his Far Eastern policy often confused and alarmed those around him. Yet, this dogged persistence saw off the waverers; Britain and her Allies would have been poorly served by a less forthright personality. He bred an undying faith in his soldiers because he demonstrated similar belief in them, with the resulting maintenance of morale so valuable, and so apparent to even the most pessimistic. And all those stirring speeches and telling one-liners – did Churchill invent the 'sound-bite'? – kept civilian and warrior alike convinced that the Allied cause was right and, fundamentally, was in the hands of someone who would see it through to success.

That the British denied Churchill the opportunity to prove himself a leader of the peace as well as of the war may have been a blessing, for his reputation remained untainted by any fading in post-war performance. It was better that he should spend these years writing his account of the war for this literature is treasure indeed. In 1940 Britain was a company facing bankruptcy needing a chief executive, a sports team requiring a coach to turn it from the threat of relegation into championship winners, and it was clear that Churchill saw his role like this. At the end of the war the demands were different, the 'trophy' was in the cabinet and the rules of the competition were hugely changed.

If it is necessary to re-affirm the essential part Winston Churchill played in defeating Nazism and its expansionist plans, it should be considered what the consequences might have been had he succumbed to one of the many journeys he made to the battlefronts or to distant conferences. A void would have been left which it is most difficult to envisage any other being suited to fill; it could have prejudiced the Anglo–American alliance and would have removed the motor from the drive for victory. He died in London on 24 January 1965.

Churchill, W. S. *Blood, Sweat and Tears*, 1941
– *The Second World War* (6 vols.), 1948–53
Churchill, R. S. *Winston S. Churchill* (2 vols.), 1966–7
Gilbert, M. *Winston S. Churchill* (8 vols.), 1971–88
Pitt, B. *Churchill and the Generals*, 1981

CHU TEH
1886–1976
Together with MAO TSE-TUNG he built up the Communist forces in China and was commander of these troops in the Japanese War of 1937–45 and the Civil War which broke out in 1945. His tenet, 'our soldiers join the Army to serve the people, not the officers', is an indication of the affinity he had with the simple soldiers and why he enjoyed their support.

General Mark Clark (left) with General Kirkham and Major General Arbuthnot. He called for the monastery of Monte Cassino to be bombed when the Allied drive through Italy was halted there. (IWM NA20784)

Count Galeazzo
CIANO
1903–1944
As Italy's foreign minister, he signed the 1939 pact with Germany although he was known to be alarmed by the possible consequences. Favoured by the dictator because of his marriage to Edda Mussolini, he remained disenchanted with the regime and resigned in February 1943. One of his most grievous misjudgements was the belief that 'the British draw back as slowly as possible but they do not want to fight'. He supported MUSSOLINI's removal in July but was himself imprisoned and exe-cuted by the Germans shortly afterwards.

General Mark
CLARK
1896–1984
After working with EISENHOWER during the Operation 'Torch' landings in North Africa, he was given command of Fifth Army which was to invade Italy. Operation 'Avalanche' began on 9 September 1943 at Salerno, and Naples was quickly taken. Operation 'Shingle' saw the Anzio landings in the following January but Clark could not advance as he wished. The terrain, with its difficult river crossings,

hampered progress and the German defence was determined, especially at Cassino where even the bombing of the famous monastery failed to break their lines. It was May before combined Allied forces removed the Germans from this stronghold and enabled Clark, contrary to ALEXANDER's orders, to head for Rome. This action allowed the Germans to retreat northwards and Clark was again halted by the regrouped enemy at Bologna four months later. Not until April 1945 did he finally secure the victory which brought the surrender.

Although Clark was guilty of some incongruous decision-making, he was a popular leader. He once claimed that award winners on the battlefield were so determined to live up to their reputation that they would be better employed training troops at home because of the danger posed by their presence on the battlefield. After the war he commanded the US occupation force in Austria and later took charge of UN forces in Korea from 1952.
Clark, M. *Calculated Risk*, 1950

Lieutenant-General 'Lightning Joe' Lawton
COLLINS
1896–1963
This dynamic battlefield leader first came to prominence at Guadalcanal in December 1942 where he led the US 25th Infantry Division in this important psychological and strategic success. He moved on to work with XIV Corps in chasing the Japanese off New Georgia.

Believing that success was the spur to progress, he next excelled in the dramas of D-Day and its aftermath, commanding VII Corps and landing on Utah Beach before thrusting forward to take Cherbourg on 24 June. After closing the Falaise Gap, Collins drove his men north and east across France and into Belgium, taking Mons, Namur and Liège, joining the counter-attack at Houffalize and tracking on to the Rhine, into Germany, through the Ruhr to the Elbe where they met up with the Russians.

Air Marshal Sir Arthur
CONINGHAM
1895–1948
A skilled exponent of long-range flying, this World War One veteran brought his expertise to the Desert campaign, becoming Commander of the Western Desert Air Force with which he supported the Eighth Army's ground movements. He was for a time in com-

Air Marshal Coningham conducts an airfield briefing with his squadron commanders. (IWM CNA2176)

mand of the British and American air units in Tunisia and used this experience when given command of 2nd Tactical Air Force which gave air support to the Allied forces in north-west Europe in the last year of the war.

Alfred Duff
COOPER
1890–1954

An energetic opponent of appeasement, he returned to government as Minister of Information in 1940, having resigned over the Munich Agreement; he became CHURCHILL's personal representative in the Far East from spring 1941 to the beginning of 1942.

Having been a staunch advocate of the French and of DE GAULLE's credentials in the early war years, he became the British delegate in the Algiers-based French Committee of National Liberation and then was appointed Ambassador in Paris from November 1944. In these positions he presented the case for close relationship with France which he saw as a major player in post-war Europe. His efforts culminated in the Treaty of Dunkirk in 1947.

Sidney
COTTON
1894–1969

Having been a pioneer of aerial photography and intelligence gathering in World War One, he returned to this work at the time of the Munich Conference, first under French auspices but later with the British. Under cover of an aviation research business, he overflew Germany, Italy and North Africa, recording troop and shipping movements and battle zone constructions. As his work developed he was graded as a commissioned squadron leader in the RAF and given command of its first dedicated photo reconnaissance unit.

Rear-Admiral Sir John
CRACE
1887–1968

A British officer who commanded the Australian naval squadron, Task Force 44, in the Coral Sea battles of 1942 and in action off the coast of New Guinea. He retired to become Superintendent of HM Dockyard, Chatham.

General Crerar (left) with Montgomery and General Dempsey at an impromptu planning meeting at Second Army HQ in September 1944. (IWM BU557)

General Henry
CRERAR
1888–1965

Originally selected by the Canadian government for work in planning training courses for that country's troops in Britain, he sacrificed his high-ranking position for the chance of combat.

After successfully leading I Corps in Sicily he returned to Britain to take charge of the motley, multi-national Canadian First Army which followed the D-Day landings to move inland before breaking north to tackle the defended ports of Le Havre, Boulogne and Calais. Within weeks Crerar was at the Scheldt estuary, with 72,000 prisoners, from where he moved on to take Antwerp and Udem to break the Siegfried Line.

Crerar moulded the Dutch, Belgian, Polish and British troops in his force and was unstinting in support of MONTGOMERY's drive through France and Belgium.

Sir Richard Stafford
CRIPPS
1889–1952

When appointed Ambassador to Moscow under CHURCHILL's coalition government in 1940, it was anticipated that the leftish stance of this Labour politician would open doors that a diplomat could not approach. Certainly his dry formality suited that post though not so obviously the negotiations he later entered into with the Indian nationalists in 1942 when Britain sought their co-operation. He was a skilful administrator and was efficient in masterminding aircraft production when he assumed that ministry in November 1942.

General Sir Alan
CUNNINGHAM
1887–1983

From Kenya, his force of East, South and West Africans invaded and overran Italian Somaliland and in May 1941 restored EMPEROR HAILE SELASSIE to the Ethiopian throne. In August he was appointed to command the Western Desert Force (now retitled Eighth Army) for Operation 'Crusader' by which AUCHINLECK planned to relieve Tobruk. Out-manoeuvred by the

Sir Stafford Cripps with Gandhi, among the adoring crowd in Delhi, April 1942. (IWM IND440)

General Cunningham sets out on a reconnaissance flight over the Western Desert. (IWM E6658)

'Desert Fox', ERWIN ROMMEL, he was replaced in November and so missed the mighty battles that were to follow.

Admiral Sir Andrew
CUNNINGHAM
1883–1963

A naval tactician and highly capable administrator who will be forever associated with the daring November 1940 raid on Taranto which saw the Fleet Air Arm's finest hour and removed the Italian naval threat from the Mediterranean. Few men would have taken the fight into the Italians' own har-

bour, let alone destroy three battleships. In November 1941 he followed this success at the Battle of Cape Matapan which saw the loss of the Italian heavy cruiser *Pola* and heroic fighting to prevent German reinforcements reaching the island of Crete.

Cunningham was then sent to Washington to talk future strategy with the Chiefs of Staff and asked by that group to serve as EISENHOWER's deputy for Operation 'Torch'. Later he supervised the naval landings on Sicily before succeeding POUND as First Sea Lord in October 1943.

Cunningham, A. B. *A Sailor's Odyssey*, 1951

John
CURTIN
1885–1945

When he took over as Prime Minister of Australia from ROBERT MENZIES, this Australian Labour Party leader had to adjust his previously stated policies which had opposed conscription and his predecessor's support of the British stance. Now, facing Japanese expansionism, he accepted the need for Australian involvement, although he was more supportive

Admiral Cunningham inspects the ruins of Anzio with other Allied naval and army officers. (IWM A21498)

Meeting at the National Press Club in Washington, John Curtin (third from left) is seen with Lord Halifax, Sir Owen Dixon and Sam O'Neill. (IWM NYP27492)

of MACARTHUR's plan than CHURCHILL's which he thought lacked commitment to the Far East theatre.

After re-election in 1943, illness cut short his active involvement in the international war management and he died in July 1944.

Edouard
DALADIER
1884–1970

This French Prime Minister was appointed in 1933 because of his acceptability to the diverse factions in French politics, but he lost much support by his signing of the Munich Agreement in September 1938 and more still when his lack of decision-making and positive action in the face of the German threat became apparent. His government fell in the spring of 1940 but he was in REYNAUD's team which replaced it.

When France was invaded he sought to work with resistance fighters in North Africa but was discovered, brought back to France and prosecuted by the Vichy authorities, the charge being one of taking his country to war without due preparation. He suffered internment in Buchenwald and Dachau.

Daladier was never suited to holding power during a time of such frenetic activity; in a different age he might have proved a capable administrator.

Kurt
DALUEGE
1897–1946

An early recruit to Nazism, he held several high-ranking posts during the pre-war years. In May 1942 he was appointed Deputy Protector of Bohemia and Moravia under NEU-RATH, after HEYDRICH's assassination. He was replaced by FRICK in August 1943 and at the end of the war was hunted down, tried and executed by the Czechs for his role in the Lidice massacre.

Sir Claude
DANSEY
1876–1947

As Assistant Chief of MI6, Britain's Secret Intelligence Service, throughout the war, his principal role became that of recruiting spies and agents from the nations of Europe via their governments-in-exile in London. In the years leading up to the war he had been 'dismissed' from the Service so as to set up the clandestine 'Z' organisation and keep it free of German infiltration.

Admiral Jean François
DARLAN
1881–1942

Had the circumstances of the land warfare turned out differently, Darlan and his mighty French fleet might well have played a different role in World War Two. As it was he was instructed by the British to prevent his ships from falling into German hands but an apparent reluctance to do so brought about the H Force bombardment – the Mers-el-Kebir incident – in July 1940 which saw an ineffectual attack in terms of damage to vessels but a significant impact on Anglo–French relations.

From his office in PÉTAIN's government Darlan sought to negotiate better living conditions from the German's but got no response. He was appointed head of the French Armed Forces and High Commissioner in French North Africa when LAVAL returned to power. EISENHOWER and CLARK led Allied talks with Darlan to secure his co-operation in getting the French forces to fight with the Allies and he did gain some recognition as head of the French Government in North Africa, though the British remained suspicious of his motives. He was assassinated by a French royalist on 24 December 1942.

Joseph
DARNAND
1897–1945

A wholehearted collaborator with the Germans, he was given office in the puppet French government and charged with setting up and controlling the hated Vichy military police. Ruthless in the use of force against the opponents of the Vichy regime, he was tried, found guilty of treason and shot at the end of the war. He maintained throughout that his liaison with the Nazis was prompted by patriotism.

Marcel
DEAT
1894–1955

In his pacifist journal *L'Oeuvre* this socialist politician railed against the Vichy regime, and PÉTAIN in particular, but then appeared to succumb to Nazi propaganda and pledge his support to LAVAL to the degree that he was appointed labour minister in the Vichy government in 1944. He fled to southern Germany with his colleagues once the Allied invasion took hold and remained outside France for the rest of his life.

General Charles
DE GAULLE
1890–1970

Had he been a British rather than a French World War One veteran, he would surely have seen major involvement in the 1939–45 war. As it was he enjoyed only brief command, albeit with some success, with 4th Armoured Division in 1940 before leaving France. From England in June of that year he broadcast a stirring message to his countrymen, declaring the creation of 'Free France' with himself as its head.

Initially neither French forces nor civilians were particularly supportive. A de Gaulle-inspired, British-led attempt to take Dakar in September was thwarted by the resistance of BOISSON's troops and an invasion in Syria in June 1941 was repelled by troops under GENERAL DENTZ's command.

Although certain lobbies among the Allies, notably the Americans, promoted GIRAUD as their preferred leader of the French, de Gaulle began to get backing at home, from Frenchmen dismayed by the acquiesence of the Vichy government. With Giraud's resignation in 1943 and an improved power base, de Gaulle returned home in June 1944 and entered a newly freed capital to general acclaim on 26 August.

If he was now undisputed leader – he was made President of the Committee of National Liberation – he did not receive the status from the Allies he had expected; he was excluded from the conferences at Yalta and Potsdam. His subsequent resentment is given by historians as reason for some of his independent, nationalistic dogma, but he was always of an arrogant demeanour and felt that he must employ such a stance to demonstrate to his coun-

De Gaulle meets General Giraud in North Africa. (IWM CNA831)

trymen at home that he was not a British puppet. He did little to rid himself of this trait during the post-war years.

His stress on the value of leadership explains his later political dominance: 'Training for war is, first and foremost, training in leadership, and it is literally true, for enemies as well as for nations that where leadership is good, the rest shall be added to them.'

Barres, P. *Charles de Gaulle*, 1941
Crawley, A. *De Gaulle*, 1941
De Gaulle, C. *The Army of the Future*, 1941
De Gaulle, C. *War Memoirs* (5 vols.), 1955–61
Kersandy, F. *Churchill and de Gaulle*, 1981
Nachin, L. *Charles de Gaulle: Général de France*, 1944

Leon
DEGRELLE
1906–1994

In the years leading up to war he had joined other Belgian Catholics to form the Rexist movement which collaborated with the Nazis at the invasion in May 1940. He created units of like-minded men to fight on the Eastern Front and was one of the few non-Germans to be awarded the Iron Cross with Oak Leaves. At the end of the war he fled to Spain and remained there to evade the death sentence passed on him by the Belgians.

Major-General Francis
DE GUINGAND
1900–1979

Every battlefield commander is made more effective when he has staff who can take the detail of planning and negotiation away from his superior once guidelines have been established. De Guingand was used in such a capacity by MONTGOMERY for whom he was Chief of Staff in North Africa and North West Europe. He was especially efficient as a reducer of tension

Major-General de Guingand with Montgomery in North Africa. (IWM E20057)

between Montgomery and the US commanders when differences occurred over the strategies employed on the advance to the Rhine and beyond.

De Guingand, F. *Operation 'Victory'*, 1964

General Jean
DE LATTRE DE TASSIGNY
1889–1952

This Frenchman, a veteran of World War One, was Chief of Staff of the French Fifth Army which faced the German invasion. After the defeat of France he worked for the Vichy government in Tunisia but remained very critical of the Germans for advance into the free zone in 1942.

This brought him imprisonment at Riom but he escaped to Britain to join DE GAULLE and became commander of the French First Army in North Africa before bringing that force back to assist the liberation. He represented his country at the signing of the German surrender.

General Sir Miles Christopher
DEMPSEY
1896–1969

A soldier admired for his practical grasp of strategies and tactics, he had been in command of 13th Infantry Brigade until the fall of France, and then formed a new armoured division before being appointed commander of XIII Corps in MONTGOMERY's Eighth Army. He demonstrated his skill on the battlefield in several difficult situations in Italy and Sicily and was promoted to command Second Army at the Normandy landings. He brought his men ashore on Juno Beach and moved inland to Caen and Bayeux, Falaise and Mortain, and joined the race across France

and the problematic Operation 'Market Garden'. The setbacks encountered there were not of Dempsey's making and he had got his army across France and Belgium to that point with great efficiency and a minimum of fuss. He was a constant supporter of Montgomery and enjoyed a close relationship with him.

Vice-Admiral Sir Norman
DENNING
1904–1979

He was the dedicated creator of the Royal Navy's Operational Intelligence Centre which provided such vital data from the ULTRA decrypts as to stultify German naval tactics. The OIC was instrumental in finding and eliminating the *Bis-*

General Dempsey and General Grishin at Mecklenburg Castle in May 1945. (IWM BU5611)

marck and certainly curtailed the U-boat threat. Denning was a masterly organiser who maximised the value of every technological advance.

General Henri
DENTZ
1871–1945

His Vichy French forces resisted the Free French and British Army invasion of Syria in June 1941, so disproving DE GAULLE's assurance to CHURCHILL that they were ready to desert the German cause. With little or no air cover and no extra assistance forthcoming, he eventually had to sign an armistice with the British, the terms of which he was later found to have broken.

Henri
DERICOURT
1909–1962

One of the more mysterious of the agents used by F Section of the Special Operations Executive, he was known to have worked for the Nazi security service before he was brought to London for training in September 1942. Once his field work, controlling air movements to and from the Resistance, began in France in January 1943 it was not long before he came under suspicion of betraying the 'Prosper' network to the Germans. He was returned to London in February 1944 but investigations of his alleged treachery were not proven.

General Devers visits a mortar position manned by French Moroccan troops. (IWM NA14284)

It remains unclear whether Dericourt was merely a rather risky SOE agent who was forced to prejudice some operations to retain his credibility, or if he were a dedicated double agent of the Germans who deliberately damaged an important SOE unit.

Eamon
DE VALERA
1882–1975

Although his stance was substantially pro-Allied, this prime minister of Eire steadfastly maintained his country's neutrality, regularly rejecting requests to send his countrymen to war. He refused the British use of Irish ports and urged them to end conscription in Northern Ireland, but remained chiefly supportive while provoking doubts as to his motives by occasionally sending encouraging notes to the Germans and Japanese.

Colonel André
DEWAURIN
1911 -

Under the code-name of 'Passy', this French officer and DE GAULLE supporter became head of the French secret service in London. Apart from liaising with similar Allied organisations and setting up many missions for others, he was twice dropped into France by night, on one occasion to assess the consequences of MOULIN's arrest.

Major James
DEVEREUX
1903–1991

His active service was brief. Commanding the minimal US garrison at Wake Island in 1941, he and his men beat off an initial Japanese approach, sinking two destroyers and knocking out some aircraft before succumbing to the second landing and being taken prisoner.

General Jacob
DEVERS
1887–1979

As MAITLAND WILSON's second in command, he commanded the Allied landings in southern France, Operation 'Dragoon', which would see the subsequent link up with the 'Overlord' forces to the north. Hitting the coast on 15 August 1944, Devers' troops had reached Grenoble by the 24th and Lyons by 3 September, the link being made shortly afterwards. Devers was then given command of 6th Army Group and was required to hold Strasbourg as the Germans attempted a counter-offensive. Once he had achieved this he swept on to Munich and Berchtesgaden.

SS General Josef 'Sepp'
DIETRICH
1892–1976

This one-time butcher rose quickly in the Nazi Party from the moment it took power in 1933. He was instrumental in the Blood Purge of 1934 and supervised many executions. He was utterly committed to his Führer, whose bodyguard he commanded and expanded to become the Waffen SS.

During the war he led a tank corps in the attack on Paris and SS troops on the Russian front. At the end of 1944 HITLER turned to this most loyal of men to take Sixth Panzer Army into the Ardennes Offensive, but Dietrich was unable to perform the miracle his leader expected; he is said to have remarked that it was called Sixth Panzer because it had six tanks! With defeat looming ever closer, Hitler vented his fury on Dietrich's troops, demanding that they be stripped of their armbands. In response, Dietrich is reported to have returned his many medals.

In 1946 he was one of 43 SS officials found guilty of murdering 71 US prisoners during the Battle of the Bulge. He was sentenced to 25 years' imprisonment but released after ten. A German court then sentenced him to 19 months for his part in the 1934 purge.

Lucas, J. *Hitler's Enforcers*, 1996
Messenger, C. *Hitler's Gladiator*, 1983

Field Marshal Sir John Greer
DILL
1881–1944

When the war began he was in command of I Corps, but succeeded EDMUND IRONSIDE as Chief of the Imperial General Staff in May 1940 where he stayed for eighteen months before being replaced by ALAN-BROOKE. He was one of the men credited with the nurturing of the vital Anglo–American relationship during the second half of the war. Certainly he was much admired in Washington – ROOSEVELT described him as the 'most important figure' in the Anglo–American accord – where the national gratitude for his work as head of the British Joint Staff Mission was recognised by his burial in the Arlington National Cemetery – a rare distinction.

General Sir William
DOBBIE
1879–1964

He was called out of retirement to become Governor of Malta in 1940. As he also took the role of Commander of Armed Forces there he was responsible for its holding out against fierce Axis pressure for the next two years during which he used his sparse military resources and the amazing fortitude of the local civilians to repel attacks, service Allied troops and equipment in transit, and maintain the island's

General Sir William Dobbie. (IWM GN786)

strategic value. Before he was succeeded by GORT, the island had been awarded the George Cross.

Kenji
DOHIHARA
1888–1948

A Japanese expert on Chinese traditions, and Asian history in general, he was nicknamed 'Lawrence of Manchuria' by Western newsmen in 1936 when he unofficially began the occupation of northern Chinese territories on the pretext of protecting Japanese trade routes. After a period spent as Principal of the Military Academy in 1940, he was successively Commander-in-Chief of the Eastern District Army, of 7th Area Army in Singapore, of 12th Area Army and, following the surrender, of 1st General Army. Shortly afterwards he was arrested as a Class A war criminal, found guilty and hanged in Sugamo prison, Tokyo on 23 December 1948.

Hans von
DOHNANYI
1902–1945

A principal opponent of HITLER who worked with the Abwehr during the war but whose true colours were revealed by the 1944 bomb plot. He was arrested and executed at Sachsenhausen concentration camp near Berlin in April 1945

Grand Admiral Karl
DÖNITZ
1891–1980

He had been taken prisoner by the British at the end of the First World War when his U-boat *U-68* was sunk in October 1918 after he had torpedoed a British merchant ship near Malta. Two decades later he was again to be the scourge of British shipping.

He was utterly faithful to the Nazi cause and to HITLER who, told a Berlin rally, foresaw everything and was incapable of errors of judgement. Just prior to Hitler's suicide he described him as 'the single statesman of stature in Europe' and in 1969 spoke of the Führer's style as 'the best method of military leadership'.

From 1939 he was responsible for U-boat strategy, and evolved the 'Wolf Pack' tactic which so ter-rorised Allied shipping for a time. He was made an Admiral in 1942 and Grand Admiral in January 1943 when he succeeded RAEDER as Supreme Commander of the Navy.

His U-boats held sway in the early years of the war, but once the Allies got more long-range air patrols working, and became more efficient at tracking the U-boat fleets, Dönitz began to lose the Battle of the Atlantic, losing in fact one U-boat for every merchantman sunk. When informed that Dönitz had recalled his boats, Hitler raged that he was being stripped of his first line of defence in the west, and he was right; convoys were now sailing virtually unmolested across the Atlantic that had seen 175 warship losses and 2,603 merchant ships damaged, although the Germans had paid a high price with 784 U-boats and 28,000 men lost.

Despite the failure of his navy to help Germany win the war, Hitler declared Dönitz his successor. He assumed the leadership on 30 April 1945 and held it for the 23 days of freedom he enjoyed before capture by the British. The Nuremberg trial found him guilty on two counts and sentenced him to 10 years, which he served. His defence at the trial was based on his assertion that he was merely a professional naval officer following instructions.

Although he had been responsible for one of the most effective strategies in the history of sea warfare, Dönitz has been criticised for paying too much attention to the increasing strength of the Allies' forces ranged against him, but he was handicapped by the lack of air and surface vessel support. He felt that professional skill alone would not compensate a lack of morale and or belief in the cause.

Dönitz, K. *Mein Weckselrolles Leben*, 1968
– *Memoirs*, 1959
Edwards, B. *Dönitz and the Wolf Packs*, 1996
Padfield, P. *Dönitz: The Last Führer*, 1984

The dapper and sycophantic Karl Dönitz inspecting German forces. He briefly succeeded Hitler on 30 April 1945. (IWM A26643)

William Joseph
DONOVAN
1883–1959

Many commentators feel that the work of the British SOE (Special Operations Executive) and the American OSS (Office of Strategic Services) contributed as much to the defeat of the Germans in Europe and the Japanese in the Far East as many a large-scale military action. Certainly the agents recruited by these organisations and the resistance workers they deployed, caused countless disruptions and reversals to the Axis powers.

Early in the war Frank Knox, US Secretary of the Navy, sent a lawyer to visit and report on the actions of resistance movements in France. His mission was a huge success, giving him a knowledge of European affairs almost unique in American political and military circles; he had

Lieutenant General Doolittle with Princess Elizabeth, during a visit to a US Eighth Air Force base.
(IWM PL29127)

also impressed those he met, including CHURCHILL.

This man was 'Wild Bill' Donovan who, when working as an intelligence co-ordinator, was called to head the OSS when it was created in the summer of 1942. Under his command it recruited American and foreign personnel for covert operations in Europe, Africa and Asia. In a very short time it became a huge, complex network of clandestine activity, proving Donovan as a man of great vigour and organisational ability. He never saw eye-to-eye with FBI chief J. EDGAR HOOVER and their antagonism limited the exchange of information and views between the formative OSS and Hoover's large crime-busting operation.

Brown, A. C. *The Last Hero: Wild Bill Donovan*, 1982
Dear, I. *Sabotage and Subversion*, 1996

Lieutenant General James
DOOLITTLE
1896–1995

Beginning his military flying career in the US Army Air Service in 1917, and broadening his experience to encompass endurance and racing flights during the inter-war years, Jimmy Doolittle returned to the air force at the beginning of the war to organise the American automotive industry's move to aircraft production.

By 1942 he was on active flying duty, leading an air raid on Tokyo which undoubtedly led Japan to strike at Midway and for which he received the Congessional Medal of Honor. He then returned to the European theatre to command the US Fifteenth Air Force and then the North-west Africa Strategic Air Force. In 1944 he took command of the Eighth Air Force for the Allied bombing offensive before moving

with the Eighth to the Pacific. Doolittle was certainly one of the giants of air force command in World War Two, having proved himself as an inspirational leader as well as an efficient organiser and tactician. In 1949 he stated that 'the function of the army and navy in any future war will be to support the air arm'.

Jacques
DORIOT
1898–1945

Even after the Vichy government was forced to move to southern Germany, this French politician remained obstinately pro-Nazi and vehemently opposed the Free French movement led by DE GAULLE. He had earlier formed French volunteer units to fight for the Germans on the Eastern Front.

Air Marshal Sir William Sholto
DOUGLAS
1893–1969

He took over from HUGH DOWDING when the latter was controversially removed from the RAF Fighter Command after the Battle of Britain. The two had seldom seen eye-to-eye when Douglas was having to present the Air Ministry case

Air Marshal Sholto Douglas watching Empire-trained pilots on a Spitfire operational training course. (IWM CH4215)

during Dowding's determined stance to keep his aircraft in Britain in early 1940. Once in control of a now offensive force, Douglas was able to deploy his aircraft across the Channel. From July 1943 he headed RAF Middle East Command and a year later Coastal Command as it geared up to support the D-Day landings.

Sir Hugh
DOWDING
1882–1970

At the outbreak of war he was due for retirement but was kept on to command RAF Fighter Command during its 'finest hour'.

Early in the 1930s he had led RAF research and development towards the building programme which would produce the Spitfire and the Hurricane, and ensure that radar technologies were advanced at best pace. Although he might have expected to become Chief of the Air Staff in 1937, he approached his subsequent appointment as head of Fighter Command with typical single-mindedness, bringing it -to a national defence system based on the single-seater fighter despite theoretical and economic restraints.

When his command was threatened by the reversals of the first year of war, Dowding found himself increasingly unpopular as he insisted on retaining the defensive mission for his fighters rather than send them piecemeal into the skirmishes over mainland Europe. With CHURCHILL and the RAF hierarchy determined to divide up his pilots and aircraft, 'Stuffy' Dowding was on increasingly shaky ground until the Luftwaffe offensives in the late summer of 1940 proved his stand to have been a correct one and saw the men and machines he had so zealously guarded take on and beat the

best of the German fighters in the Battle of Britain.

Such was the animosity felt towards Dowding in the Air Force and political circles that even this greatest of air warfare successes was insufficient to save his career. His 'reward' was removal to posts of low importance and a continued lack of thanks or recognition. There can be little doubt that but for Hugh Dowding's dogged fight to keep his aircraft in Britain, the nation would have lost those battles with the Luftwaffe and the course of the war could have been fundamentally changed. Only since his death has Dowding's value been truly accepted and recorded; his reluctance to employ the 'Big Wing' strategy is now better understood and the plotting and intrigue which worked towards his removal is now fully documented.

Ray, J. *Battle of Britain: New Perspectives* ,1994
Wright, R. *Dowding and the Battle of Britain*, 1969

Sir Hugh Dowding and Sir Trafford Leigh-Mallory at the third Battle of Britain anniversary. (IWM CH11054)

Allan Welsh
DULLES
1893–1969

As Chief of the OSS (Office of Strategic Services) in neutral Switzerland, this experienced diplomat was the motivating force behind the rapid build-up of agents and resistance units across Europe, often in co-ordination with the British SOE network. He started from a position of strength, having extensive knowledge of Europe and its leaders; he had met MUSSOLINI as early as 1932 and HITLER in 1933. Many of his business associates were recruited by Dulles to work for the OSS. He secured the surrender of German forces in Italy in the spring of 1945 and by so doing prevented a bloody, haphazard end to war in that region.

Dulles, A. W. *Conspiracy in Germany.*
– *The Craft of Intelligence*, 1963
– *Germany's Underground*, 1947
Grose, P. *Gentleman Spy (Dulles),* 1994

General Ira
EAKER
1898–1987

To him fell the distinction of leading the first US bombing raid in Europe in August 1942; he remained in the European theatre throughout the war. Commanding the 8th Air Force, Eaker was committed to the strategic bombing tactic and strongly argued his case at the Casablanca Conference. He succeeded ARTHUR TEDDER as Commander of the Mediterranean Area Command where he continued bombing raids into German-held areas and in spring 1944 ordered the air attack on the monastery at Monte Cassino at the request of MARK CLARK, though this did little to break the stalemate there. Later he was Air Commander-in-Chief of Operation 'Dragoon' which saw Allied forces come ashore in southern France.

Anthony
EDEN
1897–1977

Having resigned as Foreign Secretary because of CHAMBERLAIN's appeasement policy, he returned to office in CHURCHILL's administration and remained there for most of the war.

Churchill quickly reinstated his friend in the Foreign Office and

General Ira Eaker at the door of a B-17 Flying Fortress. (IWM HU36703)

Anthony Eden with Canadian Prime Minister, Mackenzie King , at a meeting in Ottawa. IWM (CAN2405)

used him extensively on overseas missions to various Allied seats of power. His reservations about STALIN and the Soviet hierarchy delayed Churchill making any offers on Eastern Europe. but he could not prevent the formation of the Morgenthau Plan in September 1944.

He had always been seen by Churchill as his natural successor and it can only be wondered which of his many talents Eden could have brought to the first post-war government had his party been elected. Eden, A. *Memoirs*, 1962

Lieutenant-General Robert Lawrence
EICHELBERGER
1886–1961

Quoted as having said, 'surprises are commonplace in war – and reconsidered opinions too', he made sure that views as to his ability as a war commander remained unaltered. He commanded US I Corps which held back the Japanese advance through New Guinea; his significant victory at Buna in January 1943 against the odds and in terrible conditions was strategically important. By the autumn of 1944 he was commanding US Eighth Army in its successful invasion of the Philippines before going on to the occupation of Japan.

Adolf
EICHMANN
1906–1962

As a child he had been moody and withdrawn, and was referred to as 'the little Jew'. He may have had Jewish relatives, but he was fanatical in his anti-Semitic crusade. An SS officer, he was assigned the responsibility of implementing the extermination policy agreed by the Wannsee Conference early in 1942. Once BORMANN had signed the decree that removed the right of appeal to Jews, he began their mass transportation to the camps and gas chambers.

As a disciple of Nazi doctrine from its early days, he had sought employment in HIMMLER's Gestapo information centre; he was briefly in Palestine in 1937 to liaise with Arab leaders before the British were alerted to his presence and ordered him to leave. After his return he was promoted rapidly through the SS ranks eventually to head Subsection IV-B4 of the Reich Central Security Office. He was responsible for selecting the gas chamber as the principal means of murder and was able to report to Himmler in August 1944 that four million Jews had been killed in the camps and half as many again hunted down outside.

He was captured and imprisoned at the end of the war but escaped to South America where the Israeli Secret Service eventually tracked him down in 1960. He was smuggled back to Jerusalem where he was very publicly tried, found guilty and hanged on 31 May 1962.
Aharoni, Z. *Operation Eichmann*, 1997

General Dwight David
EISENHOWER
1890–1969

Of humble Texan origins, the 34th US President undoubtedly benefited in this highest office from his military career which began at West Point and ended with the glory of Allied victory in World War Two. Although without battlefield experience, his ability to direct staff, negotiate and adjudicate, and provide a focal point – and a listening ear – for disparate views, marked him as a man of special quality.

At military college he was an excellent student, successful at sports and popular with his peers. A training officer during World War One, in the inter-war years he served as a staff officer under MACARTHUR and then caught the eye of the Chief of Staff, GENERAL MARSHALL, who took him to Washington to head the Operations Branch.

The theorising of discussion groups in the capital soon gave way for the realities of an active war theatre when he was sent to London to lead the American staff there and was quickly given command of Operation 'Torch', the landings in North Africa. There he came into his own; his deftness in co-ordinating contrary views, diplomacy in steering conflicting endeavours on to a single course, and calm, clear judgement when required, meant a successful campaign just when multi-national Allied effort needed it.

Now he was the natural choice to become Supreme Allied Commander for the entire European theatre and in this role he quickly had to apply his management skills to the rift which was developing between his chief commanders. With MONTGOMERY and PATTON each wanting to lead a narrow front advance against the retreating German forces, and both of them promising prompt results given extra supplies, Eisenhower chose a steadier, broader strategy which he hoped would see both men advancing at a more modest pace – and in harmony.

Whatever a different policy might have achieved, Eisenhower's decision saw the British and American forces advance to victory in true alliance, with support from both national 'home fronts' being undiluted and demonstrable. At this point a more adventurous, less equable decision

Eisenhower watches Montgomery in full flow at a meeting in March 1945, shortly after Allied troops had crossed the Rhine. (IWM EA59461)

General Eisenhower with Lieutenant General Bucknell, General Dempsey and Air Chief Marshal Tedder. (IWM5571)

could have brought much disruption and consternation, at least to one of the major Allied forces, and those who claim that a narrow, short and sharp advance would have ended the war more speedily should take this into account.

Eisenhower allowed Montgomery his airborne operation 'Market Garden', without incurring too much ill-feeling among the Americans to the south; and he later gave him charge of the counter-offensive in Belgium in December 1944.

His successful prosecution of the Allied advance to Berlin won him the admiration of military and civilians alike. He was a firm but democratic man-manager whose admirable equanimity hid a deep resolve to achieve the desired result; he knew his commanders well, listened to them carefully, pushed them hard and got the very best out of them.

Ambrose, S. *Eisenhower the Soldier*, 1984
– *The Supreme Commander*, 1970
Chandler, A., and Ambrose, S. *The Papers of Dwight David Eisenhower*, 1970
Davis, K. *Eisenhower: American Hero*, 1969
Eisenhower, D. *At Ease*, 1967
– *Crusade in Europe*, 1948

Air Chief Marshal Sir Basil
EMBRY
1902–1977

Commanding a bomber squadron early in the war, he received awards for his performance in the actions in Norway and against the German western offensives. He was shot down over France in May 1940 but escaped to return to active service with night-fighters in the Battle of Britain. In the summer of 1943 he moved to command No 2 Bomber Group but still flew missions himself including raids over Holland and Denmark.

Commander Eugene
ESMONDE
1909–1942

He is notable for having led two great naval air operations during the war, in the second of which he lost his life. In May 1941 he led a flight of Fairey Swordfish from HMS *Victorious* to attack the *Bismarck*, and in February 1942 he led an unsuccessful and, for him, fatal attack against the 'Channel Dash' of the warships, *Scharnhorst*, *Gneisenau* and *Prinz Eugen*.

Herbert V.
EVATT
1894–1965

Attorney-General in CURTIN's government, he represented Australia in the British War Cabinet and became highly regarded for his debating acumen and foresight in planning. This ability eroded the early reluctance on the part of some American officials who were inclined to be more respectful towards the London political leaders than to those 'from British colonies'. Evatt went on to help produce the Charter of the United Nations and from 1948 was President of the UN for a short time.

General Alexander von
FALKENHAUSEN
1878–1966

This infantry expert counted ROMMEL among his students during the inter-war years. His wartime commands were chiefly in Belgium and France, but further advancement was no doubt held back by his unconvincing commitment to the Nazi cause. And while he was known to have sympathy for the Resistance he was never trusted by them. After the bomb plot of July 1944 he was arrested by the Gestapo and sent to Dachau concentration camp. After the liberation of the camp the US forces handed him over to the Belgians who tried, convicted and imprisoned him.

Colonel General Nikolaus von
FALKENHORST
1885–1968

Chosen at the last minute to command the invasion of Norway, he achieved his task with a very small force. He remained in Norway for most of the war where his oppressive attitude caused great ill feeling. In 1945 he was sentenced to death, but it was waived, he was released in 1953.

Nancy
FIOCCA
1916–

Nancy Wake was an Australian writer whose marriage to Henri Fiocca found her in Paris at the time of the German invasion. She fled south and began working for ALBERT GUERISSE in assisting the escape and evasion of British servicemen from the Mediterranean coast. She eventually made her way to London where she was trained by BUCKMASTER and his SOE team. Early in 1944 she was parachuted back into France where she came to manage a large group of Resistance fighters, showing great resilience in all her work and proving an outstanding leader of these teams.

Rear-Admiral Aubrey
FITCH
1883–1978

This commander of Task Force 11 at the Battle of the Coral Sea was later an effective deployer of new tactics and strategies, particularly in the Solomons theatre, where he helped to evolve new methods of assault, invasion and the use of captured facilities.

Vice Admiral Frank
FLETCHER
1885–1973

At the Battle of the Coral Sea he achieved mixed success when his aircraft strike force sank the carrier *Shoho* but he lost the carrier *Lexington* and his own flagship, *Yorktown*, was badly damaged. He might have hoped for better fortunes at Midway, having removed the two Japanese carriers, but his ship was torpedoed and sank on 7 June. Two months later his cautious deployment off Guadalcanal meant that his force of three carriers was not used in support of the ground operation. That same month, in the Battle of the Eastern Solomons, his carrier group disposed of the carrier *Ryujo* and more than 90 Japanese aircraft.

James
FORRESTAL
1892–1949

A great motivator and pursuer of causes, he was responsible for the US Navy's securing funds for the massive building programme required to give the Allies control of the seas; he was also instrumental in setting up the vital Lend-Lease deal with Britain. He was critical of the hurried reductions in forces at the end of the war.

Lieutenant-General Charles
FOULKES
1903–1968

Although he began his war as a brigade major, he was commanding Canadian 2nd Division by the time of the Normandy landings. He then led Canadian I Corps in Italy and in north-west Europe where he received the German surrender in the Netherlands. He returned to Canada as Chief of Staff in May 1945.

Francisco
FRANCO
1892–1975

When he became regent and head of state in 1939 it was feared that his indebtedness to HITLER for his assistance in the Spanish Civil War would cause him to ally his country with the Axis powers. He did this, but his involvement was a passive one; he rejected the Führer's advances with a resolve few other national leaders showed, thus depriving the German navy of the freedom of the waters off northern Spain and on his Mediterranean coast, which left them vulnerable to Allied activity.

Anne
FRANK
1929–1945

Stories such as that of this young girl are thrown up by all wars, especially when countries have been invaded and inhabitants violated. *The Diary of Anne Frank* has been published in many languages and been made into a stage play, so bringing to millions a realisation of the terrors of living under German occupation and being of Jewish origin; it has recently been re-released in English. The Frank family feared the worst when the Germans overran Amsterdam, but for more than two years they hid from the enemy in the attic above the father's office. Anne and her sister Margot died in Belsen after they were discovered in 1944; only her father survived the war and it was he who found the diary. It is a work of incredible depth and emotion for one so young and has earned its place among classic literature on its own merit.

Frank, A. *Anne Frank: The Diary of a Young Girl*, 1952

Hans
FRANK
1900–1946

The sector of Poland that was not handed over to the USSR after the German invasion was governed by Hans Frank, whose wretched treatment of the nationals was implemented by the SS and others from the occupying forces. He was instrumental in hunting out Jews

Admiral Fraser (left) at the time of the Normandy landings. (IWM A24860)

and sending them to camps such as Auschwitz and Treblinka; he also looted art treasures and enjoyed a lavish lifestyle amid the poverty in Poland at the time. When the Russians invaded in 1944 he tried to take his own life but was eventually captured and tried at Nuremberg where he announced his conversion to Catholicism and showed some remorse (including an attack on HITLER). He was hanged in October 1946.

Piotrowski, S. *Hans Frank's Diary*, 1961

Karl Hermann FRANK
1898–1946

After Germany's invasion of Czechoslovakia, Frank was made Secretary of State for Bohemia and Moravia and assisted in many of HEYDRICH's wretched crimes against dissidents. When Heydrich was assassinated Frank led the reprisal atrocity against the village of Lidice, believing its inhabitants to have harboured the assassins.

Admiral Sir Bruce FRASER
1888–1981

Commander-in-Chief, British Home Fleet, he directed the action which saw the *Scharnhorst* intercepted and destroyed on 26 December 1943. He was later made Commander-in-Chief, Eastern Fleet, and in September 1945 he was Britain's representative at the signing of the Japanese surrender.

Peter FRASER
1884–1950

When New Zealand prime minister, Michael Savage, fell ill at the outbreak of war, it was his deputy, Peter Fraser, a Scottish emigrant, who led the country in support of

New Zealander General Bernard Freyberg gains a better perspective during the Italian campaign. (IWM NA9245)

the Allied war plan. He succeeded Savage on his death in March 1940 and played a full role in war cabinet meetings and the regular liaison with other Allied leaders. He occasionally baulked at requests for New Zealand troops, but was highly regarded by CHURCHILL.

General Sir Bernard Cyril FREYBERG
1889–1963

Freyberg and the New Zealand troops he commanded so capably were unsung heroes of the war, with battle honours from delaying actions against the Germans in Greece and successful battles against STUDENT's paratroopers on Crete to many feats in the desert at Tobruk and Second Alamein, before moving on to Italy and the awesome conflict at Monte Cassino. His insistence on the bombing of the latter strategic position probably delayed rather than hastened its taking. He was at the head of his men when they entered Trieste in May 1945 at the completion of, for him, a long war.

Wilhelm FRICK
1877–1946

A close confidant of HITLER's during his early quest for power, he had limited influence during the war years. He drafted much of the legislation that implemented the Nazi doctrine, but HIMMLER and other more dominant wartime leaders kept him in posts of lesser status. The Nuremberg trial found him guilty of administering anti-Jewish laws and other offences and he was hanged on 16 October 1946.

Admiral Hans von FRIEDEBURG
1895–1945

He was one of the German party on Luneburg Heath on 3 May 1945 at the signing of the surrender, having been appointed Commander-in-Chief of the German Navy just eight days previously when DÖNITZ was made Chancellor by HITLER's political testament. He committed suicide later that month.

Colonel William Frederick FRIEDMAN
1891–1969

A cryptanalyst in the War Department in Washington, he headed the Special Intelligence Service team which broke the Japanese diplomatic code (Code Purple) in 1940. His continuing work with Japanese ciphers did much to keep the US commanders in the Pacific one jump ahead of the Japanese.

General Werner von FRITSCH
1880–1939

The dismissal of BLOMBERG in February 1938 should have brought von Fritsch, then Commander-in-Chief of the Army, the post of Minister of War, but his background of silent disenchantment with HITLER's militarism counted against him and charges of homosexuality were brought against him by a Gestapo-inspired plot. His subsequent resignation removed his dissenting voice from Army High Command and enabled Hitler to bring an abrupt halt to the advancement of his and several other careers. Although the accusations were soon proved to be false, Fritsch remained in modest commands until he was killed in combat near Warsaw on 22 September 1939.

General Friedrich FROMM
1888–1945

As Commander of the Reserve Army, Fromm became aware of the plan of its Chief of Staff, VON STAUFFENBERG, and BECK, to assassinate HITLER. Without fully signing up to the plot, Fromm did nothing to prevent its happening and only when he heard of the

Wilhelm Frick in Nazi Party uniform. (IWM HU7219)

General Werner von Fritsch whose dismissal, with Blomberg, brought about wholesale changes in the German military hierarchy. He was accused of homosexuality by a bribed witness put up by the Gestapo. (IWM MH13142)

John F. C. FULLER
1878–1964

Although not an active personality in World War Two, this British general and military theorist, veteran of the Boer War and a staff officer for much of World War One, certainly had an influence over the strategies and tactics employed because many of those planning the Allied efforts, and some of the German military hierarchy, had learnt much from his textbooks. He had formulated his battlefield practices in France at the end of the 1914–18 war, and the impact of his writing is demonstrated by the fact that GUDERIAN was one of his most enthusiastic readers.

Graf Clemens von GALEN
1878–1946

Archbishop of Münster, he was an outspoken critic of the inhumanities of the Nazis, though he did not rail against the military expansionism of HITLER to the same degree. He not only preached his condemnation of the racism, cruelty and murder of the regime, but published a paper arguing against the theories that ROSENBERG propagated in articles, pamphlets and books. It seems that Galen's brave stand caused a rethink on the euthanasia programme and his status in the

Führer's survival moments before von Stauffenberg arrived to report to him of the success of the bombing, did he demonstrate his turncoat tendencies. He was arrested by the conspirators but loyalists quickly reversed the situation and enabled Fromm to show his true colours with the summary execution of von Stauffenberg and three others before persuading Beck to commit suicide. Fromm himself was arrested by the Gestapo and tried before a People's Court. He was hanged at Brandenburg on 19 March 1945

Commander Mitsuo FUCHIDA
1902–1976

Forever remembered as the pilot who led the air attack on Pearl Harbor, he was also closely involved with the strategic planning for the Battle of Midway, though illness prevented him from taking part. After the war Fuchida became a Christian and spent much time in North America before becoming a US citizen in 1966.

Fuchida, M. *Midway: The Battle that Doomed Japan*, 1955

Church appears to have kept him immune from arrest, although he was sent to Sachsenhausen briefly as part of the round-up of suspects after the bomb plot of 1944. He was released before the Allies reached Münster and was there to welcome the liberating forces.

Lieutenant-General Adolf GALLAND
1912–1996

Having honed his flying skill in the Spanish Civil War and then in the 1939 Polish Campaign, he came to the fore as a consequence of his many dogfights when leading III Gruppe of Jagdgeschwader 27 against RAF fighters during the Battle of Britain. In November 1941 he succeeded MOLDERS as Commander of the Fighter Arm and led fighter operations on the Eastern Front, the Balkans and the Mediterranean, but regular arguments over the quality and quantity of available aircraft saw him fall from favour and be dismissed early in 1945. His final posting was to the command of a jet fighter squadron and it was during operations with them that he was shot down by a P–51 Mustang, captured and taken to England. He was credited with 104 aerial victories. After his release he worked with the Argentinian Air Force before returning to Germany to work in commercial aviation.

Galland, A. *The First and the Last*, 1955

General Maurice Gustave GAMELIN
1872–1958

Although he had been Commander-in-Chief of the French Army during the inter-war years, he was unable, as Commander of Land Forces in 1940, to co-ordinate the defence of France, and the forces at his disposal, with the necessary resolve and energy. He was removed from office shortly after the German invasion.

Mohandas Karamchand GANDHI
1869–1948

Realising Britain's need for support in the war, he urged her representatives to link this to a quicker move to autonomy and independence for India. Failure in this led to violence which the Mahatma was unable to prevent, and to his arrest.

Reinhard GEHLEN
1902–1979

His early military career was as an artillery staff officer in France and then on the Eastern Front. It was in the latter theatre that he developed his expertise in intelligence matters and in December 1944 was given senior rank to enable him to report directly to the top commanders.

At this stage of the war HITLER should have used all the battlefield

Adolf Galland honed his flying talent during the Spanish Civil War.
(IWM MH6038)

intelligence at his disposal but too often he could not bring himself to believe the information, since much of it was bad news, and he dismissed the valuable data out of hand. By April 1945 the Führer had tired of the constant warnings from Gehlen and his staff and dismissed him.

Unknown to his superiors Gehlen had been privately storing many files and much photographic material. When he surrendered to the American forces with his staff on 22 May he could offer intelli-gence riches beyond their dreams and it was not surprising that he was whisked away to the US. He later returned to Germany to re-activate an intelligence organisation in Soviet-occupied territories.
Gehlen, R. *The Service*, 1972

Major General Roy
GEIGER
1885–1947

This hard-fighting Marine com-mander was prominent in the actions at Guadalcanal, Bougainville, Guam and Okinawa. At the latter he became the first Marine general to command an army in the field

Donald S.
GENTILE
1920–1951

Having been rejected by the US Army Air Corps, he became one of America's air aces of World War Two. After serving with No 71 (Eagle) Squadron, RAF, he was employed on training duties before transferring to No 133 Squadron which was to become the 336th Squadron, USAAF, flying Thun-derbolts and Mustangs. With his wingman, John Godfrey, he was soon terrorising Luftwaffe pilots with his outstanding flying skill and bravery. By the end of the war he had chalked up 36 victories; he lost his life on a post-war training flight.

King
GEORGE II of Greece
1890–1947

After his forces had pushed the Ital-ians back into Albania, the short-lived peace was brought to an end by the German invasion. He went to London where he set up a govern-ment-in-exile and kept in commu-nication with his homeland. In the spring of 1943 he moved his organi-sation to Cairo. At the end of the war it was his Prime Minister, George Papandreou, who first took control of Greece.

King
GEORGE VI of Great Britain
1895–1952

Rejecting the proposal that they should remove to Canada for the duration of the war, King George and Queen Elizabeth chose to remain in Britain, staying in Lon-don during the constant air raids,

Mahatma Gandhi with Britain's Secretary of State for India, Lord Pethwick-Lawrence. (IWM IND5083)

King George VI in Malta, being shown bomb damage by the parish priest of Sengles. (IWM NA3742)

visiting bomb-shattered towns and cities and paying morale-boosting visits to factories, farms and Home Front forces. Although he had to be dissuaded from getting as close a view of the front lines as he wished, the King survived bombs that exploded a matter of yards from Buckingham Palace. His people admired the courage that overcame his natural shyness and were inspired by him. His intimate support for CHURCHILL undoubtedly gave the latter strength in his negotiations with military and political leaders at home and abroad.

Devere-Summers, A. *War and the Royal Houses of Europe*, 1996

General Joseph GEORGES

1875–1951

Neither he nor GAMELIN, his superior, seemed the right men to command the forces set to repel the German advances. In May 1940 he had many French troops and the British Expeditionary Force at his

King George VI presenting an award to a Canadian major-general. (IWM B5617)

gators and bomb-aimers eventually achieved their goal. The 'dambusters raid' entered British folklore but also marked an advance in air bombing techniques. Gibson was awarded the Victoria Cross; he was killed on a mission over Holland in September 1944.

General Sir George
GIFFARD
1886–1964

An Africa and Middle East specialist, he was made Commander of the Eastern Army in India at a time when it was preparing for the offensives in Burma. From August 1943 he was given charge of all forces destined for that theatre when he was made Commander-in-Chief, South-East Asia Command. Inheriting a difficult task, Giffard found himself in accord with GENERAL SLIM but less comfortable with JOE STILWELL; many were surprised when he was replaced by OLIVER LEESE at the end of 1944 and after the desperate battles at Imphal and Kohima.

General Henri
GIRAUD
1879–1949

His chequered war years began with the annihilation of his Seventh Army by the invading German forces in the spring of 1940. He was taken captive on 19 May and imprisoned, but escaped two years later and made his way down to Vichy France. Now he was seen by the US as a potential representative of his country and was smuggled out of France and taken to Gibraltar just ahead of the 'Torch' landings in North Africa. After the death of DARLAN, Giraud was appointed High Commissioner of French North and West Africa but there now began a power struggle between DE GAULLE, popular with

disposal but remained cautious in the face of the German onslaught. At PÉTAIN's trial after the war, Georges maintained that he believed France could have fought on.

Vice Admiral Robert Lee
GHORMLEY
1883–1958

This US officer worked with the Royal Navy planners in London until the spring 1942 when he was sent to command the US naval forces in the South Pacific. He was ordered to attack Guadalcanal and Tulagi simultaneously in August, a tall order for a force which was under-trained and poorly equipped; the operation was aptly named 'Shoestring'. Ghormley's decision

to release FLETCHER's carriers after the landing saw the disastrous Battle of Savo Island and the loss of valuable cruisers. This, and his negativity throughout the mission, brought his replacement by HALSEY.

Wing Commander Guy
GIBSON
1918–1944

A nation at war needs its heroes and in Guy Gibson the British found a charismatic and brave airman they could acclaim. In May 1943 he was given command of 617 Squadron which had been created to drop the BARNES WALLIS-designed 'bouncing bomb' on dams in Germany. The targets presented immense difficulties, but Gibson's pilots, navi-

his countrymen but not with the Americans, and Giraud, unable to influence his people but more malleable for the Allies. The two men were forced to become Joint Presidents of the Committee of National Liberation in June 1943, but the personality and drive of de Gaulle held sway and Giraud faded from the scene.

Dr Joseph
GOEBBELS
1897–1945

From humble beginnings, he went on to secure a university education and developed a keen intellect, but was unable to rid himself of the anguish brought about by a crippled foot and permanent limp, which not only prevented him from serving in the armed forces but also set him incongruously distant from the perfect Aryan race he came to espouse. Although not initially a supporter of HITLER, he became a convert in 1926 and thereafter was one of the Führer's closest allies.

Charged with maintaining morale on the Home Front Goebbels, as much as anyone, was unsettled by changing fortunes after the Battle of Britain and the Russian Front reversals. In a last-ditch effort to stave off defeat, Hitler authorised him to use every means he chose to secure human, monetary and mechanical reserves. With the cause lost, Goebbels witnessed Hitler's marriage in the Berlin bunker, was nearby at the Führer's suicide and, on 1 May 1945, supervised the death by poisoning of his children, wife and himself.

It will forever be argued as to whether Goebbels was another Hitler stooge or a sharp-minded, able man who, in different circumstances, could have been a leader of considerable stature.

Joachimsthaler, A. *The Last Days of Hitler*, 1996
Manvell, R., and Frankel, H. *Doctor Goebbels: His Life and Death*, 1960
Reiss, K. *Joseph Goebbels: A Biography*, 1948
Semmler, R. *Goebbels: The Man Next to Hitler*, 1947
Taylor, F. *The Goebbels Diaries 1939–41*, 1982

Goebbels meets Alessandro Pavolini, the Italian Minister of Culture, in June 1941. (IWM MH20031)

Reichsmarshall Hermann
GÖRING
1893–1946

Like other infantrymen in World War One, he transferred to the Air Force; in his case, to become an ace with 22 'kills' to his name.

He was an early recruit to the Nazi Party, much to HITLER'S delight because he brought with him his status as a national flying hero. He was injured in the Munich Putsch but managed to escape, and after the 1926 amnesty he was able to return to Hitler's side.

Throughout the 1930s he acquired ever higher rank and greater wealth to the point where, at the outbreak of war, he was Chairman of the Reichs Council for National Defence and designated as Hitler's successor. Although not convinced by his leader's rampant expansionism, the ex-fighter ace commanded the Luftwaffe in the Blitzkrieg attacks on Poland and France and was able to boast a perfect performance.

The evacuation of the British Expeditionary Force from Dunkirk and the reversals in the Battle of Britain dented Göring's reputation of invincibility, and his failure to keep PAULUS supplied at Stalingrad harmed him further. Thereafter, seeing Hitler's loss of confidence in him, Göring dropped out of the limelight, finding himself overtaken by more able and determined associates.

His late attempt to reinstate his standing as successor infuriated the Führer who ordered his arrest. Shortly afterwards he was captured by the Americans and brought to trial at Nuremberg. On 15 October 1945, just hours before his death sentence was to be carried out, he committed suicide by swallowing a capsule of poison which he had kept hidden or which had been smuggled to him.

Hermann Göring seen with Werner Mölders in France in 1940. (IWM HU4481)

Bewley, C. *Hermann Göring and the Third Reich*, 1962
Frischauer, W. *The Rise and Fall of Hermann Göring*, 1951
Gritzbach, E . *Hermann Göring: The Man and his Work*, 1939
Lee, A. *Göring: Air Leader*, 1946
Overy, R. J. *Göring: The Iron Man*, 1984

Chief Marshal Aleksandr
GOLOVANOV
1903–1987

He commanded the 81st Long Range Division in the defence of Moscow in 1941, but thereafter was put in control of the Soviet Air Force for long-range operations and, working closely with ZHUKOV, planned the multi-force movements for the Belorussian campaign in 1944.

Field Marshal John
GORT
1886–1946

The tactical awareness shown by John Gort, albeit involving the ignoring of instructions from his seniors, enabled the evacuation of Dunkirk to be achieved at the last moment. Ordered to remain in position, he chose an opportune time to withdraw to prevent further futile loss. He had become Commander-in-Chief of the British Expeditionary Force in 1939 and after Dunkirk was placed in non-combatant posts as Governor of Gibraltar, Governor-General of Malta and finally High Commissioner in Palestine. In Malta this rather dry, unadventurous man showed his mettle when master-minding with great resolve the defence of this strategically vital island.

Marshal Leonid
GOVOROV
1897–1955

After serving on Russia's Western Front and witnessing the débâcle caused by the German advance, he was able to help reverse the trend when given control of Fifth Army at Moscow and savoured the 1941 counter-strike which saved the city. At Leningrad he broke the siege by forcing a route from Ladoga to Schlusselburg. His units blitzed across to the Baltic and linked up with CHERNYAKHOVSKY to isolate German Army Group North in East Prussia.

Count Dino
GRANDI
1895–1988

This former foreign minister and ambassador to London was too much the diplomat to be able to swallow MUSSOLINI's dictatorial policies and he became disillusioned with the Duce in about 1941.

He began to plot his downfall and, after being dismissed from office in February 1943, accelerated his efforts. In July he presented the motion to the Grand Council which brought matters to a head and caused Mussolini's arrest. Grandi left the country for Brazil, but returned home in 1973.

Marshal Rodolfo
GRAZIANI
1882–1955

Known as the 'Butcher of the Desert' this Italian marshal did not live up to his record as an achiever in the colonial situation when he was confronted with action on a larger, more complex scale. He left active command in February 1941 but remained a supporter of the Fascist cause.

Group Captain Colin Falkland
GRAY
1914–1995

He and his brother Kenneth were among the many excellent airmen from New Zealand who swelled the ranks of the RAF. Ken was awarded the DFC but died on 1 May 1940 when flying a Whitley bomber to collect his brother and others. Colin flew fighters, first with No 54 Squadron over Europe in 1940 and during the Battle of Britain, then with No 1 Squadron flying Hurricanes and, by the end of 1941, commanding No 616 Squadron. After backroom duties he moved to No 81 Squadron in North Africa and then to command of 322 Wing. He was still flying operational tours by VE-Day and finally clocked-up 633 hours with 27 confirmed victories.

Marshal Andrey A
GRECHKO
1903–1976

Grechko advanced swiftly after graduating from the military academy in 1941. He quickly took charge of a cavalry division and then a corps before being chosen to lead 12th Army in the spring of 1942. He played an important role in the defence of the Transcaucasus and led the liberation of the Taman peninsula.

In 1943 he was at Kiev and was made commander of 1st Army which he took to the Carpathians in 1944 and Mor Ostrava in 1945. He continued to serve in the armed forces long after the end of the war.

General Robert Ritter von
GREIM
1892–1945

He was appointed Chief of Personnel of the Luftwaffe by GÖRING in 1939, but was still leading fighter sorties during the early years of the war. From early in 1943 he commanded air forces on the Eastern Front. He was commanding Luftflotte VI in Munich when, on 24 April 1945, he received a telegram from HITLER recalling him to the Chancellery. He made the trip in an aircraft flown by Hanna Reitsch, by hedge-hopping across enemy territory, though the aircraft was hit by a Russian AA shell and one of his feet was shattered. Lying on a cot in the sugery at Hitler's bunker, he was told that he was to replace the disgraced Göring and was promoted to field marshal, the Führer's last appointment at that level. All present were perplexed by the appointment and also by the fact that three days later Hitler ordered him to return to Luftwaffe HQ. After another dangerous flight from a Berlin in flames, he reached DÖNITZ's HQ but got no further and within the month he had committed suicide.

Joseph Clark
GREW
1880–1965

An American career diplomat, he had held posts in Russia, South America, Egypt and Berlin before being appointed Ambassador to Japan in 1932. Although he had worked hard to smooth relationships between the two countries during the inter-war years, he supported the US sanctions against Japan in 1940 and warned his superiors of the likelihood of a surprise strike against American territory. After the Pearl Harbor attack he was held in Japan until an exchange with Japanese diplomats was arranged after several months.

Major General Oscar
GRISWOLD
1886–1954

As Commander of XIV Corps at Guadalcanal, New Georgia and the Philippines, this American officer was resolute in his pursuit of the strategic aim. While he may have lacked the dynamism seen in other Pacific theatre leaders, his steady completion of each task saw important successes at Luzon in January 1945 and at Manila.

General Leslie
GROVES
1898–1970

As much the 'father' of the atomic bomb as any scientist, Groves, a West Point engineering graduate, was the controller of the Manhattan Project which was to see into existence this ultimate weapon. His commitment to the cause was complete and was the reason for the pace of development and the priority status it achieved. His enthusiasm quelled the fears of the scientists

and annulled many of the administrative blocks which their research put in his way.

Major-General Colin
GUBBINS
1896–1976

A veteran of World War One and an intelligence officer in Britain and India during the inter-war years, he was Chief of Staff of the military mission in Poland in the summer of 1939. After some work with early Commando units in Norway, he joined the Special Operations Executive in November 1940 and immediately had an impact on its

increasing activities; from September 1943 he was Executive Director. An inspirational man, he trusted his own judgement of people when selecting agents and talking to representatives of governments-in-exile in London. Fundamentally, he understood what he was asking his operatives to do and was convinced of the results they could achieve.

General Heinz Wilhelm
GUDERIAN
1888–1954

Not only was he a principal leader in the armoured drive through the Low Countries and into France in

A cheerful Heinz Guderian, battle plans in hand. (IWM MH9404)

1940, but it was his own tactical theories that were being put into practice. After service in World War One his inter-war years had been spent setting out the future of armoured land warfare as he saw it and his writings on the subject remain in print and are studied to this day.

Although he was a quiet supporter of National Socialism and undoubtedly nationalist, Guderian was too much of an individualist to avoid run-ins with superiors including FIELD MARSHAL VON KLUGE and HITLER himself. This rebellious nature saw him lose command from December 1941 until February 1943 when Hitler charged him with pushing forward the new programme of land armour development. In this position his natural drive brought some progress but the construction of submarines and rockets saw investment drained from new tank construction.

When Hitler made him Chief of Staff of the German Army in the summer of 1944, it was in the hope that the man's enthusiasm would change Germany's fortunes on the Eastern Front, but he again felt the lack of resources despite applying his best efforts to the job. His long-standing relationship with the Führer reached breaking point in March 1945 when he found his leader supporting DÖNITZ's demand for resources ahead of his own.

It should have been of huge benefit to Hitler to have a battlefield theorist of such substance at his disposal, but he was under-used and misused. Having practically demonstrated the practical potency of his ideas, he should have been given a freer rein rather than be removed from direct involvement in the fighting for the whole of 1942. His maverick disregard of von Kluge undoubtedly sent warning signals to

the Führer, but it is difficult to imagine that his talents would not have been better used by a more reasonable regime.

His classic 1937 text, *Achtung–Panzer!* (recently translated into English) remains as Guderian's legacy together with *Panzer Leader* which he wrote after the war. That these books are still studied in defence colleges around the world is testament to his deep appreciation of mechanised warfare strategy. His character is well summed up by a statement attributed to him that 'When the situation is obscure, attack.' In *Panzer Leader* he claims, 'It is not the habit of politicians to appear in conspicuous places when the bullets begin to fly.'
Guderian, H. *Achtung–Panzer!*, 1994
– *Panzer Leader*, 1952

Albert
GUERISSE
1911–1989

When he fled to Britain after the Dunkirk evacuation, this Belgian doctor assumed a new identity – Pat O'Leary, a French Canadian. He joined the Royal Navy but was left behind during an SOE operation in southern France and was captured. Escaping, he was resourceful enough to link up with Ian Garrow's organisation which was concerned with sheltering and returning stray British personnel left in France after the BEF's departure. When this team lost its leader, Guerisse assumed control and was instrumental in returning many hundreds of Allied troops to Britain. He was betrayed in the spring of 1943 and was imprisoned at Dachau where he remained until that camp was liberated. A determined, action-orientated man, Guerisse was awarded the George Cross.

King
HAAKON VII of Norway
1872–1957

Throughout the war Norway's king remained staunchly anti-Nazi and led the resistance from a London base. From there he made broadcasts and saw to it that the true state of the war was made known to his subjects. He returned to Norway in June 1945.

Emil
HACHA
1872–1945

He succeeded the Czech PRESIDENT BENES when the latter resigned after the Munich Agreement. He had no political experience or acumen and was unable to maintain his independence when faced with pressure from HITLER. From March 1939 he lost all power and VON NEURATH assumed administrative control of Czechoslovakia.

Emperor
HAILE SELASSIE
1891–1976

The Italians drove him out of Ethiopia in 1936, shortly after he had been crowned. From Britain he planned his return and by 1940 was leading forces back on to home soil. With the support of CUNNINGHAM and Platt he had reclaimed the

Haile Selassie in conversation with President Roosevelt. (IWM NYF58500)

country by the end of 1941 and shortly afterwards declared independence. A wiry little man, he was a respected national leader who developed his country.

General Franz
HALDER
1884–1971

Replacing BECK as Chief of the General Staff in 1938, he was the skilled strategist and planner who could have been much more use to HITLER had his views, too often too moderate for his leader, been listened to. He was instrumental in the successful Blitzkrieg campaigns to the east and west, but remained concerned at Hitler's blind desire for more and quicker expansion.

General Franz Halder, a conspirator against Hitler. (IWM MH10933)

When VON BRAUCHITSCH was removed, Hitler's increasing role in all military direction reduced Halder's role and he was eventually replaced by ZEITZLER in September 1942. Although arrested after the bomb plot of 1944 and sent to Dachau, he survived to contribute significantly to the Nuremberg trials.

Earl of
HALIFAX
1881–1959

A dedicated appeaser, he was a member of Britain's war cabinet throughout the war, and at one point had been expected to succeed CHAMBERLAIN as prime minister. His support for the appeasement policy meant that he was 'tarred' by its failure and he had to content himself with remaining Foreign Secretary before becoming Britain's Ambassador to the USA, a post in which he proved an excellent organiser and supporter of Allied co-operation.

Vice Admiral William
HALSEY
1882–1959

'Bull' Halsey was a charismatic, sparky commander who embraced the values of naval aviation in time to use it with skill and efficiency in the Pacific Theatre. Where SPRUANCE was reserved, Halsey was all-action; each achieved much in their own ways.

NIMITZ charged Halsey with creating some momentum in the stagnating Solomons campaign but early reversals did not augur well. He sought to use every technical advantage the USA could claim over their Japanese opposition and began to turn the tide, first with successes at Guadalcanal on 12/13 November 1942 and then operating by night to rupture the Japanese supply line.

His proposal to by-pass Japanese troops and head for more important targets, rather than fight for every island, was implemented and undoubtedly saved time and lives, but initially he was outmanoeuvred by Admirals OZAWA and KURITA at the Battle of Leyte Gulf and only the presence of KINKAID's 7th Fleet saved the day. But Halsey raced after Ozawa's carriers and sank or damaged all of them. He had been misled by Japanese decoy runs but came out on top.

William Averell
HARRIMAN
1891–1986

From the ranks of high business, he emerged to play an important role

Vice Admiral 'Bull' Halsey in November 1943. (IWM EN11611)

as a roving diplomat/negotiator. First, in March 1941, he began the discussions which led to the Lend-Lease agreement between the USA and Britain and then, in the same year and after HITLER's invasion of Russia, he journeyed with BEAVERBROOK to Moscow to establish aid deals and develop relations with STALIN.

From 1943 he became US Ambassador to Moscow and now

had to tread the thin line between ensuring Soviet empathy with the total Allied war effort and showing US support in return, and reporting back to ROOSEVELT on Stalin's moods and political aims. His concerns about the Soviet desire for influence in eastern Europe were confirmed by Stalin's attitude to the Polish unrest and eventual uprising. His best negotiating skills had only marginal effect over Soviet thinking, but it is impossible to gauge how much worse matters would have become had a less able man been in Harriman's post at the time.

Air Chief Marshal Sir Arthur
HARRIS
1892 -1984

'Bomber' Harris will forever be assessed from the divergent points of view of those who believed his 'carpet bombing' policy won the war and others who question its morality. He had seen the ineffectiveness of precision bombing when he was in command of No 5 Bomber Group early in the war and, once appointed head of Bomber Command, he promptly advocated that if slow bomber aircraft were to fly over Germany, to take the war back to the Reich, they must do so in numbers and without the restraint of unnecessary accuracy. The ensuing saturation raids by as many as 1,000 aircraft destroyed a great deal of manufacturing output and dented public morale.

Saward, D. *Bomber Harris*, 1984
Sweetman, J. *The Dambusters Raid*, 1990

Major General Millard
HARMON
1888–1945

This American army officer had a diverse war. From the summer of 1941 until early 1942 he com-

manded 2nd Air Force before being given charge of US non-naval operations in the South Pacific. He led his troops in the bitter fighting for Guadalcanal and by July 1944, after serving as 'Bull' HALSEY's deputy, was Commander of the USAAF for the Pacific Ocean. Towards the end of the war he was presumed dead after his aircraft disappeared during a routine flight.

Admiral Thomas
HART
1877–1971

Before the Pacific War developed he was commanding the small US Asiatic Fleet off the Philippines, and after the Japanese invasion his role was not expanded as might have been expected, principally as a result of MACARTHUR's apparent lack of faith in him. His force was withdrawn from the theatre, and after a brief period commanding the combined Australian, British, Dutch and American unit (ABDA), he retired to Washington where he served on the Naval Board until the end of the war.

Baron Ulrich von
HASSELL
1881–1944

Because of his high profile – he was of aristocratic background and Germany's Ambassador in Rome until 1939 – he was obliged to keep his opposition to HITLER within bounds. He did all he could to encourage resistance to the dictator and associated with BECK and likeminded critics of the war regime. His attempts to broker a peace deal failed to get the support of Army generals who sought that solution, leaving him to encourage while not openly assist the plans for assassinating Hitler. After the failure of the bomb plot in 1944 he was implicated by papers which were recov-

ered; he was tried, found guilty and hanged in public.

Major Kenji
HATANAKA
1912–1945

On 14 August 1945, when the Japanese were about to agree surrender terms and the Emperor had recorded his broadcast to the nation, Hatanaka led a coup which had as its main aim the recovery of the recording and the prevention of the broadcast. He shot his commander, General Mori, for his refusal to co-operate, and recruited members of the Imperial Guards Division to assist in the storming of the Emperor's Palace. He failed in his mission and committed suicide before he could be captured.

Ernst
HEINKEL
1888–1958

This brilliant aircraft designer saw his company expand in tandem with Nazi ambitions and the growth of the Luftwaffe. His He–111 was one of the most effective bombers of the early war years, but later types performed less well. This, and other factors, accelerated his disenchantment with the German leadership and fuelled his criticism of it. GÖRING's response was to remove Heinkel from day-to-day control of his company and ignore his new designs. His opposition to the regime in these later stages of the war saved him from prosecution at its end and he returned to the aviation industry.

Colonel General Gotthard
HEINRICI
1886–1971

Typical of some of the fine strategists who were under-used or discarded too early by HITLER, Heinrici conducted a masterly defence on the Eastern Front, but, unable to meet the Führer's ludicrous demands, fell out of favour and was not given the commands his ability merited. In the autumn of 1943 he resisted all Russian attempts to break his lines at Orsha by rotating his minimal resources to keep them fresh and ensure that they were all battle hardened. When he questioned the validity of Hitler's instructions not to retreat he found himself brusquely transferred to command First Panzer Army in Slovakia. Although he was brought back to head Army Group Vistula, a move probably urged by GUDERIAN, it was too late to turn the campaign.

Sir Neville
HENDERSON
1882–1942

Sadly under-estimating HITLER's ambitions, despite his closeness to the German situation as Britain's Ambassador to Berlin, he encouraged CHAMBERLAIN in the appeasement policy. He socialised with the German hierarchy – he went hunting with GÖRING and others – and appeared to be convinced that British military might was a sufficient threat to prevent Germany making war. Having constantly flouted official Government and Foreign Office advice, he was a reluctant messenger when he handed RIBBENTROP Britain's war ultimatum at 9 a.m. on 3 September 1939.
Henderson, N. *Failure of a Mission*, 1941

Konrad
HENLEIN
1898–1945

He had founded the Sudeten German Party in 1933 and, funded and guided by the National Socialists in Germany, was used to fuel the crises as they developed in Czechoslovakia. When the Czech government moved to accept Sudeten demands and thereby call HITLER's bluff, he moved to Germany to avoid the March 1939 invasion. He was made head of the Civil government of Bohemia and Moravia. In 1945 he was captured by US forces but committed suicide before being brought to trial.

Major Hajo
HERRMANN
1913–1988

With the failure of the German anti-aircraft defences to arrest the Allied bombing raids, Herrmann came up with the simple and daring idea of using day fighters to attack the bomber fleets by the combined light of flares, searchlights and ground fires. The scheme was first tried in July 1943 with immediate success. Allocated new aircraft and new technologies, he continued his experiments and, apart from almost falling foul of his own flak on occasions, his aircraft enjoyed sufficient success as to cause HARRIS to review his bombing strategies.

Rudolf
HESS
1896–1987

According to CHURCHILL nobody knew HITLER better than Hess, or saw him more often in moments

Rudolf Hess making a pre-war speech. (IWM FLM1534)

when he was not playing the leadership role for subordinates or reporters. Nominally HITLER's deputy in the Nazi Party, he had acted as his secretary for the writing of *Mein Kampf*, and had been associated with him for 20 years, and yet Hess sought peace in May 1941 when he undertook a remarkable solo flight in a Bf-110 and crash-landed in Scotland. He wanted to reach the Duke of Hamilton, whom he hoped would persuade CHURCHILL to surrender or, at least, make peace moves. Thwarted in his intent, he was interned until the end of the war and was sentenced to life imprisonment at the Nuremberg trials. He lived out his life in controversial confinement in Berlin's Spandau Prison.

Rear-Admiral Kent
HEWITT
1887–1972

It seemed that whenever a major amphibious landing was required the Americans turned to Hewitt, a master of amphibious strategy and logistic support. In November 1942 he sailed from the East Coast of the USA with 102 vessels to accomplish the North Africa landings where more than 24,000 men under GEORGE PATTON were got ashore in three runs. Next it was 580 ships and command of the Western Naval Task Force for the landing in Sicily in July 1943 where he overcame unfavourable sea conditions to maintain the element of surprise. A few weeks later he controlled the US landings at Salerno where German resistance nearly brought failure. Finally, for the last important amphibious operation in Europe, he organised the landings in the South of France, Operation 'Dragoon'. Hewitt was the complete organiser, a master not only of amphibious strategy but of the logistical support

which such complex operations demanded.

Cresswell, J. *Generals and Admirals: The Story of Amphibious Commanders*, 1952

Polmar, N., and Mersky, P. *Amphibious Warfare: An Illustrated History*, 1988

Obergruppenführer Reinhard
HEYDRICH
1904–1942

This specialist in Nazi terror had enjoyed an upper class upbringing, but by the early 1930s, after his naval career had been cut short by a court-martial involving the daughter of a superior, he was committed to the new order, was rising to the top of the SS organisation and attracting the attention of HEINRICH HIMMLER.

He was responsible for the development of a German espionage system beyond its borders and was, by the time of his appointment as an SS General in 1941, wholly supportive of the anti-Jewish campaign, even though there was a hint that his father had Jewish blood. He became the first administrator of the concentration camps and in January 1942 was selected to put in hand the 'Final Solution' to eliminate Jews from the whole of Europe.

His unbridled cruelty left him with few friends and many enemies. As Reichs Protector of Bohemia–Moravia his systematic murder campaign found much resistance and on 29 May 1942 Jan Kubis and a fellow member of the Czech resistance threw a bomb at Heydrich's car as it travelled through Prague. He was wounded and died a week later. In reprisal the entire population of the village of Lidice was executed or driven out because they had sheltered the assassins.

Heydrich was a complex character in that his love of fine music, no

doubt inherited from his father, seemed incongruous with his contempt for human life and his heartless sadism. Forbidding calmness could be shattered by sudden rages; his demeanour was said to have frightened even HITLER and HIMMLER.

Reichsführer-SS Heinrich
HIMMLER
1900–1945

His ruthless pursuit of power and his complete disregard for those who stood in his way ensured that he rose to become effective deputy to HITLER; he was also head of the SS, with all the influence that implied, and Minister of the Interior.

He chose those who were to be killed or imprisoned in the Blood Purge of 1934 and its success advanced Himmler and his beloved SS. Appointed Reichsführer of the SS and Leader of the Gestapo, he became the drive behind every element of oppression throughout the Reich, including the elimination of any ethnic group that, in his view, posed a threat to Gemany's path to dominance. Rapid expansion of the SS – to a size where it almost matched the Wehrmacht – went unchecked, concentration camps proliferated, extermination programmes abounded, crude medical experiments were authorised on the hapless inmates.

Hitler drew Himmler even closer after the assassination attempt in July 1944 and charged him with defending Berlin as the Allied forces closed in. But for the first time Himmler's bravado wavered and he made a futile approach to the Allies via COUNT BERNADOTTE. A furious Hitler ordered his arrest, but, in a further example of a confidence destroyed, he made a pathetic attempt to escape after the surren-

Heinrich Himmler in dour mood. (IWM PIC65669)

Manvell, R., and Frankel, H. *Heinrich Himmler*, 1962
Whiting, C. *Heinrich Himmler*, 1971

Emperor
HIROHITO of Japan
1901–1987

From a position which saw him revered as a deity by his people but without power in the administration of his country, the Emperor urged caution on TOJO when it seemed certain his actions would bring war. Once his nation was at war, however, he moved even farther into the background despite the fact that his troops still fought with oaths of allegiance to him on their lips. When he saw the war turning against Japan, witnessed the bombing of Tokyo and saw the effects of the two atomic bombs, Hirohito was driven to act. Although as aware as his generals that it could prejudice the very existence of his imperial status, he agreed to surrender and, breaking with tradition, personally addressed the nation. The country, he said, must 'accept the unacceptable, endure the unendurable'. In the event Hirohito remained in his figurehead position because the Allies feared that his removal would cause continuing unrest.

Adolf
HITLER
1889–1945

The majority of people see Hitler as the cause of World War Two; none can deny his status as the leading player and the stimulus in its drama and dreadfulness.

The young Adolf Hitler had been a reluctant soldier in the First World War, having first sought to avoid service in the Austro–Hungarian Army before volunteering for the Bavarian Army. The horror of the conflict and the peace-making tendency of the leadership in

der before being captured by the British at Bremervorde. It was while he was being examined by British medics that he swallowed a cyanide capsule and died immediately.

The timidity of his actions in these last days was to some degree indica-tive of his character. The power he had sought and enjoyed was a drug that changed him into a cruel, callous and vindictive killer; apparently colourless and diffident, his persona was altered by the Nazi regime into a merciless, sadistic tyrant.

Hitler studies a map. Is there a look of resignation on his face? (IWM HU2792)

his adopted Germany – he was Austrian by birth – drove his vulnerable young mind towards nationalism and, in a short time, to the top of the small National Socialist Party.

When this group and their allies saw their ill-conceived coup fail in Munich in November 1923, it could have drained enthusiasm for the cause from some, but Hitler, who used his consequent period of imprisonment to write *Mein Kampf*, quickly set about increasing his power base with determination and ruthlessness. His drive came from his racist beliefs which had, as their ideal, an expansion of national possessions and influence, and a Germany, it must be said, populated by those of selected lineage.

Less than ten years after the coup he won power in a national election and within months had secured parliamentary approval for an increasingly dictatorial style of government. Re-armament was rampant and the grand plan of acquisition of territory by force was fully developed. His manic proposals were endorsed by the populace at large and, more remarkably, by many who could boast a greater intelligence, and deeper experience of government and high office.

By 1938 Hitler was ready to move. He deemed the leading European nations to be ill-prepared for the sacrifices of war, the lesser countries ripe for picking and America too introspective to become involved. He annexed Austria and the Czech Sudetenland before turning on the remainder of Czechoslovakia, but when he looked to move on Poland he found France and Britain uniting against him and guaranteeing Poland's protection; Hitler sought to align himself with the Soviet Union to weaken Polish resolve.

Having pledged their support for Poland, the occupation of that land caused Britain and France to declare war and now Hitler faced larger strategic questions. He backed RAEDER's proposal to invade Norway and so free the sea lanes into the North Atlantic for the Kriegsmarine, and supported VON MANSTEIN'S suggestion to take a southerly route on the drive west. Initially the Blitzkrieg techniques were mightily effective, bringing Belgium and Holland to their knees and tearing into much of France; Hitler basked in the glow of a conqueror supreme. Now, however, indecision allowed the evacuation of the British Expeditionary Force from Dunkirk and, from this point of apparent invincibility, Hitler began to waver.

Nervous about the strength of the Soviet Union and uncertain in his alliance with STALIN, he ordered the build-up to an attack on a new Eastern Front, at first set for late 1940 but delayed until the late spring of 1941. At this point the Germans required three successes: the removal of Britain's defensive strengths, a successful subsequent invasion if need be, and a decisive thrust against Moscow. Thereafter attention could be paid, with Japanese help, to America. None of these objectives would be fully met and America would never become more than an impossible objective.

After early achievements the Eastern Front became a major headache and, like Napoleon before him, he found his resources overstretched as his troops struggled against a Russian winter. His air raids on Britain failed to breach the air defences or break public morale, and now his famed Luftwaffe tasted its first reversals. With the war beginning to turn against him he

lost his confidence and much of his rationality; a decade of unchecked advancement had concealed many weaknesses, he became ever more extreme in his oppression of dissent, more selective in his choice of advisers, and ruthless – and foolish – in discarding those he considered guilty of failure irrespective of their experience or obvious qualities.

Operating ever more as a lone Commander-in-Chief, the dictator set policy by decree despite the lack of battle zone feedback that his attitude created; he tolerated no debate and chose to disregard such information as did reach his desk. Although he showed resolve in the defensive measures he was now obliged to adopt, he put too great a faith in the new weaponry he fondly believed would save the day, in his inherent belief in his cause and naïve conviction that those nations ranged against him could not maintain their unity.

With the Americans now in the war, Axis powers weakening, Allied forces planning landings in German-occupied territory and the loss of personnel and manufacturing power worsening daily, he threw fresh effort into the Eastern Front, only to suffer the wretched defeat at Kursk and find the Red Army now on the offensive. His commanders were at a loss to stem the retreats now forced upon their men and seldom showed the bravado required to act on their own instinct and independent of the ignorantly absurd instructions coming from their leader. DÖNITZ and his U-boats were still hitting at Allied shipping but soon he would be starved of resources and lose his effectiveness.

The ultimate indignity of an assassination attempt by Army officers in July 1944 only served to push Hitler into greater isolation and now, refusing to accept the negative reports which arrived daily and believing his instructions could and should be executed, he placed all his hope in the wonder weapons being developed and in one great counter-offensive which would buy him time to bring them on-stream. He resolved to stop the rampaging Allied advance across France and Belgium in the Ardennes with the Battle of the Bulge. Allied veterans have testified to the tough fight the Germans put up in the Belgian forests but it did not bring the breathing-space he needed. Within four months his eastern and western borders were crossed and the cause was lost. Rejecting the chance of escape taken by some of his senior officers, he remained in Berlin until hand-to-hand fighting could be heard from his underground bunker. Although he had remained in his command post to the end, he did not allow the Allies the glory of his capture, choosing suicide along-side his mistress of long standing and wife of a few hours, EVA BRAUN.

Most historians will refuse to place Hitler among any list of great commanders; he had no battlefield experience at high rank and had never led his men in a battle zone. What cannot be ignored, however, is that this man of modest background and limited natural intellect found the wherewithal to motivate a nation to allow him to take it towards a degree of international domination which still shocks and perplexes us. Many of the men who led his forces and fought in them showed great skill and courage; the success they and their leader enjoyed in the early years of the war caused other men of stature to rise against them and ensure their defeat.

Dietrich, O. *The Hitler I Knew*, 1955

Gilbert, F. *Hitler Directs his War*, 1950

Gosset, P., and Gosset, R. *Adolf Hitler: a Biography*, 1961

Martienssen, A. *Hitler and his Admirals*, 1948

Trevor-Roper, H. R. *Hitler's War Directives*, 1964

Smith, B. F. *Adolf Hitler: his Family, his Childhood and Youth*, 1967

HO CHI MINH
1890–1969

Bearing in mind their experiences in the area during the post-war years, it is ironic that it was America's own Office of Strategic Services (OSS) which pressured CHIANG KAI-SHEK to release Minh so that he could continue to lead the Viet-namese resistance against the Japan-ese. It had been from this position that the Chinese leader had cap-tured and interned him in 1942 after he had worked in China to set up his Communist-inspired movement, the Viet Minh. Furthermore, his group benefited from US supplies of arms and equipment. Rather than take the fight to the Japanese, how-ever, Minh was content to allow their defeat to be brought about by other forces, leaving him and his men strong and well enough armed to march on Hanoi and create the beginnings of the Democratic Republic of Vietnam.

General Courtney Hicks
HODGES
1887–1966

An expert infantryman, this under-rated American commander found himself Chief of Intelligence at the entry of the USA into World War Two. By the end of 1942, however, he was back in army command, lead-ing Tenth Army, before promotion to Lieutenant-General and command of Third Army and subsequent appointment as second-in-command

to OMAR BRADLEY as he prepared for the invasion of Europe in 1944. At this point he took command of US First Army and drove it forward to success in breaching the Siegfried Line, capturing Aachen and playing a major role in the victory in the Battle of the Bulge; his men went on to cap-ture the bridge at Remagen and con-tribute to the encirclement of German forces.

General Erich
HOEPNER
1886–1944

As with GUDERIAN, this tank expert was somewhat misused and undervalued by HITLER who, at the first sign of failure on his part, dismissed him; the General, never a supporter of the Nazi regime, sought revenge by joining STAUF-FENBERG's July plot. Leading Fourth Panzer Group on to Soviet territory in June 1941, he was diverted from the moves on Leningrad to join the drive at Moscow. Here he almost reached his goal before the Soviet counter-attacks stopped him and a severe bout of dysentery removed him from front-line command. As with several colleagues, he was blamed by Hitler for the reversal and removed from his command. At the 1944 plot he was at the Bendlerstrasse War Office ready to direct a military assumption of power, but the failure of the assas-sination attempt brought his arrest, trial and hanging.

General Masaharu
HOMMA (HONMA)
1888–1946

Although not a battle-hardened sol-dier, Homma was chosen to lead the attack on Luzon shortly after the attack on Pearl Harbor and use his experienced force to drive the weak Filipino resistance back towards Manila. After this success he had to choose whether to take Manila, which he knew to have been vacated by MACARTHUR, or seek to cut off the US and Filipino retreat to Bataan. He perhaps should have disobeyed the orders which directed him to Manila and used his Intelligence training to take the second option, but he went for Manila and sacrificed the initiative in so doing.

A second error saw him divide his forces, sending his best units to the Dutch East Indies invasion force and leaving a paltry nine battalions to move on Luzon and the under-estimated enemy forces there. His advance was halted after fierce fighting and he was left with the indignity of being replaced by General YAMASHITA. Eventual victory in April saw the surrender of 75,000 American and Filipino troops and the infamous Bataan Death March for which Homma, still seen as the nominal leader of the invading forces, was held responsible. As a consequence he was tried at the end of the war and executed by firing-squad at Luzon in April 1946.

Lieutenant-General Masaki
HONDA
1889–1964

One of Japan's principal military strategists, he had served as Military Attaché in Paris for three years at the end of World War One. By the time of the Burma Campaign of 1944 he was Commander of 33rd Army and a much admired leader. After failing to take Kohima and Imphal he was urged to hold a position between Lashio and Mandalay early in 1945, but went farther than this to disrupt the US and Chinese forces trying to open up the Burma Road. Now, in a series of dramatic battlefield strategies, Honda came

face to face with SLIM and his Fourteenth Army. Both generals enjoyed some success before the extra manpower of the British held sway leaving Honda to fight a gallant but doomed retreat through southern Burma before surrendering at Rangoon on 25 August.

J. Edgar
HOOVER
1895–1972

By the time the USA entered World War Two, Hoover had been associated with the American justice system for 25 years and had been the Director of the FBI since its founding in 1935. He had reluctantly accepted that British intelligence officers should be allowed to operate in America in a co-operative exercise with his men to track down German agents there.

He was by-passed when it came to the increasing need for collaboration once the Allied structure had become established; ROOSEVELT showed preference for the more accommodating BILL DONOVAN and, since Hoover was not even on speaking terms with Donovan and the President surely knew of this, the ramifications are clear.

When the British identified their double agent Dusko Popov to the FBI in August 1941, Hoover found himself unable to believe the spy's first employers, the Abwehr, had been outwitted by the British and treated Popov as a genuine, German-only employee and thereby failed to utilise the planted information he carried.

At the end of the war Hoover still found himself with limited influence at the White House. TRUMAN took little notice of his anti-Donovan stance and liaison between the civil and military intelligence agencies in America remained lukewarm while Hoover remained FBI Director.

Harry
HOPKINS
1890–1946

A behind-the-scenes master of organisation, administration and forward planning, he was a major player in the ROOSEVELT team. Both as Secretary for Commerce and Chairman of the Munitions Assignment Board as well as other groups directing the war effort, Hopkins enjoyed his President's trust and transferred ably to the work of a roving ambassador/negotiator when, in 1942, he was sent to Britain to line up the Lend-Lease Agreement and to Moscow to chart Russia's war needs. He became Roosevelt's spokesman at many of the Allied Conferences which were to follow. At Casablanca he sought to bring DE GAULLE and GIRAUD together, and at Yalta and Tehran applied himself to the post-war allocation of European territory. Throughout the war he did not enjoy good health but kept at his post and, even on his last mission when working for the new US President, HARRY TRUMAN, he secured an agreement with STALIN on Poland.

Leslie
HORE-BELISHA
1893–1957

As Secretary of State for War in CHAMBERLAIN's cabinet, he was not popular with the military hierarchy of the time and yet had considerable impact on the state of the nation's armed forces at the start of the war. He introduced conscription and expanded the Territorial Army as part of his modernisation plans, and improved static defences around Britain's coastlines, but he was not entirely in accord with the demands of the military professionals who were conscious of his ignorance of war tactics and strategy. He was quick to dismiss contrary views and though much of what he did prepared Britain for war, it can be argued that he ignored the need to re-equip all three forces.

General Sir Brian
HORROCKS
1895–1984

A firm supporter of MONT-GOMERY, whom he praised for his careful planning of the El Alamein battle when ROMMEL was spending time leading his men in fruitless skirmishes, Horrocks was highly regarded by Montgomery and other Allied commanders. He referred to the forward edge of the battlefield as the 'most exclusive club in the world', and this typically eye-catching quotation demonstrates his willingness to join his men at the front when the situation required it. Montgomery charged Horrocks with command of XIII Corps at Alam Halfa and El Alamein and then of XXX Corps for Normandy, the Brussels drive, Operation 'Market Garden' and the advance into Germany.

Horrocks, B. *A Full Life*, 1960

Admiral Mikos
HORTHY
1868–1946

As Regent of Hungary at the outset of the war, he sought to keep his country poised between the main protagonists rather than be overly influenced by either of them. Although nominally siding with the Axis powers because of his fear of the USSR, he was reluctant to commit even the small forces he did, and when HITLER rejected his pleas to remove them from the action his position was further weakened. When Romania collapsed and changed course in

August 1944 he tried to gain favour with the Allies, but Hitler sent SKORZENY to kidnap his son and take the Budapest citadel. Now Horthy surrendered, abdicated and was taken to Germany where he was held until May 1945. By backing the losing side in the war, Horthy unwittingly consigned Hungary to a Communist surge to power.

Admiral Sir Max
HORTON
1883–1951

After commands of the Northern Patrol and the position of Flag Officer Submarines, he was made Commander-in-Chief, Western Approaches where his primary task was to defeat the hundreds of U-boats seeking to destroy the convoys carrying supplies between America and Europe and Africa. Improving air cover, additional escort support, reducing German investment in new vessels and Horton's own clever use of resources and strategy saw the U-boat menace diminish.

Rudolf
HOSS
1900–1947

He was commandant of the Auschwitz extermination camp and the first to use the Zyklon-B gas for his killings. He had worked at the Dachau and Sachsenhausen camps and, not surprisingly, was renowned for awesome brutality. He became Deputy Inspector-General of Camps in 1944, evaded capture at the end of the war but was located and hanged at Auschwitz in 1947.

General Hermann
HOTH
1885–1971

Together with GUDERIAN and his group, Hoth and Third Panzer Army made successful drives into

the USSR in June 1941. Within weeks they had cornered 290,000 Soviet troops at Bialystok. Thereafter, however, they began to fall foul of the Russian winter and, though they got to the outskirts of Moscow, the Soviet counter-attacks repulsed them. Hoth escaped HITLER's fury which saw Guderian and HOEPNER dismissed, and was directed towards Stalingrad with Fourth Panzer Army. There he sought to reach PAULUS' trapped forces but failed. At Kursk he pushed his men in an audacious move to the south of the battle zone but was unable to sustain the move because of a shortage of heavy weapons. The loss of Kiev in November finally brought his dismissal.

Cordell
HULL
1871–1955

For much of 1941 Hull, as US Secretary of State, was set on keeping Japan out of the war. Although decoded signals and intelligence reports ensured that he knew of Japanese intentions, he still pushed proposals through in the hope that settlement could be achieved. When an interim agreement involving gradual Japanese withdrawal from Indo–China and China was put forward only to be scuppered by the Chinese, and a last-ditch suggestion requiring them to move out of all mainland Asia was rejected by the Japanese, the die was cast. Not until the attack on Pearl Harbor had begun was he handed the Japanese Declaration of War.

Although he turned his attention to the situation in France he was somewhat overlooked by ROOSEVELT, who undertook much of the normal Secretary of State's work himself or used specially appointed envoys, such as HARRI-MAN. He remained in office long enough to have influence at the Moscow Conference of Foreign Ministers and to implement the Dumbarton Oaks meetings in Washington which began the process of setting up the United Nations.

Amin el
HUSSEINI
1893–1974

This Muslim leader was a primary instigator in the overthrow of the pro-British government in Iraq in 1941. After British occupation he was exiled to Germany where he was employed by HITLER to create Muslim military units in Axis-occupied lands.

General Haruyoshi
HYAKUTAKE
1888–1947

When the US troops on Guadalcanal dug in, he was charged with recapturing it. His first attack with only 900 men of 2nd Division was a disaster and even a stronger force, of 4,000 men three weeks later, was destroyed, at the Battle of Bloody Ridge. After these reversals, with Ichiki and Kawaguchi in charge, Hyakutake took control himself and led 30,000 men in a complex raid. The attack was doomed by poor communications and a failure to follow the battle plan. When the US Navy mounted their assault, Hyakutake found his poorly-fed troops unable to do more than skirmish with the better supported Americans and he was withdrawn with his remaining forces at the beginning of 1943. Although the naval confrontations around Guadalcanal had been a close run affair, Hyakutake's land forces had been thoroughly routed by the Americans.

General Hitoshi
IMAMURA
1886–1968

He master-minded the Japanese invasion of Java and then commanded 17th and 18th Armies in the tortuous efforts to maintain Guadalcanal against the American assaults. Although he was eventually forced to retreat, he used great resourcefulness to hold out as long as he did. During his Java command he was forced to swim for his life when, in a 'friendly fire' incident, his ship was sunk by four torpedoes misdirected by the cruiser *Chikuma*.

Noor
INAYAT KHAN
1914–1944

This remarkable woman, born in Russia of Indian and American parentage and resident in Paris, was recruited by SOE, trained in Britain and returned to France with the code-name 'Madeleine' to work with the 'Cinema' network in and around Paris. She was betrayed and captured in September 1943, badly mistreated in prison before being taken to Dachau and shot. She was posthumously awarded the George Cross.

Ismet
INONU
1884–1973

As President of Turkey, he was determined to retain neutrality for his country despite constant overtures from both sides. Not until August 1944 did he finally sever all contacts with Berlin and declare war on Germany, though he had previously assisted the Allied cause by reducing exports of raw materials to HITLER. Had he taken Turkey into treaty with either of the warring parties at an earlier date the ramifications could have been substantial.

Field Marshal Sir Edmund
IRONSIDE
1880–1959

This linguist certainly saw himself as a battlefield soldier rather than a behind-the-scenes staff officer, but this view was not held by his superiors. Although HORE-BELISHA replaced JOHN GORT by Ironside as Chief of the Imperial General Staff, it was Gort who got command of the British Expeditionary Force, a post which would have suited Ironside better. He was replaced as CIGS by JOHN DILL and given an unrewarding role as Commander-in-Chief Home Forces.

General Sir Hastings
ISMAY
1887–1965

A hugely popular man but truly an unsung hero of the war. As a captain of industry needs a good PA or a sports team coach a second-in-command who can deal with routine administration, so CHURCHILL, driven by maintaining the war strategy, needed a 'buffer' to stand between him and the unending inward communications, briefings, advice and administrative matters; from May 1940, when he became Prime Minister, Churchill employed Ismay in this role and it was an ideal choice.

Not only did Ismay sieve lesser data from the vital and the note written in anger or haste from the properly crafted memo, but he handled troublesome personal meetings, freeing Churchill from such tiresome duties. In the same way he would pass on Churchillian directives and not shy away from rephrasing them into a style which might be clearer or less contentious. High representatives of Allied nations were particularly grateful for Ismay's diplomatic nature and tactful performance. His work undoubtedly smoothed the running of the war, and to an extent which has often been underestimated.

General Seishiro
ITAGAKI
1885–1948

His war ended on 4 September 1945 when he surrendered Singapore to CHRISTISON aboard HMS *Sussex*, and he was subsequently found guilty of war crimes and hanged in December 1948. He had ardently supported Japan's entering the war on the Axis side, but like many he was appalled by the German–Soviet Pact of August 1939. He commanded forces in China and Korea before becoming commander of Seventh Area Army in Malaya.

Rear-Admiral Sanji
IWABUCHI
1893–1945

Typical of his nation's military ethic, he needed no second bidding to sacrifice himself and his charges for the cause of his country. Although YAMASHITA had ordered a withdrawal from Manila, the naval troops under Iwabuchi did not conform. They did not officially report to Yamashita and their independent move kept the US 37th Division in the city for some weeks before close-quarter fighting finally quenched Japanese resistance. None of the Japanese survived what they had accepted from the start would be a suicide stand.

General Hans
JESCHONNEK
1899–1943

Not alone among German leaders who struggled to come to terms with fighting a defensive war after some years of advance and success, he was found wanting when he could not come up with tactics to

General Ismay talking to Sir John Simon. (IWM HU69125)

counter the Allied bombing raids. Having shared with GÖRING the dream and reality of building up the Luftwaffe, he was an understandable choice for Chief of the Air Staff in 1939, but the reversals to come would see Göring lose faith in him. When Jeschonnek gave orders to the air defence units in Berlin to fire on German fighters which had landed there in error during an enemy raid on the Peenemünde rocket base, he must have been aware of the likely repercussions for he committed suicide shortly afterwards.

General Alfred
JODL
1890–1946

He was nearly always at HITLER's side when strategies were discussed and decided upon. As Chief of Staff to the head of the Oberkommando der Wehrmacht, the uninspiring Field Marshal KEITEL, Jodl was able to show all the energy and dynamism his superior did not and, for this reason, was usually 'the mouthpiece and implementor for directives stemming from the daily planning conferences. He was one of the few officers who retained his position during the years of reversal and it was he who signed the surrender of the German Army at Reims. He was convicted at the Nuremberg trials and hanged in 1946.

Group Captain James Edgar
JOHNSON
1916–

With his war record ranging from the Battle of Britain, through the Dieppe Raid, the D-Day air support, and other Allied air offensives, 'Johnnie' Johnson was one of the top fighter pilots of the Royal Air Force. His 38 'kills' reflected a mastery of dogfight tactics and the ability to utilise weather conditions and every element of his aircraft's performance.

Air Chief Marshal Sir Philip
JOUBERT DE LA FERTE
1897–1965

During his time as Commander of RAF Coastal Command – from 1941 to 1943 – this fine tactical theorist suffered for lack of manpower and equipment but advanced the performance of his units by using every technological aid available and planning his operations with great efficiency.

General Jodl arriving to sign the surrender documents on 7 May 1945. (IWM EA65734)

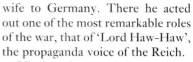

Regrettably, it was only when he was succeeded by SLESSOR that greater priority was accorded to Coastal Command and its deterrent and combat capability truly proven. From 1943 Joubert served with MOUNTBATTEN in South-east Asia Command.

William
JOYCE
1906–1946

Though spending the first 15 years of his life in New York, Joyce then came to London and then, at the outbreak of war, journeyed with his wife to Germany. There he acted out one of the most remarkable roles of the war, that of 'Lord Haw-Haw', the propaganda voice of the Reich.

His broadcasts had a considerable effect on his British audience. They contained a mixture of weak fact and believable fiction, all presented in a 'BBC voice' to add to their sense of reality. He used liberal amounts of humour, lashings of ridicule and dire tales of terror and danger; his messages, for all their wretchedness, were infuriatingly fascinating.

Reviled by his 'audience,' Joyce could not have expected much sympathy when he was arrested by the British at the end of the war. He was tried for treason at the Central Criminal Court, was found guilty and executed in 1946. His appeal on the basis of his being a US citizen was annulled by the fact that he had chosen to carry a British passport at the start of the war. Fifty years after the war, recordings of 'Lord Haw-Haw' at his most arrogant still chill the blood of those who remember his broadcasts.

Marshal Alphonse Pierre
JUIN
1888–1967

Released from German imprisonment at the intervention of PÉTAIN, this military academy classmate of DE GAULLE was never content in the ranks of the Vichy government. Offered the position of Minister of War, he instead took the post of Commander-in-Chief in North Africa. Further disenchantment with Vichy policies drove Juin into the Allied camp at the end of 1942 and now he showed his battlefield prowess in North Africa and Italy. Appointed Chief of Staff of the French National Defence Committee, this fine commander, who at the beginning of the war had led First

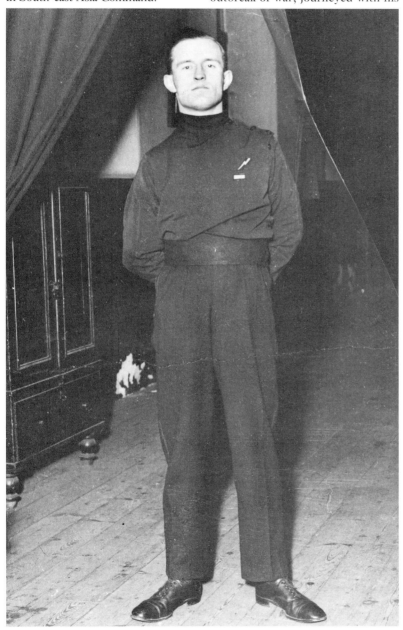

William Joyce, 'Lord Haw-Haw'. (IWM HU7036)

Marshal Juin watches de Gaulle shake hands with Mark Clark in Siena.
(IWM NA16574)

Army in an endeavour to prevent the occupation of his country, finished by helping to liberate France from German control.

Hans V. KALTENBORN
1878–1965

This American broadcaster brought the war into American living-rooms by his vivid reports from every battlefront and all theatres. For many Americans they were geography and history lessons as much as war bulletins.

Dr Ernst KALTENBRUNNER
1902–1946

Tall and imposing, with piercing eyes and a deep facial scar, he was physically daunting and his wartime actions increased people's fear of him. When HEYDRICH was assassinated, Kaltenbrunner replaced him and with it became the overseer of the Gestapo, Security Service, the extermination programme and the prison camps. Not only did he authorise his own men to commit atrocities in the name of the Nazi Party but also encouraged the public to kill any Allied airmen they

Ernst Kaltenbrunner at the Nuremberg trials. (IWM MH17454)

found. A callous and intimidating man, he protested innocence at the Nuremberg trials, claiming that he did not feel any guilt because he had only been doing his duty, and refused to be a substitute for HITLER in the court. He suffered a cerebral haemorrhage just prior to his trial, but was present when found guilty on two counts; he was hanged on 16 October, his last words being, 'Germany, good luck!'

Jan
KARSKI
1914–

Jan Kozielewski (his real name) worked with the Polish Socialist Party and the country's government-in-exile to infiltrate the Nazi death camp at Belzac and then escaped, one of only two to do so, to tell of its horror, including its capacity to dispose of 1,500 prisoners a day. When Western leaders and legal personnel heard his story – he met ROOSEVELT and gave testimony in a New York court – they initially doubted its authenticity, but, having become convinced, arranged for the governments of the Allied countries to condemn the 'Final Solution' policy being followed in such camps.

Lieutenant-General Masakuzu
KAWABE
1886–1965

Chief of Staff of all Japanese forces in China in August 1942, he assumed command of the Army in Burma in March 1943. Operation 'A-Go' to take Kohima and Imphal was planned by him and he constantly assured his superiors of its certain success, but by June 1944 he was having to admit to major problems. Ill health forced his replacement by Kimura in September.

Field Marshal Wilhelm
KEITEL
1882–1946

He owed his appointment to the BLOMBERG–FRITSCH scandal which saw better men dismissed. HITLER himself assumed ultimate responsibility for the armed forces and made Keitel head of the newly unified War Ministry and Army Command. Although he was no doubt selected for his acquiescent nature and was often ignored by Hitler in favour of his deputy, JODL, he did try to dissuade the Führer from invading Russia. Such was his devotion to his leader that he signed evil directives with apparent equanimity. He acknowledged his weakness, but retained his admiration of Hitler to the last. He was hanged at Nuremberg on 16 October 1946

Gorlitz, W. *Memoirs of Field Marshal Keitel*, 1966

Lieutenant-General George
KENNEDY
1889–1977

As US commander of air operations in New Guinea and the Solomons, Kennedy advanced the use of air transport for ground troops and used napalm bombs at Corregidor. He promptly dealt with the US/Australian rivalry in the Pacific air war by separating the USAAF and RAAF at command level.

Field Marshal Keitel carried out Hitler's orders without dispute. (IWM 13149)

Joseph **KENNEDY**
1888–1969

Until 1941 he was US Ambassador to London and had a businesslike rather than diplomatic attitude to the war in Europe. Rabidly anti-British, he approved of Germany's stance and tried by all means to persuade ROOSEVELT to keep out of it. He was recalled, still urging an isolationist policy, but the Japanese attack on Pearl Harbor destroyed that possibility and reduced the influence of those who proposed it.

Field Marshal Albert **KESSELRING**
1885–1960

A loyal Nazi, he maintained subservience to HITLER and, not surprisingly, held high rank throughout the war. An artillery officer who transferred to the Luftwaffe, he was returned to Army commands halfway through the war. For the invasion of France and the Battle of Britain he led Second Air Force, having commanded Luftflotte I in the Polish Campaign; by the end of the war he was trying to stem the Allied land advance back across the ground he had seen taken.

In December 1941 he was made Commander-in-Chief, Armed Forces South, operating in North Africa, where he initially worked closely with ROMMEL, and then Italy. He was quick to see that the increasing lack of air support would prejudice supply to front-line troops. Despite isolation and despair, he built an impressive defence line in Italy once Allied strength concentrated there, and even in retreat was still able to hamper and damage the Allied drive north. His treatment of the Italians, his one-time Axis partners, was callous and unsympathetic, entirely in keeping with his commitment to the Nazi cause, though some of the worst atrocities in Italy were committed by men of the SS who were not answerable to him.

In March 1945 Hitler sent Kesselring to France to replace VON RUNDSTEDT. Despite his criticism of his predecessor for his failure to visit the front line, this was now not a feature of Kesselring's style of command either, and he could do nothing to stem the Allied push into Germany. He was imprisoned for war crimes against Italian civilians but released because of ill health in 1952.

Lucas, J. *Hitler's Enforcers*, 1996
Kesselring, A. *Memoirs*, 1953
Macksey, K. *Kesselring: The Making of the Luftwaffe*, 1978

Field Marshal Kesselring after his surrender. (IWM AP66412)

Admiral King – 'Hold what you've got and hit them when you can.'
(IWM NYF21633)

Tyler
KENT
1911–1988

An American employed at the US Embassy in London during the war, he passed confidential documents to a pro-German group, including very sensitive communications between CHURCHILL and EISENHOWER before America had entered the war. When he was arrested in May 1940 almost 2,000 official notes and papers were found at his home as well as names and addresses, and keys to the Embassy code room. With his accomplice, Anna Wolkoff, he was tried (in camera); he was imprisoned in Britain until the end of the war and then deported.

Nikita
KHRUSHCHEV
1894–1973

During the war his job was to implement STALIN's directives concerning the military and industry, requiring him, after the initial reversals for example, to see to the destruction of manufacturing machinery and important structures such as the Dnieper dam, that might be of use to the advancing Germans. When the progress of the war gradually began to favour the Russians, he worked closely with YEREMENKO on the Ukrainian Front.

Marquis Kotcho
KIDO
1886–1977

As HIROHITO's adviser it fell to him to acknowledge the impending defeat and put in hand a premiership to negotiate a surrender that would maintain the Emperor's divine status.

Admiral Ernest Joseph
KING
1878 -1956

Although he fought his war from Washington, this did not prevent his having an uncanny affinity with the war zone; he had an immense impact on American naval strategies and was the principal policy maker and a major stimulus for getting the US on to a war footing.

As Commander-in-Chief and Chief of Naval Operations, he attended the main Allied planning conferences where he pressed long and hard for resources with which to meet the US obligations in the Pacific. In this he was outvoted by his colleagues who were pursuing the 'Europe First' agenda, but he accepted the decisions with good grace and continued to apply all his energies to winning the war.

An early convert to naval aviation, he recognised the aircraft carrier as being a vital factor in modern warfare. He built up the US fleet very swiftly into a diverse force capable of rapid deployment in a variety of locations on different missions and was always aware that victory in the Pacific would come through the actions of all elements of the armed forces working with the very best possible logistical support.

After the ignominy of Pearl Harbor he resurrected the Fleet and instilled in the naval leaders a belief in their new ships and their capability for counter-offensive in the Pacific. Although often at odds with MACARTHUR on tactical matters and the choice of priorities, there is no doubt that NIMITZ and his fellow naval commanders swept through the Pacific with the certain knowledge of the backing they enjoyed from King in Washington.

ROOSEVELT saw King as 'the shrewdest of strategists' and someone who brought him answers rather than questions. His creation of the Tenth Fleet, an anti-submarine force dedicated to winning the Battle of the Atlantic, showed his concern for all theatres of the war. Despite his staff responsibilities, his skilful delegation and management enabled him to oversee the work of the greatest naval fleet in history. His almost brutal insistence on excellence from those who worked for him probably contributed to the enormous success of his achievements.

Buell, T. *Master of Sea Power*, 1980
King, E. *Fleet Admiral King*, 1952

William MacKenzie
KING
1874–1950

Starting from an isolationist programme, this Liberal Canadian Prime Minister was persuaded by Pearl Harbor, the example of other British Commonwealth nations, and the exhortations of the British and American leaders he respected, to set up conscription and truly enter the war. He hosted Allied conferences at Quebec in August 1943 and September 1944, but within months of the second meeting was under pressure from fellow Canadians concerning the casualties they were suffering. Evidence of victory on the horizon quelled the crisis, but he also used the resignation of his defence minister to deflect complaints.

Admiral Thomas
KINKAID
1888–1972

Highly regarded for his determination in the heat of battle, he fought at Coral Sea, Midway, Guadalcanal and Santa Cruz Island where, despite losing a ship, his

Admiral Thomas Kinkaid at the time of the Luzon invasion. (IWM HU55387)

force shot down many Japanese aircraft. Later, as commander of the cruiser squadron, Task Force 67, he used advanced night-fighting tactics to reduce the logistically valuable performance of the Japanese 'Tokyo Express' supply line. After a spell commanding the North Pacific Fleet, he transferred to take charge of 7th Fleet, a convoy and support force, which took troops to Leyte and worked alongside MACARTHUR's forces there and at Luzon.

Colonel General Mikhail
KIRPONOS
1892–1941

After command of Soviet units in the war against Finland, he found himself in charge of Kiev in June 1941 when VON KLEIST led VON RUNDSTEDT's advance on the city, and died during the desperate defence of the stronghold.

Field Marshal Paul Ewald von
KLEIST
1881–1954

Although he had been brought out of retirement in 1939, aged 58, to take command of XXII Corps, he was to be a major player in German land warfare for much of the war. He led an important advance on the Western Front, breaking through defences near Abbeville, and then captured Belgrade when he was sent to the Balkans. He took First Panzer Army to Russia in 1941 but was thwarted in his progress by the early onset of winter. HITLER then ordered him to capture the oil refineries in the Caucasus. Although he ignored official Party policy and recruited many local Russians to his forces, his early gains were annulled when he ran out of fuel – in an oil-rich area – and was forced into a long, tortuous retreat.

Field Marshal von Kleist, a reliable panzer commander. (IWM GER1269)

A noted anti-Nazi, he was immediately under suspicion after the bomb plot of 1944 but escaped trial because of his high profile and seniority. He was taken prisoner by the British and subsequently handed over to the Russians in 1948. He died in a Soviet prison in 1954. A more formal, less maverick character than GUDERIAN, he was one of the few skilled Army commanders that Hitler stayed with throughout the war.

Field Marshal Günther von
KLUGE
1882–1944

One of HITLER's discards in the wake of the BLOMBERG–FRITSCH purge, he was 58 when recalled to command Fourth Army in 1939. He took his men to Poland and into France before being sent to north-west Russia in 1941; he was given command of Army Group Centre in 1942.

An astute tactician, he benefited in his relationship with Hitler by the very deference that GUDERIAN could not summon and would not show. He regularly referred decisions to the Führer for authorisation or, some would claim, to pass the glory for making a move on to Hitler. He was above all a soldier and, though not an avid Nazi, tolerated the advances to him made by those who conspired against the dictator without outwardly supporting them.

When VON RUNDSTEDT's failure to halt the Normandy invasion saw him drummed out of office, von Kluge was called from convalescence after a motoring accident to take his place. He lasted only as long as it took the Allies to force their way through the Falaise Gap. On his journey back to Berlin in disgrace, he committed suicide rather than face a showdown with Hitler.

W. Frank
KNOX
1874–1944

Another testament to President ROOSEVELT's ability to appoint

Field Marshal Günther von Kluge (left) with staff officers in France in 1940. (IWM GER1270)

able people, this publisher and Republican politician was to show the right mix of drive, judicious choice and masterful organisation in overseeing America's unprecedented growth in naval power while he was Secretary of the Navy, from July 1940 to April 1944

Simon E.
KOEDEL
1881–1957

Born in Germany, he went to America in his twenties, became an American citizen and served in the US Army. During the 1930s he returned to Germany to offer himself as a spy. He was trained by the Abwehr and returned to America as a sleeper. With the invasion of Poland he was activated and ordered to join the American Ordnance Association from where he supplied details about weapons development and shipments, even recruiting his daughter to gain further data from New York dock workers. Caught and imprisoned in October 1944, he was deported after the war.

General Marie Pierre
KOENIG
1898–1970

This French General served in the French Colonial Wars and then in Norway. In 1940 he returned to France, and then joined DE GAULLE in London; one of the few senior ranks to 'sign up' with the future President so early.

Sent with the Free French forces to North Africa, he held off a determined armoured strike from the Afrika Corps in a celebrated defence at Bir Hacheim. Once the Allies were back in France, Koenig became commander of the Forces of the Interior which were chiefly concerned with formalising the unco-ordinated strands of the Resistance movement.

Admiral Mineichi
KOGA
1885–1943

When YAMAMOTO died in April 1943 he was succeeded as Commander-in-Chief, Combined Fleet by this less charismatic, more traditional naval leader. He was unable to influence the pace of war against the Japanese, but organised defence in an orderly if futile way. Indeed he continued to plan for one last mighty confrontation with the Allied navies – code-named Operation Z – and was working on it when he was killed in an air accident during the Philippines withdrawal.

Lieutenant-General Kuniaki
KOISO
1880–1950

For a period of less than a year, but it was one which saw the most momentous events in its history, Koiso was nominally Prime Minister of Japan. He replaced TOJO and served in association with Admiral Yonai, but his position was far from satisfactory because he had little support from those who wanted more war effort or from the element who were seeking peace. He clearly believed that Japan could not win the war, but continued to state publicly that it would; his greatest fear was that any peace agreement would impoverish his people. His generals were dismissive of his pleas for greater consultation and left him with no choice but to resign in favour of SUZUKI in April 1945. He was sentenced to life imprisonment by the International Military Tribunal.

Vice-Admiral Nobutake
KONDO
1886–1953

It was he who sent out the aircraft from his patrolling Southern Fleet on the long-distance raid to sink

Repulse and *Prince of Wales* on 10 December 1941. He enjoyed less success at Midway, having to withdraw without having confronted the enemy. At the Battle of Santa Cruz Island on 26 October 1942 he sank *Hornet* and during sea action off Guadalcanal on 14 November the US ships *Preston* and *Walke* in which 191 men were lost.

Marshal Ivan
KONEV
1898–1973

A master of battlefield tactics, this World War One veteran survived STALIN's 1937 purges to serve first in the Smolensk sector and, from October 1941, commanding the Kalinin Front which was so crucial in holding the German advance on Moscow. The counter-offensives drove the Germans back more than 100 miles in a series of hard battles to take Orel, Belgorod and Poltava. Once in command of 2nd Ukrainian Front and cleared to counter-attack, he linked up with ZHUKOV's 1st Ukrainian Front to envelop the Germans south of Kiev. He could not prevent a breakout, but the Germans lost 20,000 men in achieving it. Konev then drove on into Poland, marshalled his forces – now more than one million strong, with 17,000 guns and 3,500 tanks – for the battle for Berlin, and moved through to the Elbe to join up with US forces.

Prince Fumimaro
KONOYE (KONOE)
1981–1945

A peace-seeker by conviction, he wanted a stronger Japan but sought this by diplomatic rather than military means. He became prime minister for the third time in July 1940, but was powerless to halt the militarists. He was replaced by GENERAL TOJO, his

General Walter Krueger, a major player in the Pacific Theatre. (IWM USB264)

minister of war, and faded from the scene until Tojo also fell, in July 1944. Faced with an American threat to try him as a war criminal, he committed suicide by poisoning.

Korvettenkapitän Otto
KRETSCHMER
1912–1995

Until he surrendered and scuttled his ocean-going U-boat, *U99*, when it was enveloped by HMS *Walker* and *Vanoc* on 17 March 1941, he had terrorised Allied shipping, sinking 44 vessels for a total of 266,629 tons. He developed a technique of weaving his way into convoys and making a surface attack; it caused havoc and, but for Kretschmer's capture, would surely have had a still greater effect on the sea war. As it was, the loss of *U99* and her companion *U100* prompted DÖNITZ to improve training and this delayed U-boat deployments.

Edwards, B. *Dönitz and the Wolf Packs*, 1996

General Hans
KREBS
1898–1945

As the Allied forces surrounded the remnant of the Reich, just a month before HITLER's death, Krebs replaced KESSELRING to become the last Chief of General Staff. He was sent by DÖNITZ to negotiate an armistice with the Russians but returned to report their rejection of anything other than unconditional surrender. He committed suicide shortly before the Führer's bunker fell.

General Walter
KRUEGER
1881–1967

He led the US forces in the recapture of the Philippines. From mid-1943 he was effectively in control of all south-west Pacific land troops, having been given command of Sixth Army under MACARTHUR. His Pacific offensive had been given the code-name 'Alamo Force' to distinguish it from other operations, and it was intended that control of it be kept well away from the Australian generals. At the time of the Japanese surrender Krueger was planning an amphibious landing in Japan.

Alfried
KRUPP
1907–1967

The son of Baron Gustav Krupp von Bohlen und Halbach, a principal sponsor of HITLER's, he took over the family business during the war and continued the policies his father had begun. The manufacturing giant had taken control of many similar concerns in the countries occupied by the Germans, and soon started building new factories at concentration camps; a large fuse factory was erected at Auschwitz where Jews were worked to exhaustion and then gassed to death. For this noble enterprise Krupp was awarded the Nazi Cross! He was arrested in 1944, tried in 1948 and sentenced to twelve years' imprisonment and confiscation of all his property. He was freed in 1951 and two years later was back in charge of the family firm.

Lieutenant-General Tadamichi
KURIBAYASHI
1885–1945

He turned Iwo Jima into a crude but effective fortress by means of constructing caves, tunnels and pillboxes. His efforts certainly delayed the American invasion and caused much US ordnance to be expended. When the island was invaded on 19 February 1945, Kuribayashi and his men fought with great bravery and resolve, even mounting suicide attacks. To avoid its capture he ordered the burning of the 145th Regiment's flag. Most of his positions had been taken by mid-March and he committed the traditional suicide on 27 March, aged 60.

Vice-Admiral Takeo
KURITA
1889–1977

Although attacked, delayed and weakened by US forces on his way to Leyte Gulf, he managed to take the Americans by surprise, sinking three destroyers and an escort carrier. He had gained an advantage but it was not sufficient to achieve victory, so he withdrew.

Admiral Nikolay
KUZNETSOV
1902–1974

A member of the Soviet High Command throughout the war, this STALIN favourite never saw active service but was responsible for the rapid growth of the cruiser and submarine fleets. He attended the Potsdam and Yalta Conferences.

General Vasiliy
KUZNETSOV
1894–1964

STALIN's purges had stripped the Army, but they left space for other stars to emerge. Although Kuznetsov was held responsible, with BUDENNY, for the failure to hold Kiev in 1941, his record thereafter was good, with excellent results at Stalingrad and on the advances through Poland and the final push for Berlin. He, with the likes of KONEV and ROKOSSOVSKY, emerged from the ranks of the younger Army officers to become true leaders.

Captain Hans
LANGSDORFF
1890–1939

His war ended in December 1939 but the manner of his departure was to have an impact on the whole question of neutral ports and neutrality in general. By the time his pocket battleship *Graf Spee* had been caught and surrounded by the Royal Navy cruisers, *Ajax*, *Exeter* and *Achilles* off the River Plate, he had sunk nine merchantmen, though on each occasion he had ensured that none of their crews perished.

He put into the neutral port of Montevideo for repairs, but realising that he was trapped, landed his crew and 300 prisoners, and scuttled his ship before committing suicide.

Pierre
LAVAL
1883–1945

Although he had served in World War One, he had done so with notable reluctance. Shortly after the war he became Minister of Foreign Affairs and set in train an agreement which gave Italy a free hand in Ethiopia, though further concessions to Italy implemented with British connivance, caused him and his British counterpart, Sir Samuel Hoare, to resign. He was back in power after the fall of France, first

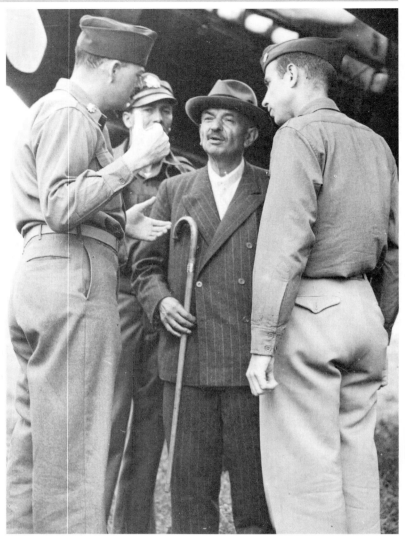

Seen here with members of 79th Fighter Group, Ninth Air Force, who took him into custody in Austria, Pierre Laval had been expelled from Spain where he had fled after the liberation of France. (IWM FRA205292)

as Vice Premier and then Foreign Minister for PÉTAIN.

Once again his overt collaboration with HITLER brought dismissal but German pressure saw him made Premier in place of DARLAN. As an obedient servant of Berlin he created a French Army for Hitler's use, allowed the Nazis to rob his country of art treasures and other national heirlooms, and

stood by while his countrymen were wretchedly mistreated.

At the liberation of France he fled to Germany and thence to Spain. Discovered there, he was expelled and was tracked down by US troops in Austria on 31 July 1945. He was taken to Paris, tried and, after an unsuccessful suicide bid, shot by a firing-squad on 15 October.

General Leclerc talks with a tank crew during a lull in the fighting. (IWM KY33826)

Major-General Robert
LAYCOCK
1907–1968

From as early as 1940 he had been a prime mover in the development of British Commando units. Initially he and his teams operated in the North Africa and Mediterranean Theatres. In 1943 he replaced MOUNTBATTEN as Chief of Combined Operations and was a principal planner for the Allied conquest of north-west Europe.

Admiral William
LEAHY
1875–1959

As CHURCHILL had ISMAY, so ROOSEVELT, from 1942, had Leahy. The Admiral chaired the

Joint Chiefs of Staff meetings but was principally a conduit through which messages were passed to and from the President. At Roosevelt's death he was able to ensure continuity by serving TRUMAN in a similar role.

General Philippe François Marie
LECLERC
1902–1947

Escaping twice from the Germans, the charismatic Leclerc reached Britain where he worked with DE GAULLE and other French patriots. Sent to Africa as Military Governor of Chad and Cameroun, and General Officer Commanding in French Equatorial Africa, he was in a posi-

tion to lead a Free French force on a 1,500-mile trek across the Sahara to link up with British Eighth Army in Libya. Later he led French troops in Normandy and was involved in several of the campaigns on the road to Berlin.

Field Marshal Wilhelm Ritter von
LEEB
1876–1956

One of the sixteen officers held responsible for the BLOMBERG–FRITSCH fiasco of 1938, he was recalled to lead Army Group Centre on the Western Front. When, against his advice, Russia was invaded, he was given command of Army Group North. Early success was short-lived

The determined face of Field Marshal von Leeb, a fine military theorist and practitioner. (IWM GER1272)

General Sir Oliver LEESE
1894–1978

Having begun his war as Deputy Chief of Staff of the British Expeditionary Force during the Dunkirk evacuations, he was brought forward by MONTGOMERY to command XXX Corps in Eighth Army for Second Alamein and thereafter for the landings in Sicily and mainland Italy. He succeeded Montgomery as Commander-in-Chief Eighth Army in January 1944, but shortly afterwards transferred to command the Allied land forces in South East Asia. In all his commands, Leese showed great purpose and was skilful in the issuing of clear directives.

Curtis E. LeMAY
1906–1990

He arrived in the European Theatre in 1942, to take command of the US 305th Bomb Group, Eighth Air Force. He quickly set out new methods of daylight bombing, using tiered height formations and leading some missions himself to see the theories put into practice. Under his guidance, bombing effectiveness was improved.

In the summer of 1944 he was transferred to the Pacific where he introduced other innovative schemes including long-distance flights and low-level fire-bombing raids by night. One mission, on 10 March 1945, had a devastating effect on Tokyo, destroying buildings and public morale. Although his solutions to problems were often controversial they were usually effective. He went on to play a major role in post-war military aviation until his retirement in 1965.

LeMay, C. E. *Mission with LeMay*, 1965

and when he proposed retreat from his Leningrad position, HITLER retired him in disgust. By now he was 66 years old. He had served his country in World War One and had been selected by General von Seckt to maintain German Army strength between the wars.

General Leese and General Freyberg during the Italian campaign. (IWM NZ1245)

Air Marshal Sir Trafford
LEIGH-MALLORY
1892–1944

Inevitably touched by the divisive debates which raged throughout the Royal Air Force during the time of PARK and DOWDING, Leigh-Mallory was prevented from implementing the Big Wing strategy he favoured by the tactical policy of the other two. Once Dowding had been replaced by DOUGLAS and Leigh-Mallory had command of No 11 Group, the more offensive role was implemented. In November 1942 he became head of Fighter Command and was later made Commander-in-Chief Allied Expeditionary Air Force to co-ordinate air support for the Normandy invasion.

Unable to take control of the Allied bomber fleets because HARRIS and SPAATZ could not bring themselves to pass them over to a fighter commander, he continued to cause friction, but his determination to attack German communication

Air Marshal Leigh-Mallory talking to pilots of Ninth Air Force in France. (IWM NY29310)

King Leopold of the Belgians taking the salute at a march past of his troops prior to the German invasion in May 1940. (IWM FLM616)

Laeken Palace. At the liberation in 1944 he was taken back to Germany by the retreating Wehrmacht. Freed by the Americans at the end of the war, he was not accepted back by his countrymen for a further five years.

Robert
LEY
1890–1945
By his early support of HITLER this politician, who had had a training in chemistry, enjoyed the sponsorship of the Führer, though he was less admired by others including GOEBBELS. He created a role for himself in the pre-war years by using force to take over existing labour organisations, imprisoning their leaders and bringing such unions under the *Deutsche Arbeits-front*, a new national group with himself at its head. Under the guise of protecting workers' rights he ensured that the labour force could be directed by the Nazi Party. He was never given sufficient scope to use this power in any way other than in support of Hitler's war ambitions, and he remained loyal to the end. He committed suicide before the Nuremberg judgement could be passed on him.

Charles
LINDBERGH
1902–1974
But for his status as an aviation pioneer and national hero, he would not have secured the attention he did for his protestations at America's anti-Nazi stance. Having been warmly greeted by the German aviation industry before the war, he formed the impression that the potential there was so great that it would swamp any British forces that could be ranged against it. His dire warnings were taken as treason by some of the US administration and even the President voiced

routes to Normandy undoubtedly helped the success of the D-Day landings and the drive inland. He also kept the skies above the English Channel clear of German aircraft throughout the crucial time.

Having commanded No 12 Group of Fighter Command in the Battle of Britain, Leigh-Mallory was to have ended his war as Commander-in-Chief South-East Asia Command, but he was killed in an air crash en route.

Ray, J. *The Battle of Britain: New Perspectives*, 1994

King of the Belgians
LEOPOLD III
1901–1983
Many of his subjects thought that he had surrendered the country too early. He had taken control of the Army at the German invasion on 10 May 1940 and sought urgent Allied support, but within two weeks his forces had been driven into a pocket. Prime Minister Perlot led the Army and the people in opposition to what they saw as premature capitulation, and the Germans kept Leopold out of harm's way in the

doubts as to the man's true allegiances. This meant that his flying skill was under-used, and he flew only a few missions in the Pacific in an advisory capacity.

Mosley, L. *Lindbergh*, 1976

Christiaan
LINDEMANS
1910–1946

A Dutch car mechanic known as 'King Kong', Lindemans was a double agent who ran one of the more successful Allied escape routes which transported evaders through Holland and France to Paris and the SOE/Resistance operation there. After considerable achievements for the Allied airmen, he switched allegiance to the Germans in March 1944 when his

brother fell into the hands of the Gestapo. The move, sudden and unexpected, compromised several agents and the lives of some escapees.

Field Marshal Wilhelm
LIST
1880–1971

Another of HITLER'S field marshals who found glory in the defeat of France and disgrace, in the Führer's eyes, for failure on the Eastern Front. After France, he was Commander-in-Chief of German forces for the invasion of Greece, but it was his transfer to command of Army Group A in July 1942 which led, after early advances to the Caucasus and the capture of the Maykop oilfield, to

stagnation, defeat and his dismissal. He was sentenced to life imprisonment at Nuremberg but released after five years.

Maxim
LITVINOV
1876–1952

His pre-war plan for co-operation with the West was brought to nothing by his replacement by MOLOTOV and the German–Soviet Pact of August 1939. Although he remained outside the sphere of influence until the invasion of the USSR, he did thereafter serve as Ambassador to Washington together with the nominal role of deputy commissar for foreign affairs. It can never be known what role he might have played or what international stature

Anthony Eden and Lord Halifax greeted by Ambassador Litvinov at the Soviet Embassy in Washington. (IWM NY6958)

he might have achieved had Soviet foreign policy not been re-aligned as it was.

Major General John
LUCAS
1890–1949

When commanding US 5th Army's landing at Anzio on 22 June 1944, he chose to consolidate his landing position, which he had gained unopposed, rather than take advantage of the absence of substantial resistance to drive inland and gain more ground. Although supported in this by his commander MARK CLARK, he was criticised for lack of initiative, and removed. It will never be certain whether a more adventurous decision would have benefited the Allied campaign; the Germans inland were awaiting reinforcements and equipment, but could have moved against such an incursion.

General Douglas
MacARTHUR
1880–1964

Whatever he did in his life, he did loudly and determinedly. Had it not been for a military career and the war, he could have been a marketing guru or international publicist. He encountered, and defeated, many opponents but his maverick demeanour leads one to suppose that he was his own worst enemy.

General Douglas MacArthur with Richard Sutherland, his Chief of Staff, preparing for the Leyte landing. (IWM NYP43162)

At the end of the war he had won some grudging admirers, but had turned potential friends against him; EISENHOWER, MARSHALL, NIMITZ and even ROOSEVELT would not have cast a vote for him, though they would have been bound to acknowledge his achievements.

It was in the summer of 1941 that his expertise in the Pacific – he had been adviser to the Philippines government – brought him forward as the prime candidate to prepare forces there for war, but though he raised more than 175,000 men in a few months, they were mostly untrained, ill-equipped and poorly motivated. Without battle-hardened troops or air and sea back-up, his Filipino army could not resist the Japanese invasion and were soon cowering in the Bataan peninsula, with even that position relinquished in May 1942 after more rigorous resistance.

Now MacArthur had to persuade Allied High Command that the Pacific Theatre should be given equal, if not higher, priority than the defeat of Germany. He had left the Philippines with the cry, 'I will return', and he would not rest until given the men and equipment to do so. The limited support offered by ADMIRAL KING and his Joint Chiefs enabled NIMITZ to try for the recapture of Guadalcanal, with General Mac-Arthur then moving through the Solomons and taking New Guinea. The slow pace of this advance, and the losses incurred, prompted him to employ an island-hopping strategy which not only avoided time-consuming land battles but saw Japanese forces cut-off from their supplies when air cover drained away. New Guinea had been secured by the summer of 1944 and MacArthur could now press to be allowed to return to the Philippines.

In the second week of January 1945, at the head of the largest amphibious operation seen to date, he waded ashore on Luzon. Within a month he was fighting for Manila and, with that city taken, he was able to plan his further advance, even though pockets of Japanese resistance held out.

The dropping of the atomic bombs brought the capitulation quicker than MacArthur could have expected. He had anticipated a longer conflict and yet, by 2 September, he was accepting the formal surrender aboard USS *Missouri* in

Tokyo Bay. For such a soldier the relief that the war was over may well have been tempered by the fact that he had not been allowed to win by traditional methods.

World War Two brought out the best and worst in MacArthur. For all his huff and bluster, his vocal demands for greater support and autonomy, and his black moods when not allowed full rein, he was a highly committed, attack-minded soldier who could not bear to retreat. Having been forced to do so, his egocentric personality gloried in retrieving lost ground.

MacArthur D. *Reminiscences*, 1964
Clayton, J. D. *The Years of MacArthur* (2 vols.), 1970–5
Gunther, J. *The Riddle of MacArthur*, 1951
Long, G. *MacArthur as Military Commander*, 1969
Willoughby, C., and Chamberlain, J. *MacArthur, 1941–51*, 1954

General Anthony C. McAULIFFE
1898–1975

During a temporary envelopment of American troops at Bastogne, during the Battle of the Bulge, General Lüttwitz urged this divisional commander of 101st Airborne Division to surrender. 'Nuts!' was his reported reply. Bastogne was relieved on 26 December 1945 and within the month this short delay in the Allied advance had been resolved.

General Sir Richard McCREERY
1898–1967

After a stormy start, McCreery had a successful war. He suffered the ignominy of defeat and retreat with the British Expeditionary Force and then proved a less than satisfactory Chief of Staff to AUCHINLECK, but thereafter proved his value in every appointment.

General Sir Richard McCreery, who led X Corps at Salerno. (IWM NA10507)

Given fresh standing as ALEXANDER's Chief of Staff in August 1942, he took a key role in devising a successful Alamein campaign for which he was acclaimed by his boss. He then led X Corps at the Salerno landings and on the drive against KESSELRING, especially during the awesome Battle for Cassino. Promoted to the command of Eighth Army, replacing LEESE, he chased the Germans north until their surrender on 2 May 1945.

Ivan
MAISKY
1884–1975

The German–Soviet Pact of 1939 and Soviet action against Finland put great strain on the good relationship Maisky had established with Britain during his seven years as Ambassador to London. Once the Germans had reneged on the terms of the pact and invaded Russia, he was able to regain his credibility and was a vital link in Allied discussions on aid, co-ordinated strategies and with governments-in-exile based in London. He was recalled to the Foreign Affairs Ministry in Moscow in 1943 and attended the Potsdam and Yalta Conferences.

Georgi
MALENKOV
1902–1988

When Germany invaded the Soviet Union, he was appointed to the Soviet State Defence Committee where he was made responsible for the technical equipping of the Army and Air Force. In this post he also master-minded the dismantling and removal of vital industrial plant that was in danger of falling into German hands. A close associate of STALIN's before and during the 1937–8 purges, he briefly assumed power after Stalin's death before being out-manoeuvred by KHRUSHCHEV.

Marshal Rodion
MALINOVSKY
1898–1967

After commanding an army at Odessa after the Germans had invaded, and being given charge of the South West Front there in December 1941 after BUDENNY's errors, he won the day when he stopped VON MANSTEIN from reaching PAULUS' beleaguered Sixth Army. Later he directed 3rd and 2nd Ukranian Fronts in the drive into the Ukraine, Hungary and, in April 1945, Slovakia. Transferred to the Transbaykal Front in August, he successfully campaigned against the Japanese in Siberia.

Group Captain Adolph Gysbert
MALAN
1910–1963

'Sailor' Malan – so called because of his time with the Merchant Marine – was a South African who joined the Royal Air Force in 1936. He was soon posted to No 74 Squadron with whom he quickly set out new fighter flying techniques, especially for attacks using pairs and 'finger-four' formations. Leading from the front, he shot down 29 enemy aircraft during the Battle of Britain.
Walker, O. *Sailor Malan*, 1953

Marshal Carl von
MANNERHEIM
1867–1951

His war years began, at the age of 72, with a valiant but losing battle to defend Finland against the Soviet Army in 1939 when the latter moved to safeguard its Baltic approaches. His brave resistance at least brought more reasonable settlement terms than a more complete defeat would have done. He then joined the German invasion of Russia so as to reclaim his country's former territory. When the war turned against Germany von Mannerheim negotiated equable terms with the Russians. His skill in such discussions made him a natural choice as President, but he retired in 1946. He was a positive fighter and a shrewd statesman. 'An adversary who feels inferior is in reality so', was a von Mannerheim quote which demonstrated his wisdom.
Mannerheim, C. von. *Memoirs of Marshal Mannerheim*, 1953
Screen, J. E. *Mannerheim: The Years of Preparation*, 1970

Field Marshal Fritz Erich von
MANSTEIN
1887–1973

HITLER undoubtedly had at his disposal some brilliant military minds and fine battlefield strategists. Von Manstein was such a man and he could boast great experience, having fought in some of the early battles on the Western Front in World War One. Like many of his colleagues, however, his effectiveness was badly hindered by the Führer's interference and poor direction.

It was von Manstein's revisions of the German High Command's invasion plan that formed the basis of the *Blitzkrieg* drive into France. The *Fall Gelb* scheme had been suppressed for a while and even when disclosed to Hitler and approved, it was 'officially' altered and re-presented by HALDER so as to dilute von Manstein's involvement. Its success, however, was sufficient to prove the excellence of its theory.

In 1941 he was given command of 56th Panzer Group for the move on Leningrad and was then charged with taking Eleventh Army through the Crimea to take Sevastopol. The following year he was put in command of Army Group Don but failed to take Stalingrad or relieve PAULUS' forces trapped there. Sending a memo to Hitler about the dire state of the forces, he quoted the manpower odds of seven to one; the telephoned response from Hitler was that there should be no retreat from 'Fortress Stalingrad' under any circumstances.

There then followed brief success with the counter-offensive which re-took Kharkov, but even von Manstein's abilities could not delay the inevitable change in the pattern of the war. In retreat he was as powerless as his fellow generals and incurred Hitler's wrath for the perceived failings, though he did propose revisions of policy which could have had some impact if followed. A year before the end of the war he was dismissed by Hitler and consigned to his country estate. He had tried to get an audience with the Führer but it was refused.

He was convicted of war crimes in 1950 but served only two years of his 18-year sentence. Ironically he was to spend part of the 1950s advising the West German government on the rebuilding of its Army to work with its former enemies against the threatening Soviet Union. Liddell Hart voiced the opinion of many when he opined that von Manstein was a considerable foe who possessed a mastery of technical detail, especially of the fluid warfare which was the *Blitzkrieg*. In different circumstances he, like GUDERIAN and others, could have earned an even greater reputation.

Lucas, J. *Hitler's Enforcers*, 1996
Manstein, E. von. *Lost Victories*, 1958, 1994
Paget, R. T. *Von Manstein: His Campaigns and His Trial*, 1951

General Hasso-Eccard von
MANTEUFFEL
1897–1978
This hard-nosed, uncompromising commander saw service in North Africa and on the Eastern Front before being given command of Fifth Panzer Army for the Ardennes campaign. Here he faced unprecedented pressures – lack of air support, diminishing supplies of ammunition, and HITLER decreeing that he should press forward to Brussels. The Allied counter-offensive removed any hope for the resourceful von Manteuffel who, having failed to secure more men and *matériel*, urged a general retreat.

Manteuffel, H. von. *The Fatal Decisions*, 1956

MAO TSE-TUNG
1893–1976
When he directed his militancy towards CHIANG KAI-SHEK in 1940 it showed a change from the policy that had caused him to ally himself with those working to contain Japanese aggression. In his campaigns he showed himself to be a skilled practitioner of guerrilla tactics, incorporating indoctrination into his taking of territory and, by doing so, gaining the support of the natives of those areas. Once Japan had been defeated and no reconciliation could be engineered between Mao and Chiang, the Civil War began.

Mao Tse-tung. *Selected Works*, 1977
Schram, S. *The Thoughts of Mao Tse-tung*, 1989

Hans Joachim
MARSEILLE
1919–1942
Rated by GALLAND as a fighter pilot of unique ability, he was a thorn in the side of British and Commonwealth airmen, against whom his record of 158 victories in nearly 400 sorties, was achieved. In the Battle of Britain and then North Africa his tactic of diving to attack served him well because he could handle the Bf 109 as no other pilot could. He died when baling out on 30 September 1942.

George
MARSHALL
1880–1959
The day that Germany invaded Poland, ROOSEVELT appointed George Marshall Chief of Staff, so demonstrating how early the USA were preparing for likely war involvement. His choice of the World War One veteran was wise because Marshall had the ability to carry through the detailed negotiations and put forward a clear, determined policy; he was a most significant player in the Allied victory.

Initially he worked on the establishing of close links with British military leaders so as to stay in touch with those who were already in action; he also led a sceptical American government and public away from isolationism and towards alliance. Once Pearl Harbor had sealed US commitment he led the faction which accepted the 'Europe First' scenario, fighting off those who believed that the USA should address the Pacific threat and leave Britain and her existing combatant allies to hold off Germany.

At all times Marshall's strategies meshed with those propagated through the CHURCHILL/ROOSEVELT liaison and fixed at the various conferences. When the Normandy landings were agreed, Marshall – still from his Washington base – supervised the delicate transfusions of American troops, equipment and command into the Allied structure and kept the combined force commanders focused on the objective. At the end of the war he became TRUMAN's Secretary of State and created the Marshall Plan to assist the depleted national economies of Europe.

Pogue, F. C. *George C. Marshall* (3 vols.), 1969

Jan Garrigue
MASARYK
1886–1946

Son of Thomas Masaryk, a figure-head of Czech independence, Jan was Ambassador in London on the partition of his country and the outbreak of war. When President BENES exiled himself in Paris and then in London, Masaryk worked closely with him and was the mouthpiece of Czech ambition and policy at diplomatic meetings and in BBC broadcasts to his countrymen. He kept the cause of Czech independence in high profile and earned the respect of national leaders.

Yosuke
MATSUOKA
1880–1946

Perhaps because of his experience of life in the West – he had been educated in America and held diplomatic posts there and in Europe – he was committed to Japan's playing a full part in the development of new power blocs. Having been his country's representative at the League of Nations in 1933, and the leader of its withdrawal from it because of the League's refusal to recognise Japan's puppet regime in Manchuria, he pursued a fiercely Nationalist agenda as Foreign Minister in KONOE's government. He took his country into the Unity Pact with Germany and Italy which proved stronger than his neutrality agreement with MOLOTOV, which he sought to rescind after Germany invaded the USSR. His strident views and independent action alienated his colleagues and he was dropped by Konoe in July 1941.

William H.
MAUDLIN
1921–

'Look into an infantryman's eyes and you can tell how much war he has seen.' Such keen observation stood Maudlin in good stead for, fighting with the 45th Infantry Division, he became known as a skilled cartoonist contributing to the magazine *Stars and Stripes*. His

The jovial and popular Robert Menzies visits Australian Air Force units in England. (IWM CH2295)

sketches, featuring 'Willie' and 'Joe', won a Pulitzer Prize in 1944.

Joseph
MENGELE
1911–1979

During the last years of the war he used his position as doctor at the Auschwitz concentration camp to conduct experiments on foreign nationals, both living and dead. He tested new methods of skin and bone grafting and organ transplantation on selected prisoners. He escaped to South America in 1945 and remained at large despite many efforts to track him down. He is believed to have drowned in Brazil.

Sir Robert Gordon
MENZIES
1894–1978

Bob Menzies endeared himself to the British by his whole-hearted support of the war effort and his regular visits to his troops in the front line and on training in England. A six-months' absence on such a trip in the first half of 1941 fuelled home opinion that his backing of CHURCHILL's policies was too unquestioning and he, and then his Party, fell from power to be replaced by a Labour government under JOHN CURTIN

Major General Sir Stewart
MENZIES
1890–1968

At the age of 25 he began an intelligence career which was to see him contribute hugely to the advance in the importance and effectiveness of clandestine action in the modern world. He was on Haig's staff in World War One and worked in MI6 during the inter-war years. In November 1939 he succeeded Admiral Hugh Sinclair as Commander of that organisation, and remained in the post for thirteen years, using the code letter 'C' for his name.

While the traditional elements of the armed forces were struggling to meet the demands of war, MI6 had to develop rapidly in order to keep up the supply of intelligence about the enemy. Work on cracking codes and placing increasing numbers of agents under cover was accelerated, and Menzies adopted an exhausting 'hands-on' style of management, while at the same time having to address the political calls on his resources and allowing for, and encouraging, the liaison with the security personnel of other Allied nations.

It was impossible for him to remain wholly popular throughout his tenure, but he earned the confidence of CHURCHILL and cleverly supervised his joint understudies, Vivian on counter-espionage and DANSEY on intelligence gathering. Although later revelations about double agents and scandals within the service tarnished his reputation to some degree, Menzies' work was acknowledged by awards from six Allied governments and a knighthood in 1943.

Marshal Kirill
MERETSKOV
1897–1968

After his replacement by ZHUKOV in January 1941, he was prominent in command of the Volkhov Front at Leningrad later that year. In 1944 he led forces of the Karelian Front in Finland, but thereafter fell out of favour and was posted to the Far Eastern Front.

Brigadier General Frank D.
MERRILL
1903–1950

The US force known as 'Merrill's Marauders' has entered the annals of military history as an early example of effective special-purpose forces when such units were in their infancy. With his men drawn from those supportive of the long-range covert operations pioneered by ORDE WINGATE, he set up his force in the summer of 1942, training them in jungle survival, small team operation and guerrilla tactics. In February 1944 they moved behind Japanese lines to sever their supply routes in the Hukawng region and in May linked up with STILWELL's Chinese units to take the airstrip at Myitkyina. Recognition of Merrill's ability came with his appointment as Deputy US Commander in Burma and India, but he has found long-lasting repute as an originator of today's élite force strategies.

Lieutenant-General Sir Frank
MESSERVY
1893–1973

This popular and successful British officer served exclusively in Southeast Asia and Africa. A brigade leader in the East Africa campaign, he led 4th Indian Division and 7th Armoured Division in the desert before moving to Burma where he was with 7th Indian Division at the Battles of Admin Box and Imphal. Later he was with IV Corps for the victory at Meiktila and then became Commander-in-Chief in Malaya.

General Giovanni
MESSE
1883–1968

This capable Italian commander had served in Libya, Ethiopia and Albania before, on the outbreak of World War Two, participating in the invasion of Greece and then leading Italian troops sent by MUSSOLINI to the Eastern Front to assist HITLER. Proving a difficult associate for his German counterparts, he was recalled in February 1943 to take over Italian First

Army which until then had been under ROMMEL's command. He surrendered with these troops in May.

Professor Willy Emil
MESSERSCHMITT

He started his aircraft manufacturing company in 1923 and its finest achievement – the Bf 109 – first flew in 1935. Its versatility and longevity proved the brilliance of the original concept and its adaptability, and gave him his world-wide reputation as a designer of great class. He remained somewhat distant from the mêlée of war and its political leaders, but still managed to secure orders for new aircraft ahead of many of his rivals.

General Joannis
METAXAS
1871–1941

During the pre-war years he forced a style of dictatorship on Greece from his position as prime minister. At the outbreak of war it was feared that he might side with the Germans, but the Italian invasion of 1940 saw him speedily and effectively range his forces against the enemy, first to force them back and then to occupy much of Albania. His death shortly after this left a void in the region which CHURCHILL and his allies hastened to fill.

King
MICHAEL
of Romania
1921–

Becoming king on his father's abdication in September 1940, he found himself being usurped by ANTONESCU's move for power. By August 1944, however, the threat of a Russian invasion and ever greater influence being exerted by Germany, enabled him to be certain of sufficient support by the generals to remove Antonescu and imprison him. War was declared on Germany and links created with the Allies; Romania moved swiftly from an Axis to an Allied power.

He reigned until 30 December 1947 when he abdicated in the face of increasing pressure for a purely Communist regime.

General Draza
MIHAILOVIC
1893–1946

When the Germans invaded the Balkans in spring 1941, two resistance groups evolved in Yugoslavia – the Communist partisans under TITO and the Serb Cetniks led by Mihailovic. Co-operation between the two was short-lived and before the year was out they were in direct opposition. When Mihailovic attacked Tito's forces he was well beaten and became a willing collaborator with the Germans and Italians against the Communist threat, while feigning support of the Yugoslav government-in-exile. When this duplicity became apparent the British severed all links with Mihailovic who, with the German defeat, went into hiding until found in March 1946, tried and executed.

Stanislaw
MIKOLAJCZYK
1901–1967

At the beginning of the war Mikolajczyk left Poland to join the government-in-exile in Paris. When this group moved to London he was made responsible for ensuring covert support for the Resistance in Poland. When SIKORSKI died, he became prime minister but found himself unable to meet the expectations of his own people, the Russians and the British, and resigned in November 1944. He returned to Poland after the war and took a seat on the Lublin Committee only to be removed and sent into exile two years later.

Field Marshal Erhard
MILCH
1892–1972

In his position as head of Lufthansa from 1926, he was the catalyst for much of the secret development of a military air force, in concert with his good friend, HERMANN GÖRING. Such was his success that HITLER had made him a field marshal by the time he led an air raid on Norway in 1940. The Führer's recognition of his abilities coincided with, and probably stimulated, a lessening of the friendship with Göring and, for a while, UDET was preferred. After his suicide, however, Milch came back into favour and tried to improve the Luftwaffe's flagging fortunes.

Like many of his colleagues, he suffered under the misguided and autocratic directives of Hitler, and his status as Air Inspector-General was rendered meaningless. Aware of the mighty aircraft production output of the Americans, he could only watch and warn as the air force he did much to create was swamped by numbers and technical superiority.

His Jewish origin was not the hindrance to his career that it might have been because Göring had persuaded his mother to attest that Erhard was a bastard son of his father. He was convicted of war crimes in 1947 but released in 1954.

Vice Admiral Marc
MITSCHER
1887–1947

He raised the profile and performance of naval aviation to new heights with his handling of the US

Field Marshal Erhard Milch, World War One fighter squadron commander, who was the first chairman of Lufthansa and a friend of Göring's. (IWM MH6070)

carrier forces in the Pacific Theatre. He was commanding USS *Hornet* when she launched JIMMY DOOLITTLE's Tokyo Raid in April 1942 and when she saw action at Midway.

From April 1943 he was commander of the Fleet Air Force based on Guadalcanal and then, early in 1944, took command of Carrier Division 3 (Fast Carrier Task Force 58) which performed brilliantly at the crucial battles of the Philippine Sea, Leyte Gulf and Okinawa. During the following months this group disposed of nearly 800 enemy ships and more than 4,400 aircraft and had a major impact on land and naval operations.

Field Marshal Otto Moritz Walther
MODEL
1891–1945

The 'Führer's Fireman', was unfalteringly loyal to HITLER and, after the failure of the July bomb plot, sent a note to him commending his survival of the assassination attempt.

Model was with IV Corps in Poland and Sixteenth Army on the drive into France. When the Eastern Front was opened he commanded 3rd Panzer Division and later Ninth Army. In this theatre he was used by Hitler to patch up the perceived failings of others; the Führer, describing him as 'the Saviour of the Eastern Front,' knew that he would faithfully follow out his ignorant and impossible orders.

When the Allies invaded Normandy he was sent there to produce more unlikely successes. He commanded Army Group B and fought manfully at Arnhem and in other confrontations, though he was eventually enveloped in the Ruhr and, though offered terms by General

Field Marshal Model, who committed suicide rather than surrender.
(IWM MH12850)

the funeral of ERNST UDET. During a difficult flight in treacherous conditions his He–111 hit a ground obstruction and he was killed instantly. ADOLF GALLAND took over his command.

Viachislav M
MOLOTOV
1890–1970

Taking over the Foreign Affairs post from LITVINOV on 3 May 1939, he continued in that position for the duration of the war and after.

As STALIN's nominee to implement the complex, shifting foreign policies of the USSR, he was the principal negotiator at the international conferences, Initially he argued for and signed the German–Soviet Non-Aggression Pact in August 1939, but once Germany's attitude to Finland became apparent, and his renewed discussions failed to change the situation, the pact was annulled and Molotov announced the German invasion to the Russian public.

Turning to the Allied camp, Molotov now agreed the Mutual Assistance Pact with Britain and the Lend-Lease Agreements with the USA and Britain. He attended the Tehran, Yalta, San Francisco and Potsdam Conferences where he continued to demonstrate debating skills which could be best described as terse and unyielding. Although in no way popular with his Allied counterparts – CHURCHILL referred to him as a puppet – he was acknowledged as a powerful influence on the status of the USSR at the end of the war. After Stalin's death he did not enjoy the same rapport with KHRUSHCHEV.

Ridgway, chose suicide rather than surrender, shooting himself in the woods near Düsseldorf on 21 April 1945.

Guerlitz, W. *Model*, 1978
Lucas, J. *Hitler's Enforcers*, 1996

Colonel Werner
MÖLDERS
1913–1941

Even during a brief posting to the Spanish Civil War, this excellent fighter pilot claimed fourteen kills to top the order of merit of German flyers there. In 1939 he was given command of Fighter Group 53, and then, in June 1940, of Group 51 with which he saw action in the Battle of Britain. A continuing success rate in combat saw him the first Luftwaffe winner of the Knight's Cross with Oak Leaves, Swords and Diamonds. He was in the Crimea when he was called home to attend

Field Marshal Bernard Law
MONTGOMERY
1887–1976

Even the briefest assessment of Bernard Montgomery, referring

Molotov arrives in Washington in April 1945 and is met by Secretary of State Edward Stettinius. (IWM NYP67283)

Montgomery in cheerful mood with Eisenhower. (IWM NA1696)

An impromptu office for Montgomery and Omar Bradley, the Commanders-in-Chief of 21st Army Group and Twelfth Armies respectively. (IWM BU3378)

rightly to his able leadership, supreme professionalism and undiluted commitment, must make mention of his difficulty in working cordially with Allied officers of similar rank, his dogmatic adherence to his own view however narrow and a natural immodesty which rankled with friend and foe alike.

His unhappy experiences in World War One, where he was shot in the chest and almost died, undoubtedly contributed to his cautious trait as a battlefield strategist – which often brought criticism – and his determined pursuit of good training and preparedness.

He fought against the German forces invading France and was one of the last to leave Dunkirk when his 3rd Division was evacuated.

From that time until he was sent to North Africa to replace GOTT as commander of Eighth Army, he concentrated on training the troops who would take the fight back to Germany. Once in the desert he spurred the beleaguered Eighth Army to success at Alam Halfa and El Alamein in September and October 1942; it was the first major Allied victory of the war, and Germany's first significant reversal, and the world rejoiced ... with Montgomery leading the cheering.

If his North African glory owed much to the groundwork of AUCHINLECK and ALEXANDER, he was more directly responsible for the 'Torch' offensives and the invasions of Sicily, Italy and Normandy, even though he was then effectively

under the command of EISENHOWER. The confidence of the North Africa victories showed through in Montgomery's stirring, impromptu speeches to his troops and the mark of the victor was constantly employed as he discussed logistics, support and strategies with his Allied counterparts.

The planning for the invasion of Europe was dogged by acute disagreement between Montgomery's caution and BRADLEY's belief in pace. In the event Montgomery's detailed planning brought steady progress, and success, with only suspect judgement at Caen and poor tactics at Arnhem tarnishing a superb advance which worked in tandem with Bradley's speed under Eisenhower's diplomatic management, which was doubly important when PATTON and Montgomery clashed head-on over tactics and supplies, so opening up wounds first inflicted during the Sicily operation.

Montgomery led an Anglo–American force on the northern route to the Rhine and it was he who accepted the German surrender of forces in northern Europe.

Bernard Montgomery felt able to communicate with the common soldier and few would criticise the morale-boosting value of his front-line speeches to them. With his fellow officers there was more often a failure to receive opinions or offer alternatives tactfully. His readiness to criticise failings in others but refuse to acknowledge his own can be interpreted as a weakness or a strength depending on your viewpoint. Would a less volatile, more pragmatic British commander have worked better or worse with Eisenhower? Certainly the Supreme Allied Commander recognised

Montgomery's qualities, even if he fought hard to tolerate his belligerence. 'It is the spoken word which counts, from the commander to his troops,' Montgomery said. 'Plain speech is far more effective than any written word.'

Chalfont, A. *Montgomery of Alamein*, 1976
Hamilton, N. *Monty* (3 vols.), 1981–6
Lamb, R. *Montgomery in Europe 1943–45*,1983
Montgomery, B. *Normandy to the Baltic, 1946*
– *El Alamein to the River Sangro*, 1950
– *Monty: A Life in Photographs, 1985*
Thompson, R. W. *The Montgomery Legend*, 1967

Henry
MORGENTHAU
1891–1967

ROOSEVELT's Secretary of the Treasury, he had the thankless task of generating funds for the massive war production within the framework of a routine national economy. He introduced the Defense Savings Bond and the Lend-Lease Program. His proposals to force post-war Germany to destroy its manufacturing machinery and return to agriculture was not supported by the British and American governments and was abandoned.

Herbert
MORRISON
1888–1965

From the outbreak of war until 1945 he was a leading player in British politics; his role in the British conduct of the war was considerable. As Leader of the Labour Party he was responsible for tabling the motion of 'No Confidence' which brought down CHAMBERLAIN in May 1940. CHURCHILL immediately brought Morrison into his war cabinet, first as Minister of Supply then as Home Secretary and Minister for Home

Herbert Morrison beside Churchill during a Downing Street meeting. (IWM H40529)

Security. He proved adept at dealing with the myriad policy matters on censorship of the media and internal security which were so necessary during the war years. At the end of the war his collaboration ended and he played an energetic part in the Labour election victory of 1945 and formulated the party's industrial and welfare state reforms.

Lieutenant-General Sir Leslie
MORSHEAD
1889–1959

This Australian officer was acting Commander when his 9th Australian Division confronted ROMMEL in the siege of Tobruk which lasted for more than six months from April 1941; he and his men were also at the second Battle of El Alamein when Rommel was decisively beaten. Later he was to operate in New Guinea before taking command of Australian I Corps for the Pacific amphibious operations during the last months of the war there.

Harrison, F. *Tobruk: The Great Siege Reassessed*, 1996

Moore, J. *Morshead*, 1976

Sir Oswald
MOSLEY
1896–1980

From 1918 to 1930 this British politician switched allegiance between the Conservative and Labour Parties during the course of his parliamentary career. In 1932 he founded the British Union of Fascists and his rabble-rousing rhetoric recruited some 30,000 members in two years. In 1940 he was imprisoned; his rabidly anti-Semitic rallies of 'Black Shirts' and his publicly stated admiration for the Nazi regime had become outrageous. His organisation was disbanded; controversially, CHURCHILL had him released in 1943.

Jean
MOULIN
1899–1943

Legendary French Resistance leader. Having opposed the German invasion from the start, Moulin (his *nom de guerre*) quickly proved a focal point for Resistance groups in Provence. He went to London to meet DE GAULLE and returned as his representative in Occupied France. For eighteen months he worked strenuously to unify the movement and created the *Conseil National de la Résistance*. Only a few weeks after he had chaired the first meeting of the group he was captured by the Germans and tortured to death.

Admiral Lord Louis
MOUNTBATTEN
1900–1979

Beginning his war as Commander of 5th Destroyer Flotilla which took part in the evacuation of Norway, he was soon active in the Mediterranean Theatre where his flagship HMS *Kelly* was sunk. He was quickly selected as KEYES' succes-

Mountbatten and MacArthur at a meeting in July 1945. (IWM NYP75776)

Mountbatten with Admiral Fraser and General Stilwell. (IWM A25544)

sor in charge of Combined Operations. Here, as a member of the Chiefs of Staff Committee, he planned the Dieppe and St-Nazaire raids and was involved in the early planning for Operation 'Overlord'.

He was in attendance at the Casablanca and Quebec Conferences in January and July 1943 and was chosen by CHURCHILL and ROOSEVELT as Supreme Allied Commander of the new South-East Asia sector established at the latter meeting.

In his new command his shortage of naval *matériel* forced him into a land strategy based on a secure staging-line from his HQ in India. With GENERAL SLIM, he used his sparse resources with great ingenuity to counter the Japanese offensive in Burma and turn the war around. Within eighteen months Burma was

recaptured and he received the surrender of 750,000 Japanese at Singapore.

Despite a reckless streak which brought some poor decision-making early in his war career, he had youth and a natural charisma on his side. His inspirational determination which eventually came to be proven in severe conditions stood him in good stead for his post-war diplomatic career.

Mountbatten, L. *Personal Diary*, 1988

Heinrich
MÜLLER
1896–1945

Although nominally Chief of the Gestapo during the war years, he was really HIMMLER's highest-ranking administrative clerk who implemented his superior's dictates

without demur. He was responsible for the rounding-up of Jews from January 1942 and for sealing the national borders from would-be escapees. At the end of the war he was working more independently of Himmler and showing every intention of wanting to assume his position in due course. He was with HITLER in the bunker but his subsequent fate has been disputed, claims that he had died in Berlin conflicting with sightings in South America.

Josef
MULLER
1898–1979

This lawyer was fervently anti-Nazi, but at the outbreak of war he signed up with the Abwehr and was posted to Rome. Now beyond the reach of those who knew of his rebellious nature, he was able to

Mussolini and Hitler: the dictators ride together. (IWM NYX68777)

liaise with British agents moving through Italy and working permanently from the capital, and do so without hindrance. When his activities were discovered in April 1943 he was arrested and taken to Buchenwald concentration camp where he was deprived of food and sleep and kept in chains. He survived this ordeal and a later transfer to Dachau.

Robert
MURPHY
1894–1958

Under the guise of being his political representative in the area, Bob Murphy acted as ROOSEVELT's intelligence 'eyes and ears' in North Africa from 1941 to 1943 when every scrap of information was useful in view of the Allied landings proposed for November 1942. He

later worked in Italy while the Allied forces were driving out the Germans.

Edward R.
MURROW
1908–1965

Ed Murrow was *the* voice from London for Americans at home. As European Director of CBS throughout the war, his live broadcasts during the 'Blitz' and sober portrayal of the Londoners he admired trying to carry on during the period when invasion seemed possible made a colossal impact at a time when Pearl Harbor and the presence of US troops in Europe were in the unimaginable future. Without doubt the calm authority of his reporting contributed to the American public's endorsement of US involvement when the time came.

Benito
MUSSOLINI
1883–1945

This North Italian schoolteacher sought but failed to avoid national service in World War One. After that conflict he turned to manual trades, becoming influenced by, and soon showing leadership qualities in, Socialist ideals and movements. The inter-war years began as a breeding ground for anti-Communist, pro-right wing groups which he showed skill in combining to form the Fascist Party. Election success enabled him to call for a government of the same colour and he was declared prime minister when the king eventually agreed. As HITLER rose to power Mussolini aped many of his policies, including that of anti-Semitism and absolute dictatorial control. He also concocted reports of his own achievements and used manipulative propaganda to a point where other European nations of similar persuasions began to revere him.

Although there was great mutual distrust between Mussolini and Hitler, their pursuance of such similar goals inevitably fused them together to a degree which could not be influenced by those nervous of the liaison. The German leader showed him the outward courtesies accorded to an equal, but the Italian's natural subservience was apparent whenever strategic planning took place. The Duce was allowed his delusions of grandeur through his dream of a Mediterranean–African empire while the Germans' quest was on an altogether greater scale. Hitler knew that he was Mussolini's superior and that his human and industrial resources were dramatically superior in quantity and quality.

The pact of May 1939 sealed their union, but even then the German declaration of war came after only a few days' warning to Mussolini, who was infuriated by this demonstration of his true status. He reluctantly clung to the coattails of the Reich, sharing the glory of the defeat of France and believing that he could enjoy similar success in Egypt, Greece and East Africa.

Now the wasted years of Italian drift, alongside the Reich's purposeful build-up of new weaponry and trained manpower, was demonstrated by ignominious defeats and the failure of Italian industry and the people to throw their efforts behind the national war footing. Manic directives by the Duce saw troops sent to the Eastern Front, far from the points where they were needed, and futile declarations of war on the Americans.

Undermined by political peacemaking moves by subordinates, Mussolini from early 1942 could only play out his chosen role rather than fulfil it. Hitler tolerated him while it suited his purpose, but no longer liaised with him. The Italian's gestures and decrees only served to further alienate his people. When he met Hitler in the north of Italy in the summer of 1943 he was no more capable of repelling the expected Allied invasion of his country than he had ever been. On his return to Rome his Grand Council demanded his resignation, placed him under arrest and replaced him with BADOGLIO.

Hitler was uncertain of Italian intentions for their disgraced leader so OTTO SKORZENY and a team of élite paratroopers was sent to extract him and return him to Germany where he was set up for a return to the German-occupied north of Italy to act as head of a puppet government – the Salo republic – there. Although acquiescent, Mussolini feared for his safety as the Allies drove up from the south and he sought to escape to Switzerland with his mistress. He failed even in this, the pair being captured by Italian partisans beside Lake Como on 27 April 1945. The following day they were shot and their bodies publicly displayed in Milan, hanging upside down from meat hooks on a petrol station forecourt.

Whatever intelligence and leadership qualities Mussolini might have possessed at one stage, and he did rise from modest ranks to lead a national party, they were overwhelmed by an ignorant and immature quest for glory at all costs where the perfection of power dominated any attention to the means required to hold on to it. Had Italy prepared better for war, with the same rigour as Germany, and then begun it with the same resolve, its course must have been somewhat different; it was perhaps this very weakness, however, that prevented his regime from plunging into the horrendous excesses of Hitler's.

Renya MUTAGUCHI
1888–1966

This Japanese Army officer was highly regarded for his bravery and decisiveness and, like many of his colleagues, saw action, as a major-general, in the Kwantung Army in Manchuria before the outbreak of World War Two. He was Commander of 18th Division during the invasion of Malaya, and in February 1942 for the attack on Singapore. In the spring of 1943 he faced the first Chindit raids and submitted his own plans for attacks on Imphal and Assam over the heads of his superiors; the scheme was accepted and became Operation 'U-GO'. Its eventual failure led to his transfer to staff headquarters in Tokyo and his retirement shortly afterwards.

Vice-Admiral Chuichi NAGUMO
1887–1944

He commanded 1st Air Fleet for the raids on Pearl Harbor, the Dutch East Indies, Australia, Ceylon and India. He failed to deploy his aircraft adequately to achieve his missions and at Midway he lost four carriers and all offensive impetus. From this point he took lesser commands in the forces which saw the war turning against them and he committed suicide in July 1944 when the US forces were engulfing his defences at Saipan.

Constantin Freiherr von
NEURATH
1873–1956

This diplomat was one of several skilled administrators whom HITLER allowed into high position to lend some semblance of authority to his policies. He shared this seniority with VON RIBBENTROP and ROSENBERG, but was often set in competition with these by Hitler's 'divide and rule' philosophy. He became critical of the Führer's rampant expansionism and lost favour during the BLOMBERG–FRITSCH purge, though he was kept on in the insignificant role of Minister Without Portfolio and chairman of a toothless foreign policy committee. This kept him within control of the regime he despised and demonstrated his lack of resolve.

Admiral Chester
NIMITZ
1885–1966

When ADMIRAL KIMMEL was removed after Pearl Harbor, Nimitz was tasked with rebuilding shattered naval morale and preparing the forces for offensive action. In this he had excellent support from ERNEST KING and quickly assembled a fine group of commanders including MITSCHER, HALSEY, SPRUANCE and KINKAID.

Using every scrap of naval intelligence he could muster and employing the full range of attacking operational tactics modern equipment could provide, he set about capturing the central Pacific islands, engaging the Japanese fleet and cutting enemy supply lines. Rather than reduce impetus by engaging every

Von Neurath, Goebbels, Frick, von Ribbentrop and Hess attending a conference. (IWM HU2355)

island in his path, Nimitz evolved a leap-frogging tactic which by-passed heavily defended territories in favour of smaller islands, leaving the others isolated 'to wither on the vine'. Using Spruance's 5th Fleet and Halsey's 3rd in rotation, Nimitz was able to progress at maximum pace, outwitting and outmanoeuvring the larger Japanese forces.

Backed by King, Nimitz was convinced that his means of taking the

Nimitz and MacArthur studying a map. (IWM NYP22190)

war back to Japan by amphibious attacks and island-hopping was more efficient and effective, but it was the opposite process to the one favoured by MACARTHUR who shared command of the Pacific Theatre. Once it was given the go-ahead by the Joint Chiefs of Staff, Nimitz charged on, driving the Japanese back to their home territory, his submarines decimating their merchantmen and his carrier force striking through a chain of islands from Makin and Tarawa to Guam and Palau. The mission was completed with the capture of the Philippines and victories at Leyte Gulf, Okinawa and Iwo Jima, and the achievement was recognised by Nimitz's promotion to Fleet Admiral at the end of 1944.

Although MacArthur accepted the Japanese surrender, the ceremony took place aboard Nimitz's flagship, *Missouri*. Much has been made of the competitive animosity between MacArthur and Nimitz. Both were men of huge drive and determination whose desire to outdo the other not only made for fierce debate in Washington but also spurred them on to greater and quicker actions.

The vital part played by Nimitz in lifting the US Navy from such a low ebb, instilling its leaders with clear, well-defined strategic plans, and then ensuring that they were carried through, is undeniable and has endurably marked Chester Nimitz as a great naval commander.
Potter, E. B. *Nimitz*, 1976

Colonel General Aleksandr
NOVIKOV
1900–1976

For the latter half of the war he commanded the Soviet Air Force. In that role he repaired the wreckage of the defeats at the hands of the Luftwaffe during the German advances. He deployed his aircraft at Stalingrad and Kursk, was able to mount the air barrage at Königsberg which brought General Lasch's surrender, and then brought his force up to full strength against the Kwantung Army in Manchuria.

General Sir Richard
O'CONNOR
1889–1981

He spent the middle years of the war held captive by the Germans, having been ambushed by a forward unit in the Western Desert.

In 1939 he had been commanding 7th Division in Palestine and was Governor of Jerusalem. In the summer of 1940 he and his men were sent to Egypt were he became commander of the Western Desert Force under WAVELL. When the Italians invaded Egypt, Wavell and O'Connor master-minded the counter which took Tobruk and pushed the enemy back to Benghazi and El Agheila. O'Connor was sent to join GENERAL NEAME to combat ROMMEL's arrival and it was then that he was captured. Having

Colonel General Novikov. He was commander of Russian air operations during the major set-piece land battles. (IWM RR214ε)

escaped in December 1943, he was sent to command VIII Corps in Normandy. Later he was Commander-in-Chief Eastern Command in India. O'Connor was a shrewd and resourceful leader who, but for his imprisonment, would surely have played an even greater role in the Allied success.

Colonel General Friedrich
OLBRICHT
1888–1944

He was one of the leading players in the July bomb plot of 1944. At the outbreak of war he was commanding 24th Infantry Division but thereafter was Chief of the General Staff of the German High Command and then Deputy Commander of the Reserve Army. A career soldier administrator but vehemently anti-Nazi, he worked on the scheme which would supplant HITLER and revise German politics. After the failure of the assassination attempt he was one of the first to be arrested and was shot alongside VON STAUFFENBERG.

Vice Admiral Jesse
OLDENDORF
1887–1974

In the first significant surface naval defeat of the Japanese in World War Two, he was in command of Task Force 77.2 when Nishimura's group was destroyed by torpedoes and radar-controlled gunfire during the Battle of Leyte Gulf. Later his vessels were in the forefront of the kamikaze attacks of January 1945.

Vice-Admiral Takijiro
ONISHI
1891–1945

Working with GENDA under YAMAMOTO, he prepared the plans for the Pearl Harbor raid and further damaged US aviation in the Pacific by his attack on Clark Field

in the Philippines during the early days. Towards the end of 1944 he was asked to support KURITA's attack on the Leyte invasion force. With too few aircraft to mount consistent attacks he turned to the kamikaze strategy, with considerable short-term success. Totally opposed to the surrender, Onishi committed suicide after its signing.

J. Robert
OPPENHEIMER
1904–1967

An internationally acclaimed nuclear physicist in the 1930s, when the USA entered the war he headed up the laboratory at Los Alamos which built the first bomb. The pace of his work and the ingenuity of his team made the weapon available in time to hasten the end of the war.

General Hiroshi
OSHIMA
1886–1975

'Our main basis of information regarding HITLER's intentions in Europe' was how GEORGE MARSHALL described this man, a confidant of HITLER and VON RIBBENTROP. As Japanese Ambassador to Germany, he visited many battlefronts and factories and since his many reports back to Tokyo were available to Allied code-breakers he was an unwitting source of valuable data.

Hans
OSTER
1888–1945

A deeply religious man, he spent eleven years as Chief of Staff of the Abwehr, Germany's military intelligence department; he was deputy to both VON BREDOW and CANARIS. When HITLER's ambitions became apparent, his opposition to the National Socialist agenda grew and

soon he was disclosing war plans to those countries the Führer planned to invade. He could not reconcile the Nazi aims with his own beliefs and became a prominent organiser of the resistance to Hitler. He was arrested after the failure of the July 1944 assassination attempt and executed with Canaris at Flossenburg concentration camp on 9 April 1945.

Vice-Admiral Jisaburo
OZAWA
1896–1966

The career of this astute naval officer was blighted by the loss of his own flagship, *Taiho*, other vessels and nearly 350 aircraft at the Battle of the Philippine Sea – losses exacerbated by his insistence on remaining at battle stations. But he was an able strategist and his decoy moves at Leyte Gulf nearly cost HALSEY the initiative.

General Alexander
PAPAGOS
1883–1955

As Commander-in-Chief of the Greek Army, he confronted the Italian forces when they invaded Greece via Albania. He was able to eject them but then defended a line other than that agreed between the Greek and British war leaders. As a result the Italians, now joined by German forces, proved too much for him when they attacked again on

9 March 1941. Within a few weeks Greece was occupied and Papagos had been taken off to Dachau where he remained until the American liberating troops arrived.

Air Marshal Sir Keith
PARK
1892–1975

A New Zealander, he was a resourceful and deep-thinking air strategist who, under DOWDING, worked with 11 Fighter Group at the evacuation of Dunkirk. The two worked in concert again during the Battle of Britain, but their tactics, devoted to securing Britain's defensive capabilities, incurred the wrath of LEIGH MALLORY and others in the British military hierarchy. Although their tactical foresight can

be said to have been proven by the successful outcome of that battle, both men were replaced and given lesser commands.

Even in smaller roles Park was an achiever. As AOC in Egypt and then Malta, he applied astute offensive moves to hamper Axis supply lines and aid Allied landings, and evolved excellent air support systems for Allied drives inland. During the last year of the war he was in command of Allied Air Forces in South-East Asia where his support missions were again vital in the Burma campaigns. He was disconsolate about his treatment after the Battle of Britain but did not allow this to affect his subsequent excellent performance thereafter.

General Alexander McCarrell
PATCH
1889–1945

He was in command of the Infantry Replacement Center in North Carolina when, in the spring 1942, he was tasked with aiding the French defending New Caledonia. He then led American forces in their first land success, at Guadalcanal in early 1943, before taking command of US Seventh Army for Operation 'Anvil' (originally 'Dragoon'), the Allied landings on the French Mediterranean coast.

With this force he moved up through France, to Grenoble by August, Lyons and Besançon in September and to the German border by 15 December. He crossed the Rhine on 26 March 1945 and

Air Marshal Sir Keith Park (right) talking to Air Vice Marshal Vincent and Group Captain Goddard on a Burmese airfield. (IWM CI1144)

General Patch is congratulated by Lieutenant General Devers on his Distinguished Service Medal. (IWM EA58879)

secured the formal surrender of Army Group C on 5 May. Although facing scant opposition in comparison with that encountered in Normandy, the attack from the south reduced German options during the last months of the war.

General George Smith
PATTON
1885–1945

'Old Blood 'n' Guts', as he was known, both affectionately and caustically, to his colleagues and his men, was a bluff, no-nonsense character whose robust battlefield manner made some of his more formal associates uncomfortable but undoubtedly contributed to 'getting the job done'.

Born into a military family, he was brought up to believe that an Army career was both a duty and an expectation. In World War One he saw service in Mexico (where he reputedly acquired his ivory-handled pistols from a henchman of Pancho Villa's whom he had personally killed) and Europe, where he was seriously wounded.

He was given command of the Western Task Force for the 'Torch' landings in November 1942 and four months later was personally selected by EISENHOWER to restore the morale of US II Corps after their losses at Kasserine Pass. But it was his performance with US Seventh Army in Sicily which brought him to prominence, and into some conflict with MONTGOMERY and other British officers, and made him the logical leader of American forces for the Normandy landings.

With US Third Army he thrust out from the Normandy bridgehead and tore across France at an unexpected pace which, in turn, exacerbated the continuity of supplies to keep his progress going and, in his view, prolonged the war. Required to delay further advances he became embroiled in static battles until the German counter-offensive at the Battle of the Bulge brought his greatest success, and enabled fresh advances across the Rhine and onwards.

His efforts brought a post-war appointment as military governor of Bavaria, but this was no role for a soldier of his ilk and his arguments with Eisenhower brought his removal after a few months. He died in December 1945 after being severely injured in a car accident.

George Patton was not the only eccentric, maverick soldier fighting the Allied cause, but he was perhaps the most effective. His private persona was far distant from the brash, brazen style he used in negotiations with equals or the spirited urgings he used to drive his men on; he was a quiet, almost insular man when off-duty. He was not a good theorist, but he was a master practitioner who acted out of his natural character to secure the battlefield success his national loyalty demanded he should achieve. 'In war nothing is impossible, provided you use audacity', he said, yet in his private life he seldom showed this characteristic.

The only blot on his 'man-management' file – an incident when he slapped a shell-shocked soldier in hospital – surely came about because of an inner belief that every man should fight for his country to his last breath and his maximum determination. This was Patton's own code.

Blumenson, M. *The Many Faces of George S. Patton Jnr*, 1972
Essame, H. *Patton: A Study in Command*, 1974
Forty, G. *Patton's Third Army at War*, 1990
– *The Armies of Patton*, 1996
Patton, G. *The Patton Papers* (2 vols.), 1972–4
– *War As I Knew It*, 1947

General Friedrich PAULUS
1890–1957

As Deputy Chief of Staff to HALDER, he was the source of much of the theory behind the invasion of Russia, having been charged with examining the feasibility of such a move. In January 1942 he was given command of Sixth Army which was to move on Stalingrad; a year later he had surrendered his forces there. He did succeed in entering the city, but did so depleted of supplies and resources. The Luftwaffe failed to fly in requisite replenishment and VON MANSTEIN'S attempt to reach him foundered. Although a breakout from the city, in which he was continually losing ground in close-quarter combat with CHUIKOV's forces, offered him some hope, he rejected the opportunity because HITLER had forbidden a withdrawal. No sooner had the Führer promoted him to field marshal (to prevent his surrendering; no German field marshal had ever surrendered), Paulus was obliged to surrender, incurring his leader's wrath. In captivity he broadcast to German troops urging them to submit to the inevitable defeat, and later gave testimony for the Russians at Nuremberg. He lived in East Germany after the war.

Air Chief Marshal Sir Richard PEIRSE
1892–1970

He was Commander-in-Chief of Bomber Command from 1940 to 1942, but before this force came into its own during the offensive against Germany, he had transferred to South-East Asia where he led the

'Blood 'n' Guts' George Patton seen here as his troops cross the Seine. (IWM EA35720)

Allied Air Forces, reporting to MOUNTBATTEN. In this role he superintended the dramatic supply flights into China via the Himalayan route – known as 'flying the hump' – and ensured that his aircraft played a vital role in the victory in Burma in 1944.

Vladimir PENIAKOFF
1887–1951

Because of his work as a sugar manufacturer in Egypt during the interwar years, Peniakoff was used to travelling the desert terrain and adept in the requisite navigational skill. When he was commissioned into the Libyan Arab Force of the British Army at the start of World War Two he created a special-purpose unit, No 1 Long Range Demolition Squadron, for small force assault, sabotage and reconnaissance far behind enemy lines. This group became known as Popski's Private Army and even appeared as the PPA in official reports.

Lieutenant-General Arthur PERCIVAL
1887–1966

Although he was the General Officer Commanding when Malaya was invaded by the Japanese on 8 December 1941, and oversaw the retreat from there and the surrender of Singapore, he could by no means be held solely responsible. His area had been starved of quality officers, air support and clear directives, and when *Prince of Wales* and *Repulse* were sunk on route to assist the defence of Singapore, his cause was hopeless. Utterly outnumbered and facing armies of skilled jungle fighters, he withdrew his men farther south before making a stand on Singapore Island from 27 January 1942.

The Japanese landings began two weeks later and with no reinforce-

Lieutenant-General Arthur Percival was in command of the British troops in Malaya at the time of the Japanese invasion.

ments likely he and his 85,000 men lasted only a week before capitulating, though he survived imprisonment to have the pleasure of attending the Japanese surrender at the end of the war. Percival, who had started the war as Chief of Staff to GENERAL DILL, was a victim of circumstance, accident – in the form of the lost warships – and the ignorance of his military and political superiors; he could have done better, perhaps, but not much better.

Marshal Henri Philippe Omer
PÉTAIN
1856–1951

The Hero of Verdun in World War One, he came to be seen as a traitor in the next conflict, though many think that this was a result of his not believing as avidly as some, in a German defeat. He felt that it would be in the best interests of the nation to side with those he foresaw as being the eventual victors.

Brought back from ambassadorial work in Spain when the Germans invaded, Pétain – acting as Deputy Premier – decried the REYNAUD/DE GAULLE/DARLAN faction which called for alliance with Britain, and with the support of Laval and others forced Reynaud's resignation. As his replacement he received the German terms for an armistice and established his new regime at Vichy, in the area of France which the Germans were to leave unoccupied. Though acquiescent in most discussions, he never succumbed to German urgings for him to declare war on Britain.

Once the Allies had invaded North Africa and so caused the German forces to move into the whole of France, the Vichy regime and Pétain in particular lost influence and purpose. He was taken into custody by the Germans but returned of his

Pétain declined to ally his country with Britain because he was sure she would lose the war. (IWM HU69903)

own free will to face trial at the end of the war. The resulting death sentence was commuted by de Gaulle who no doubt saw in Pétain a former Army colleague who was weak rather than wicked.

Ferro, M. *Pétain*, 1987
Griffiths, R . *Pétain: A Biography of Pétain of Vichy*, 1972
Lottman, H. R. *Pétain: Hero or Traitor*, 1985
Ryan, S. *Pétain the Soldier*, 1969

King
PETER II
of Yugoslavia
1923–1970

Prince Paul ruled as Regent from 1934, when Peter was only 11 years old, until 1941 when his policy of collaboration with the Germans brought about GENERAL SIMOVIC's coup which put Peter firmly on the throne. The immediate German invasion caused Peter and govern-

with deterring Japanese aggression in Malaya and helping to secure Singapore. On 8 December 1941, without air support, he sailed to attack a large Japanese supply convoy. Within 24 hours Japanese aircraft had used a window of clear weather to locate the vessels and sink them. Phillips was one of the few men lost. The fact that the Japanese naval air force could destroy one of the most modern battleships in existence while operating at the extremes of their range caused much concern in British naval circles which had barely come to terms with the Pearl Harbor raid a few days before.

Eugenio (Pacelli)
PIUS XII
1876–1958

Having earlier advised Pius XI during the setting up of the 1933 Concordat between the Roman Catholic Church and the Third Reich, Pacelli was elected Pope in March 1939 and was thereafter under constant pressure to condemn the Nazis and their atrocities. He held meetings with JOSEF MULLER and other opponents of the German regime but seemed reluctant overtly to support opposition to HITLER. But through his efforts Rome was treated as an open city, and when the Germans occupied it in September 1943 he made the Vatican into an immense asylum for countless refugees including Jews,

General Markian
POPOV
1902–1969

His principal success came when his Bryansk Front forces outmanoeuvred and inflicted heavy casualties on VON KLUGE's troops near Kursk. He had previously performed well at Leningrad and Stalingrad, but when in 1944 he was

King Peter II of Yugoslavia proudly displaying his 'Wings' in January 1944.
(IWM CM5648)

ment officials to flee to Athens and then London.

From his new base Peter gave backing to MIHAILOVIC's Cetnik guerrilla force, which did not endear him to the Allies who favoured the more reliable group under TITO. He recognised the shift in the power base of the partisan units and signed an agreement with Tito on 1 November 1944, though given the declaration of a republic at the end of the war, this did nothing to maintain him in power and he did not return to Yugoslavia.

Admiral Sir Tom
PHILLIPS
1888–1941

To Tom Phillips fell the unenviable task of commanding the new battleship *Prince of Wales* and the older vessel *Repulse*, of Force Z, charged

given command of 2nd Baltic Front and his progress west was too slow for his superiors, he was replaced by YEREMENKO; Germany's Army Group North had held Riga, Popov's objective, and STALIN, never a great admirer, saw it as a chance to dismiss him.

Marshal of the Royal Air Force Sir Charles
PORTAL
1893–1971

He enjoyed the trust and support of CHURCHILL and worked to earn the respect of his American allies. He took over RAF Bomber Command from April 1940 and was Chief of the Air Staff in Britain from October of that year until December 1945. His position on the Chiefs of Staff Committee meant that he not only had to dovetail RAF thinking into the British war strategy, but just as significantly needed to shape Allied air tactics in a manner that would satisfy both the Americans and his own commanders, *and* win the war.

The American preference for precision bombing was not easily accommodated, especially by HARRIS who was committed to area attacks. Portal struck effective compromises and displayed democratic astuteness in keeping both camps happy. When the Allied bomber forces were required to work in greater concert after the invasion of France in 1944, new pressures were encountered from the intransigent Harris, but Portal managed to ensure that the heavy bomber support required by the invasion forces was provided without huge loss to the operations against German industry. It was fortunate, or wise selection, that such an admirable strategist and able negotiator was at the helm of British air policy at this time.

Admiral of the Fleet Sir Dudley
POUND
1877–1943

There is no doubt that this veteran of the great Battle of Jutland in 1916 was a fine strategist who was capable of seeing, and acting on, the broader war zone picture. It is unfortunate that the pressures of the highest command clouded his service record with some notable errors of judgement.

Already 62 years old when recalled from command of the British Mediterranean Fleet in 1939 to become First Sea Lord, he

Marshal of the Royal Air Force Sir Charles Portal with Air Vice Marshal Broadhurst. (IWM CNA2295)

was then required to chair the British Chiefs of Staff Committee with its resultant workload. Determinedly 'hands on' in his working style, he sought to see every document and be involved in every meeting and decision with the result that he intervened too often, most notably in his decision to have Convoy PQ17 scatter. The loss of two-thirds of the vessels brought heavy criticism from the press and long-running controversy. When he resigned because of ill-health in October 1943, and died a few weeks later, there was no lessening of this severe judgement, but post-war assessment has been more prepared to recognise his capabilities as a monitor and motivator of policies which won the sea war.

Commander Günther
PRIEN
1908–1941

He planned and put into action the raiding of the Royal Naval anchorage at Scapa Flow in the Orkney Islands off the north-east tip of Scotland. In an audacious move his U-boat *U47* penetrated the narrow, murky entrance to this natural harbour on 14 October 1939 and sunk HMS *Royal Oak* with 786 men aboard. Although the greater part of the fleet had already left Scapa Flow, the resulting boost to German morale contrasted sharply with this early sign to the British of the Royal Navy's vulnerability even within its own waters. Just six weeks after entering the war, Britain could only use the event as a reason to increase the defence of the fleet. Prien's brilliant manoeuvre had been made easier by the absence of worthwhile simple defences, an error which was rectified forthwith.

Prien's war ended when *U-47* was sunk with all hands on 7 March

Admiral of the Fleet Sir Dudley Pound retained Churchill's confidence even though the two did not always agree on policy matters. (IWM A4859)

Günther Prien, the U-boat commander who sank HMS *Royal Oak*. (IWM HU40836)

1941 by HMS *Arbutus, Camellia and Wolverine.*

Juan PUJOL
1912–1988

When rejected as an agent by the British, this Spaniard signed up with the Abwehr and immediately made himself more useful to those who had turned him down. He subsequently became a double agent run by MI5 and, under the codename 'Garbo', proceeded to feed the Germans misleading information, especially in the case of false plans for the Normandy landing. Such was his effectiveness that the Germans awarded him the Iron Cross; the British made him an MBE.

Ernest PYLE
1900–1945

He was one of America's most revered war correspondents. Although he was able to discuss strategic matters with the highest-ranking commanders and presented these in simple terms to his civilian readers, hiss forte was in describing the war as experienced by the ordinary soldier, whom he seemed able to persuade to confide in him without hesitation. He was in London during the *Blitz* and followed the action through northern and southern Europe, North Africa and the Pacific. He was killed by Japanese fire on Ie Shima Island near Okinawa on 18 April 1945.

Manuel QUEZON
1878–1944

From 1935, when he became President of the Commonwealth of the Philippine Islands, his official military adviser was DOUGLAS MAC-ARTHUR. Quezon's support for a US/Philippine alliance was unstinting and made even stronger by the threat of Japanese aggression. In December 1941 he had to leave Manila, and his second inauguration took place in an air raid shelter on Corregidor. He subsequently travelled to Australia and America to urge support for his country and assure his listeners of the Filipinos' desire to play their part. He created a government-in-exile in Washington but died shortly before his country was retaken.

Vidkun QUISLING
1887–1945

Although there is evidence that this politician had his nation's interests at heart, his actions were deemed despicable by Norwegians and caused his name to enter the world's dictionaries as a synonym for traitor. Founder of the Norwegian Fascist Party, his career waned when HITLER came to power. He visited

The traitor who considered himself a patriot; Vidkun Quisling, on trial in Oslo. (IWM FOX69159)

Germany to persuade the Führer to use him as a means of gaining control of Norway, but the Germans used military might to achieve their objective and then installed him as leader of a puppet government. Existing ministers resigned and even the German hierarchy found themselves unable to work with him. He was quickly removed and given a token position under the Germans' own man, Josef Terboven. Quisling was tried and executed in 1945, having surrendered to the new government that was formed at the liberation.

of belief in its feasibility surely contributed to its cancellation. Like many of his colleagues he was used as a scapegoat for his leader's fallible decisions. Blame for the loss of the Barents Sea action in December 1942 was laid at his door, though Hitler was as much to blame. In Jan-

uary 1943 he was ordered to retire. He was not a convinced Nazi in the style of DÖNITZ, but he admired the strength of purpose shown by Hitler. At Nuremberg he was sentenced to ten years' imprisonment.

Raeder, E. *My Life*, 1960
– *Struggle for the Sea*, 1959

R

Admiral Erich
RAEDER
1876–1960

Under his tough leadership the lightly armed coastal force that was the Kriegsmarine became a large navy in the space of four years. His preference would have been for a high seas fleet capable of taking on the world's capital ships, but he recognised the need of a diverse range of surface and submarine vessels with which to damage an enemy's supply lines.

As HITLER's disappointment with his navy's performance grew and funds available for development were reduced, Raeder fell out of favour, though he was still charged with planning Operation 'Sealion', the invasion of England, and his lack

Erich Raeder, Germany's Naval Commander-in-Chief. (IWM A14906)

Admiral Sir Bertram Home
RAMSAY
1883–1945

Recalled to duty from retirement, he was a highly regarded, supremely meticulous organiser of some of the most complex amphibious operations in the European Theatre. A master of logistics and organisation, he executed the naval element of the Dunkirk evacuation in 1940 and then was CUNNINGHAM's deputy for the 'Torch' landings in North Africa in 1942. As Naval Commanding Officer, Eastern Task Force he again enjoyed success at the Sicily landing in July 1943 and then created and deployed the convoluted maritime element of 'Overlord' where even the setbacks of bad weather and the loss of some ships were overcome. On 2 January 1945 he was killed in an aircraft on the way to a meeting with MONTGOMERY.

Admiral Ramsay after his appointment as Allied Naval Commander-in-Chief.
(IWM HU69905)

Field Marshal Walther von
REICHENAU
1884–1942

Although he must have been as aware of the danger in HITLER's proposals as his Army colleagues were, he firmly nailed his colours to the Führer's mast. He came close to assuming FRITSCH's job as Commander-in-Chief of the Army, but Hitler saw much evidence of lack of support from Reichenau's colleagues. Instead he was given command of Tenth Army in Poland, Sixth Army in Belgium and in Russia where he eventually encircled Kiev. He was among those officers who fell from grace after the failure to take Moscow, but remained in command of Army Group South. A heart attack necessitated his return to Leipzig for treatment, but he was killed when his aircraft crashed en route. He was one of several Generals who were skilful in implementing the 'Blitzkrieg' against weaker opponents, but found battlefield tactics against a stronger force altogether more taxing.

Hanna
REITSCH
1912–1979

A crack test pilot, she tested the V-1 'flying bomb' in its preliminary designs before it evolved into an unmanned flying-bomb, and test flew various jet aircraft for the Luftwaffe. She demonstrated extraordinary flying skill when required to take GENERAL GREIM to HITLER's bunker in besieged Berlin in April 1945, and then flying him back out of the war-torn city three days later. A friend of Eva Braun's, she was equally besotted by Hitler and begged him not to kill himself. Hitler gave her a phial of poison and she says that she planned to share it with Greim, but evidently she thought better of it.

She was the only woman to receive the Iron Cross.

Paul
REYNAUD
1878–1966

While personally committed to resisting German expansionism and, in succeeding DALADIER on 21 March 1940, determinedly sharing this aim with CHURCHILL in a declaration of intent, he made a great mistake when seeking to strengthen his ministerial staff just before the German invasion. Two of his appointments were WEYGAND and PÉTAIN who promptly supported a policy of surrender and thus, by his own hand, Reynaud reduced his options hugely. The help he sought from Britain was not forthcoming and proposals to move the government and military hardware to North Africa came to nothing. Just eight weeks after becoming Prime Minister, Reynaud resigned to leave Pétain in charge. The Vichy government put Reynaud on trial for failure to prevent the invasion, but the case collapsed and Reynaud was taken to Germany

Lieutenant-General Sir Neil
RITCHIE
1897–1983

His job as Assistant Chief of Staff to AUCHINLECK in Cairo did little to add to his limited combat command experience. Consequently when he replaced CUNNINGHAM as Commander of Eighth Army, which was struggling to contain ROMMEL's offensive in Libya, he was unable to bring the necessary expertise to bear. He suffered reversals at Gazala and Tobruk before Auchin- leck had to resume control and, in a change to Ritchie's plan, withdraw to El Alamein.

Joachim von
RIBBENTROP
1893–1946

Whether or not HITLER appointed Ribbentrop as his Foreign Minister in 1938 because he saw in him the diplomatic characteristics he would never claim for himself, it was soon evident that this veil of courtesy and convention was a thin one. Ribbentrop had a short temper and an arrogance which riled friends and foes alike.

He set out the plan for the German–Soviet Pact which saw the partitioning of Poland and put his signature to it in August 1939, expecting that it would draw Britain into the war. Having earlier been

Von Ribbentrop leaving Hitler's Rastenburg HQ. (IWM MH9244)

Ambassador in London – he was at a farewell lunch at 10 Downing Street when Britain received notice of the invasion of Austria – he must have realised the stance that Britain would be obliged to take and, though an acute Anglophobe from his time in London and ready publicly to accuse the British of weakness and complacency – he had told CHURCHILL, 'England may be clever but this time she will not bring the world against Germany', he must surely have known the resolve of the nation. He held his position for the duration of the war but had little power or influence. Dictatorship took over from diplomacy.

He was captured by the British on 14 June 1945 and at Nuremberg was one of several of the accused who claimed their complete subservience to Hitler as a reason for their actions and in mitigation of their guilt; he sought to call Churchill as a witness. He was the first of the German hierarchy to be hanged, on 16 October 1946.

General Matthew Bunker
RIDGWAY
1895–1993

A fearless exponent of the 'new' strategy of deploying infantry from the air, he demonstrated leadership in the use of the tactic with the US 82nd Airborne Division in Sicily in 1943, where he achieved the planned result but with heavy losses brought about by poor weather and the lack of training in similar conditions. By the time of Salerno his men were even more effective, driving into Naples, and then for the D-Day operations he led the assault on the Cotentin peninsula, enjoying the advantage of a more thoroughly planned operation. He was later given command of 18th Airborne Corps for operations at Eindhoven

and in the Battle of the Bulge. By the time he and his men crossed the Elbe, he had brought airborne landings in a battle zone to a fine art.

Marshal Konstantin
ROKOSSOVSKY
1896–1968

Although he had been imprisoned during STALIN's pre-war purge, he was back in command, under ZHUKOV, in the Kiev area by the spring of 1940.

At the German invasion Rokossovsky led an early counter-offensive with tanks in the Ukraine and then moved to work with the forces surrounded at Smolensk. When Moscow came under threat he commanded Sixteenth Army with distinction and then produced the vital breakthrough at Stalingrad which culminated in the envelopment of PAULUS' Sixth Army. He offered the German general surrender terms, and defeated him when they were rejected.

It was at Kursk that he cemented his reputation as a battlefield commander of rare ability. Showing offensive determination at first, he then absorbed the might of VON KLUGE and MODEL's best attacking moves until, nursing their wounds and seeking to strengthen their resources, they were susceptible to his counter-attack which drove them back to the Polish border and beyond. His push was held at Warsaw from July until the end of 1944 as local forces joined in. Rokossovsky denied the insurgents the support of his own forces or supplies from the western Allies and only in January 1945, after the brutal crushing of the uprising by the Germans, did the Russians, with Rokossovsky commanding 2nd Belorussian Front, move into Warsaw and then on to Danzig and eventual contact with the British moving east.

Rokossovsky was a masterful organiser on the battlefield whose war was an unmitigated success save for the blemish of his inaction at Warsaw which, in any case, was surely approved or requested by his superiors.

Field Marshal Erwin
ROMMEL
1891–1944

He did as much as any German battlefield commander to raise the morale of the military and civilians alike. At the same time, however, he could be criticised for leading small actions from the front when his time might have been better spent in planning success on a grander scale.

Although he had proved a cavalier, award-winning infantry officer in World War One, and wrote an important treatise on infantry warfare afterwards, he was employed in a modest teaching position when HITLER called him to head his own Headquarters forces at the outbreak of the war. After the evident success of the Polish campaign Rommel yearned for field command and was given 7th Panzer Division for the invasion of France. Like many of his colleagues he worked the *Blitzkrieg* tactic effectively, against limited opposition, and enhanced his reputation accordingly.

He might have expected a command on the Eastern Front when 'Barbarossa' was being formulated, but instead was sent to North Africa with just two tank divisions to reinforce the struggling Italian forces there. It was a shrewd appointment; free of the shackles of a larger operation and fellow commanders to debate his strategy, he was able to supervise the employment of an amended *Blitzkrieg* scheme in the sharp, attacking moves of which he was so fond. The 'Desert Fox' came out into the open.

From the moment he set foot in Africa, early in 1941, he went on the offensive, driving back WAVELL who had not previously encountered such pace in an opposing force. Now wiser, the British – under AUCHINLECK – checked Rommel to some degree, but he generally held the upper hand and his defeat of the British forces at Gazala in May 1942, where he had many fewer tanks than Auchinleck and RITCHIE, was a great achievement. When he pressed on to Tobruk to recapture that stronghold a few days later he was promoted to field marshal

But now Allied reinforcements began to arrive in greater numbers and a turn of the tide was inevitable. The first Alamein battle was inconclusive but significant; Rommel was now suffering from over-extended supply and communication lines and losing patience with his Italian counterparts, though he was still urging new extravagant offensives. Defeat at Second Alamein in October brought massive casualties and the loss of most of his armour as MONTGOMERY successfully pulled the German forces around the battlefield in reaction to the British moves.

Even though forced to retreat, he remained active in defence but was called home by Hitler in May 1943 before the collapse of the German forces in North Africa. He was alarmed by the state of Germany, but accepted the command of Army Group B which was expected to defend France from the Allied invasion. Here he quickly fell out with VON RUNDSTEDT, his superior in this theatre, though both eventually urged the Führer to withdraw.

On 17 July he was wounded when a British fighter strafed his staff car and he was in hospital at the time of the attempted assassination of Hitler by his own officers. Some of the conspirators arrested were said to have implicated Rommel who was quickly visited by Gestapo officers. He was offered trial or suicide and chose the latter in order to save his family from public humiliation; the official announcement of his death quoted the car incident as the cause of death.

Hitler had delighted in celebrating Rommel's successes for he knew him to be a supreme soldier with no political ambition. In his enemies 'The Desert Fox' engendered only high regard and admiration, though they became thankful for his reluctance to slow the pace of his offensive or be more reserved in his adventurism. Had he spent more time at the planning table and less leading sniping attacks that should have been left to subordinates, he might have had an even greater impact; he was almost captured at advanced locations several times. Churchill referred to him in the House of Commons as 'a very daring and skilful opponent', and without doubt he was a battlefield leader of some genius who might have served his country even better had he been deployed on the Eastern Front.

Forty, G. *The Afrika Korps at War*, 1978
Liddell Hart, B. *The Rommel Papers*, 1953
Lucas, J. *Hitler's Enforcers*, 1996
Rommel, E. *Infantry Attacks* (trans.), 1956

Eleanor ROOSEVELT
1884–1962
The President's wife was a willing supporter of her husband's career in peace and war. Hugely popular with the American public, she was also warmly welcomed on her wartime visits to Europe and the Pacific. She had the official status of being a director of the Office of Civilian Defense and continued high-profile duties after her husband's death.

President Franklin Delano ROOSEVELT
1882–1945
While British politicians had been concentrating on bringing the economy and industry out of recession, Roosevelt had spent the first seven years of his Presidency building a new nation from the dire state it had reached in the mid-1930s. He had shown a devotion to this cause and had demonstrated only peace-making tendencies in his foreign policy during those early years.

With their leader bent on national renewal, his countrymen were little concerned about the fears of war being expressed in Europe. It can be argued that, from the moment Britain declared war, Roosevelt was supportive and probably expected direct American involvement to follow. Publicly the statements were of a sharing of aims without active commitment, but behind the scenes the President and his representatives were in close contact with, and making lengthy visits to, London and elsewhere in Europe.

His employment of flexible neutrality in foreign matters was already under pressure in the Pacific where Japanese adventurism was thinly veiled, so when Britain found herself almost alone to combat the advance of the Third Reich, he was able to increase the production of materiel, despite the urgings of the isolationists, under the guise of concerns for the Pacific.

Within months of renewing his mandate at the 1940 election on the stance of staying out of the Euro-

The Yalta Conference in February 1945. Roosevelt flanked by Churchill and Stalin with, behind them, Alexander, Maitland Wilson, Alanbrooke, Cunningham, Ismay, Portal, Leahy, Marshall and the Russian delegates. (IWM NAM235)

President Roosevelt being briefed by Admiral Nimitz in Hawaii. Beside him are General MacArthur and Admiral Leahy. (IWM EN33590)

pean Theatre, he had persuaded Congress to back his Lend-Lease plan to support his friend, WINSTON CHURCHILL. At the end of 1941 the Pearl Harbor attack enabled him to drop all pretence. HITLER's declaration of war on the USA meant that the President was empowered to act globally.

He recruited well; he had a gift for appointing hard-working, astute, problem-solving characters in the administrative posts and was content to use hard-nosed, belligerent officers in the field. For his part, Roosevelt embraced his new international responsibilities which brought a peculiar alliance between him, Churchill (a long-time confidant) and STALIN, whom the President could only identify as an ally in the sense that they both sought peace.

He and his chief advisers skilfully pursued an agenda which shared US resources between the Pacific, which all Americans were concerned about, and Europe which many saw as too distant to be their problem. Roosevelt agreed that defeat of Germany was a priority, that Britain was to be helped to an essential victory, but the build-up for pushing the Japanese back was developed in tandem.

Despite his poor health – he suffered badly from polio – his determination to head America's co-ordinating role took him across the world to conferences of 'the Big Three' where he began to find Churchill's dogmatic stances tiresome and Stalin's avowed fear of being isolated deserving of some sympathy. His drive appealed to the voters who awarded him a further term in 1944. Although he could now see an Allied victory on the horizon, he did not live to see the surrenders signed; the world mourned his death on 12 April 1945.

Despite some criticism of his naïvety in dealing with the Russians, the world recognised Roosevelt's qualities and did so during his lifetime. He managed to combine the commitment to victory with a light, democratic touch in negotiations, to appoint the right man to the right job, and to play the role the Allied side required at this critical time. As Churchill observed, he had an 'inflexible sense of duty' and was 'the greatest champion of freedom'.

Alfred
ROSENBERG
1893–1946

Of Estonian and Lithuanian parentage, he emigrated to Germany, settling in Munich in 1920, where he met HITLER. The young man's vehement anti-Bolshevik line and his hatred of the Jews identified him as a kindred spirit and Hitler made him Editor of *Völkischer Beobachter*, the infant Nazi newspaper. His vitriolic editorials and pamphlets fuelled the fires of National Socialism; he was responsible for the introduction of the crudest form of anti-Semitism into Germany and the Nazi Party. For a time he was given charge of the Party's agents overseas, directing their subversive intrigues and infiltration activities. Although he lacked the organisational skill which the Party system required, he remained close to the Führer and from the time of the 1923 *Putsch* was always one of the most prominent Nazi leaders. In 1933 he was Hitler's private envoy to London. He was appointed Reichs Minister for the Eastern Occupied Territories in July 1941, but he did little more than follow instructions in a routine fashion. He was the official 'philosopher' of Naziism, his book *Mythos des 20. Jahrhun-*

derts being second only to *Mein Kampf,* but despite his deep convictions he had neither charisma nor persuasive skill to maximise his role. At Nuremberg he was found guilty on all counts and was hanged on 16 October 1946.

Rosenberg, A. *Selected Writings,* 1970

Field Marshal Gerd von
RUNDSTEDT
1875–1953

Although he had been a casualty of the FRITSCH–BLOMBERG affair, the outbreak of hostilities saw him recalled to active service, and he had a busy war. He commanded Army Group South for the invasions of Poland and France – at Sedan he produced the decisive thrust which isolated the British Expeditionary Force – and was promoted to field marshal. His reticence in pursuit of the BEF retreating to Dunkirk, and the failure of the Luftwaffe to do his job for him, enabled the evacuation to take place. but remarkably did little long-term damage to his relationship with HITLER.

The Führer's plan for von Rundstedt's Army Group South in Russia – to capture the Black Sea ports and the Maykop oilfields and then head for Stalingrad – was a tough one with which he could not cope and the resulting disagreement with his leader saw his dismissal in December 1941. By the spring of 1942, however, he was replacing WITZLEBEN in command of Army Group West. This too was a daunting and hopeless task.

Adjudged to have failed to prevent the Normandy landings he was replaced by VON KLUGE only to return yet again at the latter's removal after only seven weeks. The Ardennes Offensive was never von Rundstedt's idea as some have claimed, but a directive from Berlin which he implemented under duress, as best he could.

He was a very capable field commander who lacked the inventive spark that would have made him great, and his reputation has suffered because he was ordered to carry out one impossible task after another. Although not an avowed Nazi, he was loyal to Hitler, to the point that he presided over the court which judged those responsible for the July bomb plot.

Yvonne 'Jacqueline'
RUDELLAT
1897–1945

Born Yvonne Cerneau, this frail, innocuous-looking woman was a most unlikely heroine of the French Resistance, being the first woman trained by the Special Operations Executive to work with their agents in France. Having spent some years in London her background gave her fine qualifications for the work but her age – she was a grandmother by the time she saw active service – and her slight physique might have been expected to count against her. She showed great determination to 'do something to help' her country and this made her an inspiration for many who followed; had she failed then other female agents might not have been sent to France.

Seriously wounded when eventually captured by the Germans, Yvonne – code-named Jacqueline – was imprisoned at Ravensbruck and then Belsen, where she died in April 1945 just as the camp was being liberated.

King, Stella. *Jacqueline*, 1989

Marshal Edward
RYDZ-SMIGLY
1886–1943

It is doubtful whether the Polish forces could have delayed or seri-

Field Marshal von Runstedt, who was critical of the Ardennes offensive of December 1944. (IWM MH10132)

ously hampered the German invasion of their country, but, as their Commander-in-Chief, and Prime Minister of the country, Rydz-Smigly could have reacted quicker than he did. Such moves he did make were nullified by the pace of the German advance, and when he concentrated his men and arms in the south-east he found that the Russians were invading there, and the cause was lost. SIKORSKI had steadfastly refused him a command when he was in control, and now, from his base in exile, dismissed him. He fled to Roumania, but later returned to work with the Polish underground.

Odette
SANSOM
1912–

She was recruited by SOE who sought suitable French-born, English-speaking personnel to run the Resistance circuits in France. Arriving in the south, she linked up with PETER CHURCHILL and stayed with him and his 'Spindle' network. She was arrested with him when he was taken into custody after returning from a London visit in April 1943 and spent the rest of the war being grossly ill treated in concentration camps. Her story captured the public imagination but her work had been less valuable than that of many similar SOE agents.

Fritz
SAUCKEL
1894–1946

An early recruit to the Nazi Party and an unquestioning devotee of HITLER's. Before the war he was recommended by BORMANN for a defence commissariat post with special responsibility for labour allocation. With the pressures of war he was required to produce ever more manpower to keep the war machine moving. Despite any good intentions he might have had initially, he soon dispensed with humanitarian treatment of foreign workers and resorted to kidnapping and brutal threats in a deportation plan which brought more than five million people to Germany in the greatest acquisition of slave labour ever seen. He denuded the occupied territories of policemen, office workers, farmers and teachers; in fact, anyone who fell into the clutches of his ruthless search squads. At his Nuremberg trial he claimed ignorance of the concentration camps and was still proclaiming his innocence as he mounted the gallows.

Dr. Hjalmar
SCHACHT
1877–1970

By his early 40s he was a highly respected banker and demonstrated such advanced awareness of the financial world that he was asked to come up with a solution to the inflation that was holding the country back. He was soon President of the Reichsbank.

His reading of *Mein Kampf* convinced him that HITLER could be the leader he believed the country needed and, though not a convert to Naziism as a dogma – he had helped form the German Democratic Party – he made himself available in support of its cause. Hitler was elated; the financier was a considerable coup and was immediately given higher status. As Minister of Economics he secured funds for rearmament while guarding against fresh inflation.

It was not long, however, before the excesses of the Nazi regime began to sour his commitment. The purge of the generals in 1938, and the persecution of the Jews, unsettled him and the war rantings of Hitler saw him turn towards the resistance movement, albeit without active involvement. He was arrested at the time of the 1944 bomb plot and spent the remainder of the war in concentration camps.

He was infuriated that the Nuremberg trial placed him, an international banker, alongside manic military criminals. He protested his innocence and was acquitted, but other German trials followed before he was finally given full freedom in 1950.

Schacht, H. *Confessions of 'the Old Wizard'*, 1956

General Walther
SCHELLENBERG
1911–1952

When he joined the SS and its intelligence branch, the Sicherheitdienst (SD), in 1934, he was highly prized as an able linguist and learned, worldly organiser. HEYDRICH encouraged his promotion and deployment on crucial missions, including post-invasion activity in Austria and Poland, and the infiltration of the Dutch resistance to trap British MI6 agents in Holland. In 1940 he drew up a list of more than 2,300 British citizens to be detained after the proposed German invasion, and he was even sent to Portugal with the aim of kidnapping the Duke of Windsor.

After CANARIS was arrested in 1944, Schellenberg took charge of all secret service departments and was later a motivating force behind HIMMLER's abortive efforts to secure an armistice meeting with the Allies using COUNT BERNADOTTE as a go-between. At Nuremberg he was sentenced to six years' imprisonment.

Field Marshal Friedrich
SCHOERNER
1892–1973

Without ever becoming one of the noted 'names' of the German military hierarchy, he was a vigorous, uncompromising commander who was one of the last field marshals appointed by HITLER and enjoyed

143

his leader's support to such a degree that, in the Berlin bunker after the Führer's suicide, he assumed the role of Commander-in-Chief, which he had so coveted. During 1944 he had commanded Army Group South in the Ukraine and then Army Group North, before taking charge of German Central Zone forces, including Berlin, which brought him close to Hitler at the end.

General Ronald
SCOBIE
1893–1969

He led the breakout from Tobruk on 20 November 1941, having replaced the Australian garrison commander the month before. He stayed in the Mediterranean Theatre as GOC Malta during 1942 and Chief of Staff of Middle East Command in 1943 before moving to Greece to take command of the Allied action which forced the German withdrawal from Athens. Although this removed one problem, Scobie found he had inherited another – the developing civil strife which could only be quelled by a dominant British presence. CHURCHILL urged Scobie to keep the communist usurpers in check and deprived of external support. Once this was achieved they were forced to make a truce in January 1945.

General Sir Geoffrey
SCOONES
1893–1975

In the difficult campaign in Burma he proved a determined and adaptable commander. The early war years had seen him at Allied Headquarters in India where he latterly took responsibility for Military Operations and Intelligence. In July 1942 he moved to Imphal to command IV Corps, which obliged him to operate under GENERAL STILWELL in the newly created South-East Asia Command. At the beginning of 1944 he mounted an offensive by IV Corps across the Chindwin river in order to counter a reported Japanese incursion there. In an astute withdrawal Scoones enabled his men to set up a rugged defence which held the Japanese until they ran out of ideas and supplies which, in turn, gave the Allies the chance of an advance into central Burma. Scoones ended the war as General Officer Commanding, Central India Command.

General Scobie poses with Harold Macmillan and Rear-Admiral Mansfield at the time of the liberation of Greece.

General Sir Geoffrey Scoones, one of the excellent commanders in the Burma Theatre. (IWM IND3687)

Dr Arthur von
SEYSS-INQUART
1892–1946

Before the war he acted as a 'Fifth Columnist' in Austria where the Nazi Party was illegal. When he was appointed Minister of the Interior under pressure from HITLER, he became more overtly supportive of the German cause and assisted the Nazi take-over of the country as the newly-created Chancellor of what the Germans chose to call 'Ostmark'. Thereafter he briefly served as deputy governor of the remaining Polish territories not under annexation by Germany or Russia, but in May 1940 became Reichskommisar for Holland where he employed the judicial powers given to him with a ruthlessness that appalled the Dutch people. He seized property and manufactured goods, deported more than 100,000 Jews and sent millions of Dutch nationals into forced labour. He swore repentance at Nuremberg, but was hanged on 16 October.

Dr Arthur von Seyss-Inquart attends a charity meal. His demeanour here belies his exploitative and oppressive measures against Jews and the nationals of occupied countries. (IWM MH13113)

Marshal Boris
SHAPOSHNIKOV
1882–1945

So long as his theories were pertinent to STALIN's personal strategy he was well regarded and given high office, being a member of the Soviet High Command and for a time its Chief with ZHUKOV as his subordinate. But when he urged the expediency of withdrawal in 1940 he was removed and replaced by MERETSKOV, but was reinstated after the German invasion. When he again declined to change his policy proposals he incurred his leader's wrath anew and was substituted by VASILIEVSKY though he remained active in military planning and training.

Mamoru
SHIGEMITSU
1881–1957

During the first years of the war he was Japan's Ambassador in London where he sought to allay fears about Japanese militancy. After Pearl Harbor he was moved to Paris by TOJO who later made him Foreign Minister. In April 1945 he was replaced by TOGO but was still one of the surrender party at the signing aboard USS *Missouri*. He was imprisoned for war crimes but returned to political office in the mid-1950s.

General Wladyslaw
SIKORSKI
1881–1943

Although a political leader from the days of World War One, Sikorsky was not favoured by the Polish leadership prior to World War Two. Both Pilsudski and RYDZ-SMIGLY showed reluctance to use him in high office, perhaps because of his ambitious trait but also because of the diverse nature of his support.

General Sikorski at Tobruk in November 1941. (IWM HU17589)

When Poland fell Sikorski was in Paris and remained there to head a government-in-exile and set up a fighting force to aid the Allied effort. When France was overrun he moved his organisation to London and enjoyed a close relationship with the British leaders.

When the Soviet Union was struggling to hold the German invasion in 1941, Sikorski negotiated an agreement with Moscow which had as its main points a recognition of previous borders, a rescinding of any Soviet/German partitioning and an amnesty for prisoners and

Sikorski, Churchill and de Gaulle at an armoured vehicle demonstration. (IWM H7233

deportees. A result of the collaboration was that GENERAL ANDERS was able to recruit a Polish army from his people in the Soviet Labour Camps.

This work high-lighted the unexplained disappearance of thousands of Poles from these wretched places and brought evidence of mass murders. Sikorski presented the findings to CHURCHILL but found that the British were influenced by their need to keep their alliance with the Soviets intact and thus unable to give overt support to the investigations urged by Sikorski.

When STALIN heard of Anders' reports and Sikorski's use of them he mounted a campaign against the government-in-exile and broke his agreements with it. In the midst of this complex rift Sikorski was killed in an air crash at Gibraltar on 4 July 1943.

His ability to liaise with both Churchill and Stalin gave his nation a strong profile in Allied planning, but this influence ebbed away after his death.

General Dusan
SIMOVIC
1882–1962

When PRINCE PAUL of Yugoslavia appeared to be submitting to German pressure in February 1941 – HITLER had demanded his government's agreement to allow German troops and equipment to pass

General Simovic on a visit to London. (IWM D4305)

through the country as a ruse to create a presence there – Simovic advised him of the dire consequences. He told Paul that the people and the Army would not accept such a move and, when an agreement was secretly signed on 25 May, an Army-led coup saw Paul replaced by PETER II and Simovic becoming the head of the new government.

This guaranteed Allied support and increased the urging on Simovic to involve Slav troops in the war against Hitler. The Serb preferred a neutral path, believing that this might delay a German invasion but his naïvety became apparent when the April attacks saw a thousand aircraft and seven panzer divisions thrown against Yugoslavia, the capital occupied within a week and the elimination of all resistance inside a month.

Simovic escaped to Greece with King Peter and briefly led a government-in-exile. At the end of the war any preference shown by the king to return Simovic to power was overruled by the depth of support enjoyed by TITO.

Lieutenant-Colonel Otto
SKORZENY
1908–1975

'The most dangerous man in Europe' was how some Americans described Skorzeny after his activities against their troops in the Battle of the Bulge towards the end of the war.

He was an audacious, devil-may-care extrovert whose daring exploits endeared him to HITLER and, incidentally, kept him clear of several post-war attempts to bring him to prosecution and secured him safety in Spain where he founded an organisation to assist SS escapees. Later he moved into legitimate business and even boasted a country estate in the Irish Republic and a house in Majorca.

Having been invalided out of mainstream military activities at the end of 1942, he was soon recruited to create a special commando unit. He had found his true calling.

The scarred face of Otto Skorzeny. (IWM HU46178)

ian leader, HORTHY, with the aim of bringing him to heel but actually securing his abdication; conduct daring missions into the heart of the collapsing Eastern Front; and infiltrate US troops in the midst of the Ardennes battles.

Although his exploits have been embellished by post-war retelling, he clearly achieved more than could have been expected of a single officer in the middle of such a vast war. It is right that he should have a place in the 'hall of fame' of special-purpose force practitioners. Had any of the World War Two combatants used more élite tactical units the effects could have been substantial.

Foley, C. *Commando Extraordinary*, 1954

Whiting, C . *Otto Skorzeny*, 1972

Air Marshal Sir John
SLESSOR
1897–1979

'War is never prevented by running away from it', was one of Slessor's many valid observations during an impressive career in which he never shirked the heavy demands of war management.

His war experience was three-fold. Working in Air Ministry Planning at the start, he played an important role in staff discussions in Washington which set the 'Europe First' agenda. He was made Officer Commanding 5 Bomber Group and then Assistant Chief of the Air Staff before moving into the second phase of his war in 1943, as Air Officer Commander-in-Chief of Coastal Command. Here he saw that arm through its triumphant assault on the U-boat threat where the tactic of escorting convoys from the air reduced DÖNITZ's Wolf Pack impact and kept the Atlantic and English Channel clear for supplies and for the fresh offensives headed by the D-Day Landings.

Within a year he and his team had mounted a remarkable raid on Gran Sasso, where MUSSOLINI was being held, and spirited the dictator away.

Other clandestine actions saw him kidnap the son of the Hungar-

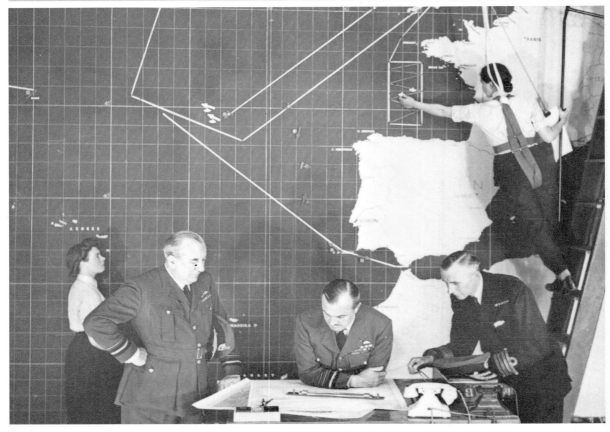

Air Marshal Sir John Slessor studies a map in an Operations Room. (IWM MU69906)

At the beginning of 1944 he moved to the Mediterranean as Commander-in-Chief of the RAF deployments there and Deputy C-in-C of the Allied Air Forces in the region.

General Sir William
SLIM
1891–1970

Having served with distinction in World War One, he proved a great commander when given the newly formed Fourteenth Army with which to reclaim Burma, and this from a man of modest background, not commonly the source for high-ranking positions in the British Army.

His war had begun with 5th Indian Division in the Sudan and,

after convalescing from injuries sustained there, with 10th Indian Division in Iraq. He remained active in Syria and Iran during 1941 with good results, and was then sent to Burma to command I Corps in 1942. It was a rude awakening for someone who had known mostly success for he had to conduct a morale-shattering retreat, but he spent the next two years planning an offensive formula which would reverse the situation.

In December 1943 he began his campaign with hard fighting to retake Arakan and then his astute planning and rigorous troop training paid off in the prolonged actions at Kohima and Imphal. He then harried the Japanese through their

retreat to Mandalay and Meiktila, forcing them to evacuate before he reached Rangoon.

In a theatre which was often forgotten amidst the concentration on the European action, Slim had reinvigorated a dispirited force and defeated the Japanese in a terrain they favoured. Lacking the support he might have expected to receive, he used diverse means, including guerrilla tactics with WINGATE and MERRILL and dangerous air-support techniques, to achieve a great land victory over the Japanese when it could not have been anticipated. His attention to maintaining morale was aided by a wry humour shown by his observation that battle always took place 'uphill and at the junction of two or more map sheets'.

Rooney, D. *Burma Victory*, 1992
Slim, W. *Courage and other Broadcasts*, 1957
– *Defeat into Victory*, 1963

General Holland 'Howlin' Mad'
SMITH
1882–1967

This tough, uncompromising US Marine general commanded amphibious actions throughout the Pacific Theatre and was instrumental in evolving the tactics of this form of warfare. He set up the Amphibious Corps at Pearl Harbor in September 1943 and from this base he trained and directed his men for the raids on the Gilbert and Marshall Islands and on Saipan and Tinian in the Marianas. His tri-service approach to the amphibious strategy and the high losses he suffered led to friction with Army commanders, especially when Smith sacked his namesake, Ralph Smith of 27th Infantry Division. In August 1944 he was given command of the new Fleet Marine Force but was sent back to the USA to take up a training command before the Japanese surrender. Smith typified the robust spirit of many American commanders. His determination overcame a succession of tough assignments.

Jan Christiaan
SMUTS
1870–1950

He had fought for the Boers against the British before becoming a British ally in his corner of their Empire. When World War Two began he urged active South African support – he had served in the British War Cabinet for part of World War One – while his colleague in the coalition government of the time, General Herzog, took a neutral stance. Smuts won the

A BBC reporter gets a first-hand account of the war from General Slim in Mandalay. (IWM SE3527)

Jan Smuts with Churchill and Alanbrooke, crossing the English Channel. (IWM 24023)

debate and assumed sole leadership, enabling Britain to benefit hugely from the considerable input of men and materiel to the Allied war effort. South Africans fought in the Mediterranean Theatre and Smuts himself became a trusted confidant and adviser of CHURCHILL and his commanders. He attended the Cairo Conference in November 1943 and the signing of the Peace Agreement at Versailles in 1946, the only person to have been present at this meeting and its equivalent in 1919.

Marshal Vasiliy
SOKOLOVSKY
1897–1968

Serving under GENERAL KONEV as Chief of Staff of the Western Front from 1941 to 1943, he was active in setting the tactics for the Battle of Kursk and then of putting them into practice. He moved forward to take Smolensk on 25 September 1943 and drove on towards Vitebsk by December, before transferring to the attacks on MODEL's forces around Lvov. When he became Chief of Staff to 1st Ukrainian Front he was criticised for a lack of offensive spirit against Army Group G in the Pripet Marshes, but survived this to join the final push for Berlin with 1st Belorussian Front under ZHUKOV.

Admiral Sir James
SOMERVILLE
1882–1949

To him fell the unenviable task, while Commander of Force H at Gibraltar, of threatening the French fleet at Oran in July 1940 with attack unless they immobilised or moved clear of Axis control. Although the French had assured the Allies that their vessels would not be allowed to fall into enemy hands, the commander of these ships seemed slow to move and, when he failed to react to a Somerville ultimatum, the British opened fire, causing the loss of nearly 1,300 lives. Later he was active in an attack on Genoa and the pursuit and sinking of the *Bismarck* on 27 May 1941. After his busy service in the Mediterranean and Atlantic, he moved to the Indian Ocean as Commander-in-Chief Eastern Fleet, operating out of Ceylon. He ended the war as head of the British naval administration in Washington.

Marshal Sokolovsky inspects the award presented to him by Montgomery at Gatow in July 1945. (IWM BU8906)

Aboard his flagship, Admiral Somerville scans the horizon with his Chief of Staff Captain William Powlett. (IWM A6259)

Richard
SORGE
1895–1944

For many years prior to World War Two, he was a spy for the USSR in Japan. Using his journalist's credentials, he enjoyed the favours of the German Embassy in Tokyo and gained information from there and from a team of agents throughout Japan. He gave STALIN warning of the proposed Operation 'Barbarossa' and enabled him to concentrate forces elsewhere by his assurances that Japan had no plans to invade Siberia. In 1941 his network was discovered by the Japanese Secret Service. He was arrested, tried and hanged in October.

General Carl
SPAATZ
1891–1974

Having been an observer in London at the time of the Battle of Britain, Carl 'Tooey' Spaatz was well placed to command 8th Air Force when it was sent to England to take part in the air offensive over Europe. His early preference for daylight bombing was prejudiced by the heavy losses incurred by his unprotected bombers. The arrival of escort fighter aircraft such as the Mustang was a step forward, but bombing was still imprecise, despite public announcements to the contrary. In the spring of 1943 he was sent to the Mediterranean Theatre as Deputy Commanding General of the Allied Air Forces there, but was back in England by January 1944 to coordinate the work of 8th Air Force in Britain and 15th Air Force in Italy.

When the time came to plan the air element for the Normandy landings he found himself in the midst of the power struggle affecting LEIGH-MALLORY, HARRIS and TEDDER over the role and management of the Allied Air Forces in the operation. Despite this his aircraft played a fundamental part in attacking German communication lines and industry once the invasion was under way.

With much of his job done in Europe, he was transferred to command US Strategic Air Force Pacific where he master-minded the

General Spaatz was an official observer during the Battle of Britain, but ended a busy war commanding the Group that carried the atom bombs to Japan.
(IWM NYT22090A)

bombing raids on Japan ending with the dropping of the atomic bombs on Hiroshima and Nagasaki.

Albert
SPEER
1905–1982

Trained as an architect, he brought his orderly mind to the planning of HITLER's pre-war rallies, to formulating Nazi policy, and redesigning the Chancellery in Berlin and the Party Palace at Nuremberg.

It was when he was chosen as the unlikely successor to Fritz Todt, the Armaments Minister who had been killed in an air crash in February 1942, that Speer truly made an impact. Now his acute attention to detail and his mental energy was directed at increasing industrial production to keep the war effort strong. Such was his success that it

can be argued that Speer did as much as anyone in the Nazi hierarchy to prolong the war; his administration of factory programmes, and relocation in the face of Allied bombing, kept output rising until the last months of 1944.

Only when his own results were affected by the lack of transport and raw materials, and he began to see defeat as inevitable, did Speer's enthusiasm subside. At Nuremberg he pleaded guilty to the use of slave labour and was sentenced to 20 years' imprisonment though even this time was used constructively, by penning *Inside the Third Reich*, the most authoritative description of the German war from one who had had Hitler's confidence throughout.

Speer, A. *Inside the Third Reich*, 1970

Field Marshal Hugo
SPERRLE
1885–1953

He had fought in the air force during World War One, stayed on active service thereafter and transferred to the infant Luftwaffe to command the first units sent to assist the Nationalists in the Spanish Civil War. In World War Two, like so many of his colleagues, he experienced the highs and lows of command. From January 1939 he commanded Luftflotte III in north-west Europe and saw its successful participation in the campaign in the Low Countries and France. He led the group throughout the Battle of Britain and, indeed, remained with it for most of the war, including its inept response to the Normandy invasion of 1944, which brought his retire-

Albert Speer tours the fortifications on the Atlantic coast in 1944. (IWM HU3045)

Under Field Marshal Hugo Sperrle communication between the various Luftwaffe commands was not as good as it should have been. (IWM MH6096)

ment. A large, intimidating man, he was well regarded by HITLER, though his working relationship with KESSELRING when the latter was commanding Luftflotte II was none too effective. He was acquitted at Nuremberg.

Admiral Raymond
SPRUANCE
1886–1969

One need look no further than Spruance for an example of the quality of determined commanders whom the American High Command employed to retake the Pacific. nor one who better demonstrates the commitment to their country's cause, for it was Spruance who said, 'If a man is not inclined to risk his life for his country he should look elsewhere until he finds a country he will risk his life for.'

At the outbreak of the war with Japan, he was commanding a cruiser division in the central Pacific and was active at the Battle of Midway where, assuming command of the US naval forces there after the loss of FLETCHER's flagship, *Yorktown*, in early June 1942, he showed effective judgement in securing the first Allied victory against the Japanese fleet.

Working later as Chief of Staff to ADMIRAL NIMITZ, he planned the operations in the Solomons before, as Commander of 5th Fleet, he led the decisive offensive through the Gilbert and Marshall Islands where he skilfully employed the leap-frogging tactic. He was promoted full Admiral in February 1944 and participated in all the major actions thereafter, including the planning of the Philippine Sea Battle and the naval elements for Iwo Jima and Okinawa.

His record was outstanding, the only question mark being the delay of offensive flights against the Japanese fleets during the Philippine Sea engagement. This showed Spruance at his most cautious, but historians are now ready to credit him with the sound reasoning of setting targets and sticking to them. Had he pursued the enemy vessels, as seemed desirable at the time, he could have been distracted from his next goal, Saipan. It was a typical adherence to a scheme by a commander who pioneered many naval war strategies involving carrier forces and amphibious landings.

Josef
STALIN
1879–1953

Of the national leaders involved in World War Two, he was surely the most complex in terms of policy and persona. As certainly as the lack of preparedness of the Soviet Army can be laid at his door, so the fact that he led his nation back from the brink of defeat is also without question, though in this he was aided by some outstanding battlefield commanders.

He had become involved in radical politics in his early twenties, was soon exiled to Siberia but returned to take part in the revolution of 1905–7 which brought further punishment. In 1914 he changed his name from Dzhugashvili to Stalin, literally 'Man of Steel', as his involvement in the Bolshevik Party grew to a point where, by 1917, he was on its central committee and five years later was its General Secretary. From this position of power he became the natural successor to Lenin.

For the next fifteen years he ruled with a rod of iron which quelled opposition, installed agrarian policies which brought hardship and death as much as food for the masses, and, just three years before HITLER invaded, purged his army of 10,000 of its best trained officers.

In 1939, affronted by the lack of readiness shown by Britain and France to include him in their alliance against Germany, he allowed his Foreign Minister MOLOTOV to sign a non-aggression pact with Hitler. The perceived benefits of a secure slice of eastern Europe and huge trading improvements began to be realised, but Stalin's ability to expand his empire foundered on his Army's poor performance in the attempted invasion of Finland in November 1939 and was then blown apart in June 1941 when Hitler invaded Russia.

The six months of German advance would have destroyed most governing structures and taken their leaders with them. With one and a half million dead and twice that number taken prisoner, Stalin had lost much of his human ammunition and most of any credibility he might have claimed as a warlord. He found his own battlefield inexperience was a handicap and his 'placed' commanders likewise ill-equipped. He called for ZHUKOV and this appointment, combined with German failings, prevented Hitler taking Moscow, enabled the Soviets to regroup and saw the invaders driven back whence they had come, and beyond.

Stalin makes a point. (IWM HU10180)

Scots Guards line the route for Stalin's arrival at a reception given by Winston Churchill during the Yalta Conference in February 1945. (IWM BU9192)

In the winter of 1941 the battle for Moscow was won by a hair's breadth, in the winter of 1942 the mighty German Sixth Army was destroyed at Stalingrad, and in the summer of 1943 the victory at Kursk saw the Germans in retreat. Army Group Centre was wiped out a year later and soon Soviet forces were linking up with American and British forces on German territory. Thereafter the Japanese incursion in Manchuria was comfortably reversed.

From the moment of the Moscow Conference of December 1941, Stalin played a full role in Allied discussion on the prosecution of the war, constantly pressing CHURCHILL and ROOSEVELT to open a second front and regularly threatening to negotiate a settlement with Germany when he was failing to get his way. He fought his corner well, managing to drive a wedge between the normally concordant British and American leaders and securing concessions with promises he probably had no intention of keeping.

If one assesses Stalin's performance on the war years alone, one might come to the conclusion that while his surviving generals openly gave him credit for strategic direction – all the more remarkable when one remembers what he did to so many of their colleagues in 1937–8 – it is more likely that victory in the Great Patriotic War, the Soviet's own description for the 1939–45 conflict, was secured by the brilliance of his commanders and the errors of Hitler. As a negotiator he was tough, devious and deliberate; as a dictator he was cruel, callous and vindictive; as a national leader he was domineering and despotic. And he was fortunate that his country's greatest weapon – its climate – served the nation as well in the defeat of Hitler's Germany as it had done for Napoleon's France.

Axell, A. *Stalin's War through the Eyes of his Commanders*, 1997
Erickson, J. *The Soviet High Command*, 1962

Tucker, R . *Stalin in Power*, 1990

Ulam, A. *Stalin: The Man and his Era*, 1974

Volkogonov, D. *Stalin: Triumph and Tragedy*, 1991

Admiral Harold
STARK
1880–1972

That the US Navy was able to show a degree of readiness for conflict when called into the war was very much down to Harold Stark, and the judgement of those who appointed him Chief of Naval Operations in 1939. Not only did he oversee the massive building programme which saw such an expansion in the operational capability, but he held lengthy clandestine meetings with the British naval strategists so as to keep abreast of tactical thinking and experience, and contributed the American point of view. Although he was officially criticised for a delay in alerting ADMIRAL KIMMEL at Pearl Harbor to the imminent attack, the validity of his preparatory work was shown by the speed of reaction thereafter. In March 1942 he was given command of US Naval Forces in the European Theatre and this caused him to ague strongly for the 'Europe First' agenda at the many Allied conferences and policy meetings. At these times, when Anglo–American co-operation was vital to the winning of the war, Stark was a masterly diplomatic fixer and assessor of priorities.

Colonel Claus von
STAUFFENBERG
1907–1944

During the successful early war record of this young Army officer there was no hint of the fatal drama in which he would eventually be involved. Having fought with distinction in Poland and France, he

Admiral Harold Stark enjoys a joke with King George VI. (IWM EN50880)

was serving in the Western Desert when in the spring of 1943 he was severely wounded by bullets from a strafing aircraft. Losing an eye and much of his right arm, he was given staff appointments at the Reserve Army Headquarters where an anti-HITLER stance became more pronounced. Now Chief of Staff to OLBRICHT, he became influenced by the views of those resisting the leadership and when required to attend a meeting in Prussia, at

Hitler's Rastenburg HQ in July 1944, he saw this as a chance to attempt an assassination. Avoiding security checks, he was able to leave a briefcase containing a bomb in the room chosen for the meeting, but as this was in a temporary building rather than the usual conference bunker, the resulting explosion was dissipated. Stauffenberg, believing the plot to have been successful, flew to Berlin to assure Olbricht, HOEPNER and BECK that Hitler was dead.

In the absence of definite evidence the conspirators hesitated in taking the control they had planned, and by evening Hitler's loyal guard had arrived to arrest them. FROMM, who had avoided complete connivance with the schemers and had telephoned Rastenburg to discover Hitler was still alive, now sided with the loyalists. The plotters first tried to arrest him but he turned the tables and saw them taken into custody. Within a matter of hours Stauffenberg and others were shot and Beck had been persuaded to commit suicide.

Edward
STETTINIUS
1900–1949

One of ROOSEVELT's prudent appointments from industry to assist the nation at war, he was first made Chairman of the War Resources Board and then Director of the Office of Production Management, where he oversaw the production of manufacturing materials required for the war and prepared industry for a war economy. From October 1941 he worked closely with the President on all matters of war production before, in the last years of the war, working on the setting up of the Dumbarton Oaks Conference which would prove to be the founding base of the United Nations. In November 1944 he replaced Cordell Hull as Secretary of State, and attended the Yalta and San Francisco Conferences, though he sacrificed this post in July 1945 to become America's first delegate to the infant UN.

General Joseph
STILWELL
1883–1946

This World War One veteran had studied Chinese before the war, and in the mid-1930s was US Military Attaché in Peking. After Pearl Har-bor GENERAL MARSHALL sought to use his expertise by appointing him commander of the US troops in China, Burma and India, with a special task of training CHIANG KAI-SHEK's forces. He became Chief of Staff to Chiang in March 1942.

Using the Chinese Fifth and Sixth Armies in Burma, he failed to hold off the Japanese advance and had to retreat. When the region was redesignated South-East Asia Command, he was appointed Deputy Supreme Allied Commander under MOUNTBATTEN. This brought diverse responsibilities and convoluted chains of command to a soldier who was fundamentally a

'Vinegar Joe' Stilwell during a visit to a front-line jungle position in northern Burma. (IWM NYP16520)

self-motivated, independent field commander. He struggled to maintain an efficient relationship with Chiang, fell foul of CHENNAULT and did not fit in well with the expanding Allied structure.

'Vinegar Joe' – the nickname he acquired because of his acerbic criticism of others and his abrasive style of command – blamed WINGATE's Chindits for some reversals and Chennault's air force for others; he was appointed Commander of all Chinese forces in an attempt to calm these disputes. His final appointment saw him replace BUCKNER as commander of US Tenth Army on Okinawa.

He was a skilled commander of small military forces and played a vital role in retaining Chinese support for the Allied effort. As a senior player in a larger force operating a mixed war over a huge area he was limited by his own difficulties with liaison and communication.

Henry
STIMPSON
1867–1950

In 1940, at the age of 72, this Republican was appointed Secretary of War by ROOSEVELT and promptly set about the organisation of mobilisation and training. This was yet another example of the President's ability to pick the man for the job; Stimpson was a strong advocate of America's playing its due role in the European War, even to setting victory against HITLER as a priority, and was able to quell the isolationist caucus with his debating skill and experience of high office. He was instrumental in securing aid for Britain and championed the collaborative cause at the major conferences and to the US media. He was a prime mover in accelerating atomic research and took personal responsibility for the Manhattan Project, America's quest for an atomic weapon. He urged its use in August 1945. He was one of Roosevelt's strong men.

Colonel David
STIRLING
1915–1990

If imitation is the most sincere form of flattery and the best indicator of endorsement, David Stirling is rightly adjudged the creator of special forces warfare; many of the tactics he devised and evolved are now, fifty years later, on the first pages of élite unit military manuals. He began his war with the Scots Guards but transferred to the new Commando units and was sent to the Middle East. There, in circumstances more obviously suitable for such schemes, he devised plans for raids far behind enemy lines to destroy aircraft and supplies. He persuaded his superiors to release personnel and began a series of attacks on installations the Germans

Colonel David Stirling, creator of many special forces concepts. (IWM E21340)

thought were safe. In 1942 the unit had become a regular regiment, the Special Air Service, and its daring exploits had earned its leader the title of the 'Phantom Major.' Such was the success of the SAS teams that the Germans set up units to operate against them and one of these captured Stirling early in 1943. Because of his determined escape attempts, he was eventually kept in Colditz until the liberation. Although the development of special-purpose forces was restricted in World War Two, it saw their birth and proved their value.

General Sir Montagu
STOPFORD
1892–1971

The eventual success of the Burma campaign was due to some outstanding British commanders; one of the finest being Montagu Stop-ford. He was posted to command XXXIII Indian Corps when the Japanese attacked across the Chindwin in early 1944. Although the Japanese had cut the Kohima–Imphal road and the tiny Kohima garrison was outnumbered and under incessant attack, Stopford raced to clear the road-block and relieve Kohima before advancing to link up with SCOONES' IV Corps and take part in the siege of Imphal. Stopford's corps maintained the advance to retake Meiktila and attack Mandalay by March 1945 and capture the Yenangyaung oil-fields. His reward was command of Fourteenth Army and the role of accepting the Japanese surrender in Burma. Like his fellow officers in this most hostile of World War Two theatres, he moved his men with a pace and tactical deftness that brought victory against heavy odds.

Julius
STREICHER
1885–1946

In him the Nazi Party found a member so cruel, sadistic and dishonest that it had to restrict his excesses on several occasions and did not reward his loyalty with high office. As early as 1919 he had created an anti-Semitic party – the Nuremberg German Socialists – and all ADOLF HITLER's persuasive powers were needed to get him to amalgamate with the National Socialist Party. It was a move which welded the two men together for life and, until the outbreak of war, Streicher was a strong ally, assisting with the Beer Hall Putsch of 1923, propagating the Hitler gospel in his anti-Jewish newspaper, *Der Sturmer*, and staging the Nuremberg rallies of 1935. In 1940 GÖRING organised an investigation

Julius Streicher was too devious and crooked for office even under Hitler's regime. (IWM FLM1533)

into Streicher's general crooked-ness and this brought his dismissal from his post as Gauleiter of Franconia, but Hitler exacted no penalty and Streicher was allowed to return to his country home. He was found guilty and executed at Nuremberg, screaming anti-Jewish invective to the last.

General Kurt
STUDENT
1890–1978

Both veterans of World War One, GÖRING and Student were each influential in the Luftwaffe when it was created in 1934, the former as its first Commander-in-Chief, and Student selected by Göring as the man to develop airborne transport and the deployment of troops made possible by the parachute and the use of gliders. He was to prove a trail-blazer, weaving the parachute infantry into the *Blitzkrieg* tactic across north-west Europe. The extraordinary drop on Crete in 1941, though a masterpiece of tactical skill, was too costly in lives to pass HITLER without notice, however, and it saw the end of large paratroop operations; the force was thereafter restricted to tactical reserve work as Germany was forced on to the defensive.

Student ended his war as a commander of ground troops, Army Group G in Holland.

Lucas, J. *Hitler's Enforcers*, 1996

General Karl von
STÜLPNAGEL
1886–1944

Although he had expressed vehement opposition to the Nazi Party since 1938, had argued against HITLER's western expansionism, and even planned a coup in November 1939, he was still entrusted with command on the Eastern Front, of Seventeenth

General Kurt Student developed the German paratroop forces. (IWM MH6100)

Army, and was then made Military Governor of occupied France from February 1942.

Even then he maintained a transparently contrary policy to that dictated from Berlin, risking his own life to argue against the work of the SS and the Gestapo and seeking to persuade ROMMEL, a long-time friend, and VON RUNDSTEDT to

General von Stülpnagel was a leading member of the groups that opposed Hitler. (IWM HU17255)

General Hajime
SUGIYAMA
1880–1945

As Minister of War in 1937–8, he was directly involved in the China campaign and, once he had been appointed Army Chief of Staff, he worked with NAGANO, his naval counterpart, to pressure the Americans into war. Once the war had begun he master-minded the Japanese efforts from Tokyo but resigned in February 1944 so as to free TOJO's route to power. Once the latter had fallen, Sugiyama worked with KOISO until the surrender, after which he committed suicide.

General Daniel
SULTAN
1885–1947

Dan Sultan succeeded STILWELL as Commander-in-Chief of the US troops in the China–Burma–India Theatre from November 1944, having been Deputy Commander since the spring of 1942. He commanded the drive south from Myitkyina to re-open the Ledo Road and reached Lashio by 7 March 1945 while the Japanese were being forced back to Mandalay and beyond.

Kantaro
SUZUKI
1867–1948

This war veteran had retired in 1927, been brought back as an adviser to the Emperor two years later, and only just escaped assassination in the Army extremists' coup of 1936. In August 1944, after the failure of the short-lived TOJO regime, he was appointed President of the Privy Council and further drawn into the political arena when made Prime Minister and asked to form a cabinet when KOISO's government fell on 5 April 1945. Although he had the stature to conduct the difficult conclusion to the

secure peace terms with the Allies. When opposition to Hitler grew, he set his own plans in train in France. On the advice that the assassination attempt was under way at Rastenburg, his men arrested 1,200 Gestapo and SS men in Paris. After the failure of STAUFFENBERG's bomb, he was recalled to Berlin to face the consequences of his actions. Choosing to travel by car rather than air as requested, he halted his convoy near Sedan, excused himself from his escort and attempted suicide. The gun shot removed an eye but did not kill him; he was put on trial in Berlin and hanged on 30 August 1944.

war – there were plenty in the armed forces wanting to fight on to the death – he was now 78 years old and proved weak in negotiations with STALIN and others. On 14 August 1945 he persuaded the government to involve the Emperor in choosing the path the nation should follow; the surrender broadcast followed, together with Suzuki's resignation.

Rear Admiral Raizo
TANAKA
1892–1969

Had this competent commander not argued his way out of favour Japanese sea power would have benefited from his expertise. He led convoy forces for invasions in the Philippines, Timor and Java, and a transport group at Midway, but his name is most associated with Guadalcanal which, though he proposed tactical abandonment of the island, he kept supplied via the daring 'Tokyo Express' night missions. On 12–14 November 1942 he tried a huge landing on Guadalcanal but could only get 2,000 men and limited supplies ashore. A few weeks later, while seeking to float fresh materiel on to the island, he inflicted a resounding defeat on a US force which had stumbled across his activities but become muddled by his nocturnal manoeuvres. In the summer of 1943 he was in turn out-

fought by the Americans during a night action off Kolombangara and lost his flagship. Having witnessed great wastage of resources and much loss of life, he did not hold back in his criticism of his superiors, with the result that he lost his command.

Air Chief Marshal Sir Arthur
TEDDER
1890–1967

He survived a chequered relationship with CHURCHILL to have a busy war and leave a major imprint on the Allied success. His strong and determined advocacy of using air superiority to damage enemy ground positions and supply routes ensured that the strategy prospered. 'Tedder's Carpet' may have been an expression born of criticism but it became a compliment.

He had headed Research and Development at the Air Ministry at the beginning of the war, but he succeeded Longmore as Commander-in-Chief Middle East in 1941 and began to prove his theories in practice during the Desert War

Air Chief Marshal Sir Arthur Tedder reads reports in his caravan in North Africa.
(IWM CNA2266)

where air attacks on enemy airfields and fuel dumps accelerated land success, a fact not lost on his colleagues in the Army hierarchy!

Appointed EISENHOWER's deputy at the Casablanca Conference in January 1943, he resumed a planning profile which saw even more sophisticated liaison between air and land units for the invasions of Sicily and Italy. It was natural that he should apply the same theories to the D-Day landings where he also needed to keep the divergent views of LEIGH-MALLORY, SPAATZ and HARRIS concentrated on the final goal. The end result of Tedder's work – the isolation of the Normandy invasion zone from the network of German supply – was a crucial element in the success of the operation.

Tedder, A. *With Prejudice* (Memoirs), 1966

Field Marshal Hisaichi
TERAUCHI
1879–1945

On 6 November 1941 this son of a former prime minister took command of the Southern Army, with YAMASHITA and HOMMA subordinate to him. From his Saigon headquarters he directed the invasion of Indo–China, Siam, Malaya and Java, and completed the task ahead of schedule. Equal haste was shown in his building of the Burma Road, where his brutal employment of prisoner-of-war labour saw more than 15,000 men die and Terauchi complaining to Homma about what he deemed to be too generous treatment of natives in the area. Although he moved from Saigon to Manila, he stayed with the Southern Army despite being a possible replacement for TOJO after his fall from power. By now however he was fighting rearguard actions, especially at Leyte where he fought on despite losing many men and vessels to enemy aircraft. In April 1945 he suffered a cerebral haemorrhage and was unable to attend the formal surrender at Singapore; he had accepted the Emperor's surrender order only after a visit from Prince Haruhito.

General Hein
TER POORTEN
1887–1948

As Commander-in-Chief of land forces there, it fell to him to take charge of the defence of the Dutch East Indies against the Japanese in January 1942. Although he had good numbers of trained troops he lacked artillery, transport and air back-up, and was not able to rely on consistent support from US bomber units because their shortage of fighter escorts rendered them vulnerable. As part of his protection of Sarawak, the Celebes and Tarakan/Borneo, he destroyed the oilfields in those territories to save them being taken by the Japanese, to whom he surrendered in March.

Colonel Paul
TIBBETS
1915–1994

He had been a noted bomber pilot in Europe, being one of the first Americans to fly over German-held territory. He piloted *Enola Gay*, the B-29 which dropped 'Little Boy' on Hiroshima on 6 August 1945 and persuaded Japan to end the war. In September 1944 he returned to the USA to train crews scheduled to fly atomic bombing missions.

Marshal Semyon
TIMOSHENKO
1895–1970

When STALIN purged the Soviet Army of thousands of its best men just three years before the German invasion, those who remained could not have been expected to perform as if these assets had not been sacrificed. Timoshenko, a long-term friend of Stalin's, and more able than many of the officers the leader retained, was involved in the occupation of Poland and the poor performance in Finland, but his efforts were deemed preferable to those of VOROSHILOV whom he replaced in May 1940 with the task of introducing a harsher training regime and the replacement of horses with tanks.

His laudable efforts were insufficient to prevent the German invasion of June 1941, but he was given command of the Western Front and lost nearly 400,000 men and 400 tanks to the massed German divisions, though he did delay them sufficiently to fall foul of the Russian winter before they reached Moscow. Replacing BUDENNY on the Southwest Front in September, he could not stop the German drive into the Crimea, but in May 1942 he was persuaded to try a counter-offensive at Kharkov. This was quickly reversed by a German attack and his forces were struck down. His subsequent transfer to the Northwest Front saw him fade from the scene and be overtaken by those commanding the forces that were now taking the fight back to the Germans.

President Joseph
TISO
1887–1946

The outcome of World War One saw Slovakia as part of the new Republic of Czechoslovakia, but a lack of power, influence and investment left the Slovaks bitter and disillusioned. Tiso, a Roman Catholic priest, was elected leader of the Slovak People's Party and became a high-profile threat to the Czech government. HITLER prevented his arrest, however, and forced the Czechs to sacrifice control of the Slovak state, a move which brought it recognition by the USSR, France and Britain. Tiso was now a puppet of Germany and his collaborative nature lost him the support of his own people. He fled into hiding in Austria but returned for trial in 1945 and was eventually sentenced to death and hanged in December 1946.

Marshal Josep Broz
TITO
1892–1980

After fighting and organisational experience during the Russian Revolution and Spanish Civil War, he moved quickly when the Germans invaded Yugoslavia. He created the partisan resistance movement without delay and set its eager saboteurs on the invading forces, with some success. He soon had control of several Serb towns and had set up an armaments manufacturing plant and a printing works.

The network of his formative organisation was Communist in nature and soon incurred the opposition of GENERAL MIHAILOVIC, the pro-Allied anti-Communist leader of the rival Cetniks. Now the value to the Allies of partisan activity against the Germans was dispelled by the vicious in-fighting. The Cetniks sided with the invasion forces and reduced Tito to sniping attacks and hasty withdrawals; the Allies looked on powerless, having previously supported Mihailovic and reluctant to back the Communist Tito.

By the summer of 1943, after Fitzroy Maclean had met Tito at his headquarters, Allied aid was made available and, with Italy dropping out of the war, the partisans grew in numbers and armed power. The Yugoslav king in exile dismissed Mihailovic and approached Tito; the Allies proffered enough air support to enable the partisans to see off a large German assault and, by 20 August, take control of Belgrade.

Tito was now effective head of the Yugoslav nation, but post-war elections sealed the fact, enabling him to abolish the monarchy and institute a Communist government of some independence. He was a leader of great resolve and inspirational ability who matured into his role of national leader in a few short years.

Sir Henry
TIZARD
1885–1959

This British scientist and administrator played an important role behind the scenes in refining operational radar, air warfare tactics, international scientific collaboration and the practical implementation of technological advance. He was an opponent of carpet bombing of German residential and manufacturing areas, believing alternative strategies to be capable of equal success.

Marshal Tito outside his mountain headquarters. (IWM NA15132)

Shigenori
TOGO
1882–1950

Having served his country in its Berlin and Washington embassies during the pre-war years, he was confident of Japan's long-term potential as a nation capable of earning world-wide respect and prestige. While the militant stance of the leaders of the armed forces and the dire demands of Prime Minister TOJO held sway, he continued to strive for peace. He was not kept informed of the Pearl Harbor attack and eventually resigned from Tojo's cabinet in September 1942, though he was brought back, again as Foreign Minister, by SUZUKI in April 1945 on the understanding that he would seek a peace settlement. Those who wished to fight on did all they could to hinder his progress; Togo urged surrender provided the Emperor's role was protected. He resigned once he had achieved his goal, in August, and was later sentenced to 20 years' imprisonment by the International Military Tribunal. A worldly intellectual who served Japan well in international circles, he was swamped by the militancy of the Tojo regime.

Dr Fritz
TODT
1882–1950

A brilliant engineer, this World War One veteran was an early recruit to the Nazi Party and spent the pre-war years organising the construction of a new road network and, later, military fortifications, notably the *Westwall* (Siegfried Line), using penal labour battalions to do the work. From 1940 he served as Minister for Armaments and Munitions but was killed in an air crash near HITLER's Eastern Front Headquarters.

General Hideki
TOJO
1884–1948

When he was appointed Minister of War by KONOYE in 1940 his uncomplicated belief in his nation's right to use force to ensure its security was given free rein. Within the year he had stimulated the signing of pacts with Germany and Italy and, by October 1941, had eased Konoye from power to assume the role of Prime Minister for himself. His appointment signalled the end of any reasoned negotiation and he rushed headlong into war. The occupation of French Indo-China, albeit with the tacit agreement of the Vichy regime, was the taster, the raid on Pearl Harbor was the true opening salvo.

Taking for himself the post of Chief of the Army Staff and War Minister in addition to the premiership, he was solely responsible for the progress of the war. Initially he gloried with his countrymen in the attacking successes, but at the first reversals his role was seen as a sham. He hurriedly devolved the war portfolio to UMEZU but continual retreats and defeats brought his resignation on 18 July 1944.

When the Americans reached Tokyo a year later Tojo attempted suicide, but he survived thanks to the treatment given by an American Army doctor, to be one of those hanged in December 1948. His drive for a military solution to Japan's quest for a place at the 'top table' was misguided, being driven by naïve ambition rather than strategic wisdom or political forethought.

Mrs Iva Toguri d'Aquino
'TOKYO ROSE'
1916–

It remains uncertain whether there was one 'Tokyo Rose' or several. The Japanese equivalent to LORD HAW HAW, was a bright, appealing female voice which broadcast propaganda to American troops in the Far East. The speaker would mix confident reports of Japanese successes and certain dominance with dark tales of infidelity by the wives and girlfriends the Americans had left at home. It is probable that Iva d'Aquino, an American citizen and university graduate, was *a* voice, if not the only voice, of Tokyo Rose who, having found herself in Japan at the outbreak of war, chose to stay there and take a job in broadcasting. After the war she was sentenced to ten years' imprisonment of which she served six, but in the mid-1970s she sought to clear her name, claiming coercion and that she was only one of Rose's voices. She did win a Presidential pardon. The truth is that the Americans serving in the Pacific found the broadcasts a light relief from war and will never know whether the only voice they heard was that of Mrs d'Aquino.

Marshal Fyodor
TOLBUKHIN
1894–1949

This Russian commander enjoyed great success against the Germans, for even in the defence of Stalingrad his 57th Army managed to out-manoeuvre and envelop German Sixth Army in the city. In April 1944 he commanded 4th Ukrainian Front to reclaim the Crimea and took 67,000 prisoners in a few weeks. He then worked with MALINOVSKY as they pushed the Germans out of the Balkans and Roumania before moving into Yugoslavia and, aided by TITO's partisans, taking Belgrade. With Malinovsky again he laid siege to Budapest and in March 1945 drove the Sixth SS Panzer Army out of Hungary and into Austria.

Tolbukhin commanded the forces that drove the Germans out of the Crimea. (IWM NA22647)

Admiral Sir John
TOVEY
1885–1971

From his Scapa Flow base he deployed his Home Fleet on missions to protect Atlantic convoys and restrict movement to and from German ports. He commanded the operation which, with SOMER-VILLE's Force H from the Mediterranean, hunted down and sank the *Bismarck* in May 1941. For the next two years the Home Fleet's priority was covering the Arctic convoys to Russia. When *Tirpitz* became a threat he sought permission to destroy her, but was never allowed the time or the ships to do so.

Admiral Soemu
TOYODA
1885–1957

When he succeeded KOGA as Commander-in-Chief of the Japanese Navy in May 1944, he was faced with a rampant American Navy

Admiral Sir John Tovey visits the newly commissioned HMS *Prince of Wales*. (IWM A3891)

steaming through the Pacific, forcing his own vessels into their home waters. His solution was the 'decisive battle' where, given advantageous conditions, he believed he could take on the entire US Pacific Fleet, but he was fooled by the American attack on the susceptible Marianas. He thought he could still lure the US fleet away from there to a point of his choosing, but this move became the Battle of the Philippine Sea and the decimation of the remaining Japanese naval and aviation strength. Toyoda made a stand at Leyte Gulf in October 1944 and came closer to success before lack of air power and a cohesive, malleable plan lost the day. He sent the *Yamato* on a suicide dash to Okinawa but she was sunk en route. Toyoda steadfastly refused any form of unconditional surrender and was aquitted of war crimes by the International Military Tribunal.

Harry S. TRUMAN
1894–1972

When he took over the US Presidency after the death of ROOSEVELT in April 1945, the war was not won but it was entering the finishing straight. He accelerated towards the winning line by deploying the atomic bomb against the Japanese and his lap of honour was only clouded by the unsatisfactory state of relations with STALIN and the Soviets.

Truman had been close to the war effort by dint of his Chairmanship of the Senate Special Committee charged with supervising the National Defense Program and guarding against potential misuse of funds. His stewardship saved money, reputations and time by high-lighting spending errors before they happened .

But he had been Vice President for only five months before assuming the top job, and he relied on Roosevelt's staff initially. By the time the Potsdam Conference had ended in July 1945 he knew the Soviet situation was beyond saving and that atomic weapons must be used to secure victory in the Pacific. He stayed in office until 1953 by which time he had seen the US drawn into a new conflict in Korea. Truman, H. S. *Memoirs*, 1954

Harry S. Truman, seen here with de Gaulle, took over the US Presidency on the death of Roosevelt. (IWM NYF76669)

Lord Trenchard visits Royal Canadian Air Force personnel in the UK. (IWM CH10979)

Lord Hugh
TRENCHARD
1873–1956

Although he had been retired for ten years when the Second World War began, this 'Father of the RAF' was consulted when the fight was resumed. He had always been a proponent of strategic bombing so it was no surprise that he recommended this policy to his successors. Allen, H. R. *The Legacy of Lord Trenchard*, 1972

Robert Ronald Stanford
TUCK
1916–1987

Bob Stanford Tuck was a hero of the Battle of Britain where, as a Flight Commander with No 92 Squadron, he recorded six consecutive victories in air combat. He was something of a rebel where official

fighter tactics were concerned, believing the official training to be antiquated and lacking in imagination. Once he was able to demonstrate success his views were more readily listened to.

He was shot down over Boulogne in 1941 and taken prisoner. Although he escaped to England in 1945 his war was over; but his brief contribution had an important impact on fighter training and tactics.

Vice Admiral R. Kelly
TURNER
1885–1961

He was a backroom planner whose theoretical expertise in amphibious operations caused him to be assigned combat postings in the Pacific. His first practical experience, at Guadalcanal, ended with

his being caught off guard by the Japanese fleet and, in the consequent Battle of Savo Island, he suffered a bad defeat. Thereafter he progressed to the invasion of New Georgia and the Gilbert Islands, where he incurred more heavy losses, before working under SPRUANCE in the Marshall Islands episode which brought a change of fortune, his promotion to Vice Admiral and a role with Spruance in the operations at Truk and Eniwetok. From there he landed Marine divisions in the Marianas and led the expeditionary force sent to Iwo Jima.

General Ivan
TYULENEV
1892–1981

Although he was unable to defend the Caucasus against the German

171

incursion in August and September 1942, this Soviet general secured strongholds in the mountains from which to launch counter-attacks. Running out of steam, the Germans were driven from the region in a matter of weeks.

Lieutenant-General Ernst
UDET
1896–1941

Benefiting from his status as a flying ace from World War One and the personal friendship of GÖRING, he was appointed head of the Luftwaffe Technical Department in 1936 and then, at the outbreak of war, of the new Office of Air Armament. His carefree lifestyle did not lend itself to the application required in this office; he failed to evaluate new technology and paid no attention to administration. He was unable to inspire the necessary drive and during his short stewardship the Luftwaffe's technical development was almost at a standstill. He permitted work on designs of low merit to go forward and failed to adapt construction to the changing needs of the air force. In 1941, with aircraft production dropping at a time when it was increasing frenetically in Britain and the USA, he was finally brought to book and ERHARD MILCH, who had lost many of his responsibilities to Udet, was brought back to confront

him with his failings and take over the reins. In November 1941 Udet committed suicide. His death was announced as accidental and he was given a funeral befitting a national hero.

General Yoshijiro
UMEZU
1880–1949

Commander-in-Chief of the Kwantung Army in Manchuria from September 1939, he replaced TOJO as Chief of Staff in July 1944 and was one of the principal enthusiasts for rejecting the surrender. With TOYODA and ANAMI he urged his countrymen to fight on, even after Hiroshima and Nagasaki, though he had been reprimanded by the Emperor on 22 June for taking this stance. He refused to join the Army coup in August and was finally persuaded by the Emperor not only accept the surrender but to attend the signing of the documents aboard USS *Missouri* on 2 September. He was sentenced to life imprisonment and died of cancer in January 1949.

Lieutenant-General Alexander
VANDEGRIFT
1887–1972

In just two months of training in New Zealand, he prepared his 1st Marine Division for the amphibious landing on Guadalcanal, and remarkably this first large-scale

offensive against the Japanese met with success from the Marine viewpoint. Although he had landed unopposed on 7 August 1942, he repelled many attempts to retake the island and, by the time they were replaced by PATCH's XIV Corps, more than a third of his force were listed as casualties. He was made commander of I Marine Amphibious Corps at the Bougainville landing in November 1943 and then returned to the USA to assume overall command of the Marine Corps and became the first four-star General from Marine ranks.

Marshal Alexander
VASILIEVSKY
1895–1977

This veteran of the Tsarist army, who enjoyed the patronage of STALIN, rose quickly through the ranks of the Red Army. First as Deputy Chief of Operations Control, then as Chief of General Staff, he was a genuine field commander whose continuing experience of the front line was invaluable to the High Command. During the Stalingrad offensive of November 1942 he, with ZHUKOV and VORONOV, drew together the efforts of the three Fronts involved and engineered the great victory which saw his elevation to Marshal.

His battlefield experience told at the Battle of Kursk – he chose to allow the Germans to attack to the point of exhaustion – and he was then given the task of organising the final push from Warsaw to Berlin. Such was his stature by this time that he deputised for Stalin when the latter attended the Yalta Conference, but he returned to field command to lead his troops over the Manchurian border at the height of the brief campaign against the Japanese.

General Nikolai **VATUTIN**
1901–1944

He was Head of General Staff Operations in 1941 and served with success at the Battle of Moscow. At Stalingrad he, ROKOSSOVSKY and YEREMENKO adopted VASILIEV-SKY's plan and cut off PAULUS'
Sixth Army before harassing the retreat. At Kursk he halted VON MANSTEIN's attack and thrust back to take Kharkov before moving into the Ukraine, retaking Kiev in January 1944. It was at this time that he was fatally wounded by a Ukrainian partisan sniper and he died on 29 February.

Vice-Admiral Sir Philip **VIAN**
1894–1968

He had his fill of hazardous operations of which the most celebrated was the daring *Altmark* raid. In February 1940, commanding a destroyer flotilla from his flagship HMS *Cossack*, he raided a German

Marshal Alexander Vasilievsky was one of the great Soviet military planners. (IWM PIC58818)

General Vatutin halted von Manstein's advance at Kursk. (IWM RU84740)

prison ship, the *Altmark*, which was at anchor in a Norwegian fiord, and rescued 299 British seamen who had been taken during *Graf Spee*'s attacks on merchant vessels. In May he led the evacuation of troops from Namos in Norway, though his ship HMS *Afridi* was lost in the effort, and a year later he was Commander of 4th Flotilla which took part in the chase and sinking of the *Bismarck*. That same summer he led the brilliant raid on Spitzbergen. Transferred to the Mediterranean, he was involved at Sirte and Salerno before returning to London to assist in Operation 'Neptune', the naval element of the D-Day invasion. After the victory in Europe he and his Eastern Task Force were sent to Ceylon and then the Pacific and were involved in the action at Okinawa.

Lieutenant-General Andrei
VLASOV
1900–1945

He had been a military adviser to CHIANG KAI-SHEK at the beginning of the war, and had fought at Kiev and Moscow in 1941. After being captured by the Germans in May 1942, his attitude and his war underwent a change. A loyal and successful Red Army officer, his anger at being taken prisoner, and fury with the Soviet High Command for leaving him defenceless, left him susceptible to German urgings that he voice his disgust in propaganda broadcasts. They even honoured him with the futile title of Chairman of the Committee for the Liberation of the Peoples of Russia, and gave him a free hand to recruit like-minded Russians among other prisoners, and then facilitated his publishing of an alternative manifesto denouncing STALIN.

His recruiting resulted in more than 50,000 recruits to the newly formed Russian Liberation Army. Although they were never accorded much status by HITLER, they were fighting against the Red Army at Frankfurt and against the SS in Prague at the end of the war. He surrendered to the Americans in May 1945 but was handed over to the Soviets who hanged him. Whether his work in Germany came from deep-seated anti-Stalin beliefs or was stimulated by capture and disillusionment is uncertain.

President Kalinin presents General Voronov with an award. (IWM RUS3886)

General Nikolai N
VORONOV
1899–1968

This traditional artilleryman was an adviser to the Soviet High Command (Stavka) throughout the war and master-minded the use and replenishment of battlefield firepower. His artillery barrages against the Mannerheim Line in Finland in 1939 and on the Leningrad front in 1941 were effective and his deployment of 2,000 guns in support of the ZHUKOV/VASILIEVSKY offensive at Stalingrad was crucial to that success.

Marshal Kliment
VOROSHILOV
1881–1969

Like STALIN and BUDENNY, he had fought with 1st Cavalry Army in the Civil War. In the mid-1930s he was charged with modernising the Red Army, a topic on which his opinion was contrary to many of the serving officers. VON MANSTEIN, who met him at the time, considered him more a politician than a soldier and this may well have been the reason for his support of STALIN's purges of the Army leadership. In the early days of the war, when Stalin surrounded himself with 'placed' colleagues from the past, he was deputy Premier and he held a position on the State Defence Committee although, after the failure to hold the German advance at Leningrad, he was only given administrative tasks. In this capacity he attended several Allied conferences.

He undoubtedly owed his status to the patronage of his friend Stalin. Following his leader's instructions was his maximum achievement; those of intellect who met him found him bereft of independent thought.

Marshal Voroshilov did much to modernise the Red Army in the years before the war. (IWM RUS393)

Lieutenant General Jonathan
WAINWRIGHT
1883–1953

He had served in the Philippines in 1909–10 and in France during World War One, but it was to the Philippines that he returned in September 1940 and was posted to defend northern Luzon against the Japanese landings from Lingayen Gulf. Unable to hold his position for fear of being cut off from other US troops, he retreated into the Bataan peninsula and, when MACARTHUR was ordered to leave, Wainwright was promoted lieutenant general and urged to hold on at all costs. His heroic defence lasted longer than expected and it was 8 April before Japanese air attacks forced a retirement to Corregidor. Once there he was again hammered by an awesome bombardment, and when the Japanese landed 2,000 men and 16,000 artillery shells on 5 May his cause was lost. The subsequent 65-mile march of the prisoners from Mariveles to San Fernando – the Bataan Death March – saw him staying with his men and surviving captivity to attend the signing of the Japanese surrender in September 1945.

Sir Barnes
WALLIS
1887–1979

Among his designs were the *R100* airship, and the geodetic fuselage construction of the Wellington bomber, but this aeronautical genius will for ever be known as the inventor of the 'bouncing bomb', or revolving depth-charge, as he would have described it. He devised the means of rotating a cylindrical mine before launching it to skip across the surface of water from an aircraft flying at very low altitude. This novel weapon was seen as a means striking at the dams in the heart of the German manufacturing area, but it needed the extraordinary daring and skilful piloting of GUY GIBSON and the crews of 617 Squadron to deploy it. The raids were successful apart from the loss of air crew, but the impact of the mission on the British and German public probably outweighed its immediate strategic value. Wallis also developed the 'Grand Slam' 10-ton bomb and the 'Tallboy' penetration bomb which knocked out *Tirpitz* in November 1944.

General Walther
WARLIMONT
1894–1980

A dedicated HITLER loyalist, he worked with KEITEL and JODL for most of the war. His report on the re-organisation of the Army had been the basis for Hitler's pre-war purge and he, with Jodl, prepared plans for Operation 'Fritz', soon changed to 'Barbarossa', the invasion of Russia. On 20 June 1944 Warlimont was with Hitler in the Rastenburg hut when STAUFFENBERG's bomb detonated, but he received only superficial injuries.

Sir Robert
WATSON-WATT
1892–1974

As inventor of the early warning radar system laid out around southern England in the late 1930s, he can be said to have contributed in no small measure to the victory in the Battle of Britain. His was the first working aircraft detection radar in the world, using the echo of approaching machines through a network of radio waves as the tracking method. Once the basic scheme was in place he expanded the value of the invention to increase anti-aircraft gun accuracy, improve inter-aircraft location efficiency, and aid the location of targets. His work was as vital as that of the code-breakers, weapons inventors and other unsung heroes behind the scenes.

Field Marshal Sir Archibald
WAVELL
1883–1950

Highly regarded by his men, and now noted by historians as a thoughtful and capable commander who was given minimal resources to complete impossible tasks, Wavell was an achiever despite the reluctance of contemporary assessors to acknowledge the fact.

In July 1939 he was appointed Commander-in-Chief, Middle East, a huge territory which needed far greater numbers of men and infinitely more equipment than he was given. Despite these drawbacks his troops drove the invading Italians out of Egypt in January 1941 and reclaimed Tobruk later the same month, Benghazi in February and Addis Ababa in April.

Having been ordered to send some of his troops to Greece, the victorious Wavell was now set back by the arrival of ROMMEL and his Afrika Korps. The rampant German advance could not be stopped by the depleted Allied forces, and CHURCHILL, impatient for results, brought in AUCHINLECK in July, moving Wavell to become Commander-in-Chief, India. In November 1941 he was put in charge of the combined Allied resources when the

Field Marshals Auchinleck and Wavell. (IWM JAR783)

Japanese began their incursions into Malaya and the Dutch East Indies, but was again left with inferior numbers to combat an enemy on the offensive. Defeat followed defeat and Wavell had no option but to return to India to regroup.

Unable to convince his superiors of the need for more men and equipment before launching a counter-offensive, and finding too many of the Allied planners ignorant of the conditions in this theatre, Wavell's pessimism was not helped by complaints about his inactivity from CHIANG KAI-SHEK, STILWELL and the Americans.

Churchill felt obliged to move him to a political post – Viceroy of India – so as to leave the way clear for fresh strategies to be employed.

Wavell suffered the fate of finding whoever replaced him being given the very support he had sought. He was admired by his opponents and those who served under him; his superiors thought that he lacked thrust, dynamism and a flexible approach to battlefield tactics.

Wavell, A. *Soldiers and Soldiering*, 1953

Major General Albert
WEDEMEYER
1897–1990

During the early years of the war he was a backroom planner and theorist with no chance of gaining practical experience at the front. In August 1943, however, he was made US Deputy Chief of Staff to MOUNTBATTEN, the Supreme Commander of the newly established South-East Asia Command. After a year in this theatre he was sent to China to replace STILWELL as Chief of Staff to CHIANG KAI-SHEK after 'Vinegar Joe' had been

Major General Wedemeyer replaced Stilwell as Chiang Kai-shek's Chief of Staff.
(IWM NYP12944)

recalled at Chiang's request. He did not assume Stilwell's role as Commander-in-Chief of land forces in China because ROOSEVELT was by now separating China from the India/Burma sector in his priorities and responsibility. Wedemeyer successfully advanced the professionalism of the Chinese Army, improving training and performance.

General Maxime
WEYGAND
1867–1965

He had been Chief of Staff to Foch in World War One and shared in the successful outcome, to become a respected officer in the French Army. Having retired prior to the outbreak of war in 1939, he was recalled to command his nation's forces in the Middle East before, on 19 May 1940, being rushed back to replace GAMELIN as Allied commander of the land forces facing the German invasion. Now 72 years old, he courageously sought to create a new front south of the Somme, blocking the German moves on Paris. The forces used to establish this barrier were not of sufficient number or calibre to hold the confident invaders and in June, within a week, the defence had proved futile.

Weygand sided with PÉTAIN in seeking the armistice that was signed on 22 June, and rejected REYNAUD's proposals to fight on together with the British plus French colonial troops. He was briefly Defence Minister in the Vichy regime and was then sent to French North Africa to command forces there, but he was removed in November 1941 because the Germans mistrusted his expressed loyalty, believing him to be fermenting anti-Axis, pro-Allied sentiments in the area.

He was imprisoned in Germany until returning to an arrest and trial in France at the end of the war. He was not sentenced; the court recognised that he had served his country as best he could and surely took into account his lifetime of achievement.

Queen
WILHELMINA
of the Netherlands
1880–1962

The Netherlands government and its sovereign fled to London when the Germans invaded the country in May 1940. From this base Wilhelmina broadcast to her subjects by radio and contrived to attend to the affairs of state *in absentia*. She spent much time with other exiled European leaders and made plans for the rehabilitation of her country after the war. She returned to The Hague in May 1945.

Wendell
WILKIE
1892–1944

Although his opponent in the Presidential election of 1940, he also acted as ROOSEVELT's envoy, tirelessly travelling the world to assure all who would listen that the enlightened American leadership had no sympathy with the isolationists and would hold sway in setting internationalist policies.

His book, *One World*, set out these beliefs. Journeying to all the continents, he provided much encouragement and fusion in the Allied cause but did not live to see the creation of the United Nations which was his ultimate ambition.

Field Marshal Sir Henry Maitland
WILSON
1881–1964

He may not have been much of a field commander, but this thor-

Queen Wilhelmina broadcasting from London in August 1941. (IWM HU47364)

Field Marshal Wilson with Eisenhower and Churchill at a Christmas Day meeting. (IWM NA10075)

ough, determined military administrator was admired by CHURCHILL and in return he dealt firmly with some very testing situations. Early in the war he was Commander-in-Chief in Egypt and then Cyrenaica where he monitored the campaigns of WAVELL and CUNNINGHAM. In March 1941 he worked on the troubled intervention in Greece and could at least claim to have kept losses down. After occupying Iraq with minimal numbers following the coup there, he intervened in Vichy-held Syria and commanded Ninth Army in the Persia/Iraq sec-

tor before succeeding ALEXANDER as Commander-in-Chief, Middle East. In early 1944 he became Supreme Allied Commander in the Mediterranean, but was soon moved to Washington as Head of the British Joint Staff Mission which saw him attending the Yalta and Potsdam Conferences.

Major-General Orde
WINGATE
1903–1944

There was nothing conventional about this soldier; his personality, training methods, tactics and atti-

tude to casualties were all controversial and the debates they caused continue long after his death. The official histories were unimpressed by his achievements and did what they could do destroy his reputation.

He had cut his teeth in guerrilla warfare in Palestine in 1936 where the operations conducted by his Special Night Squads proved many of his tactics. In 1940 his Gideon Force captured many Italian strongholds when retaking Ethiopia, and by now his reputation as an achiever was considerable. In

Major-General Orde Wingate talks with his men at an outpost on the Burma–Assam border. (IWM KY60776)

Cairo after his Ethiopian adventure, he became annoyed by the reports being given of the campaign and, at the same time, contracted malaria. His fever caused him to attempt suicide – first by shooting but his revolver misfired, and then by stabbing himself in the neck, which was not quite fatal. He was sent back to England to convalesce but soon became desperate for an overseas command.

He was sent to the Far East to create for WAVELL a new brigade-sized deep penetration unit which could be dropped behind enemy lines to disrupt communications and supplies. He called these units, Chindits, from 'Chinthe', a beast from Burmese mythology. Using British, Gurkha and Burmese troops, he was now in his element. Initial success in February 1943 on the Japanese supply lines between Myitkyina and Mandalay was followed by bad defeats which saw him lose a third of his men, with many more left unfit for further action by the time they got back to Assam.

These reversals were not enough to discourage this maverick marauder and in February 1944 a large Chindit force contributed to the saving of Kohima and of reversing the Japanese advances in northern Burma. Wingate was killed when his Mitchell aircraft crashed into a hillside on 24 March 1944.

His fighting methods and his renegade personality brought opposition from the traditional military establishment, though CHURCHILL was a supporter. His critics were unfairly condemnatory, but Wingate, hero though he was to the public, did not contribute hugely to the Allied victory.

Field Marshal von Witzleben. He was associated with Beck in the opposition to Hitler (IWM17282)

Field Marshal Erwin von
WITZLEBEN
1881–1944

Retired from active service in 1942 because of ill health, he had long been disenchanted with the Nazi regime. He had been linked with the opposition to HITLER and, with BECK, had been plotting the removal of the Führer for some years. This opposition was kept secret and did not hinder his appointment as Commander of First Army which broke the Maginot Line, and his promotion to field marshal once France had fallen. Having been invalided out, he kept contact with the conspirators and would have become Commander-in-Chief of the Army had the bomb plot of July 1944 been successful. Its failure brought his arrest at the War Ministry by FROMM on the evening of the assassination attempt. He was sentenced to death and on 8 August was strangled by a noose of piano wire suspended from a meat hook.

General Karl
WOLFF
1900–1984

He had been HIMMLER's Chief of Staff and liaison officer with Nazi Headquarters until 1943. Because of his knowledge of the region, he had visited Rome with HITLER in 1940 and, at the Italian surrender, was an obvious choice to work with Mussolini to create a loyal enclave in the north of the country. He was appointed military governor there (he created the Salo Republic in an endeavour to keep some seat of Fascist power in the country). When he realised that the defeat of Germany was certain he undertook secret negotiations with ALLEN DULLES, head of the American Office of Strategic Services in Switzerland, to arrange the surrender of the German Army in Italy. He organised the release of an OSS operative to gain Dulles' support and demonstrate his readiness to ignore instructions from Berlin while feigning loyalty to and retaining his liaison with MUSSOLINI. The surrender came into effect on 2 May 1945.

Admiral Isoroku
YAMAMOTO
1884–1943

Japan's great naval officer, he carried with him into World War Two injuries sustained very early in his career; he had lost two fingers from his left hand and received a serious thigh wound in the great Battle of Tsushima during the Russo–Japanese war of 1905.

An early convert to the value of naval aviation, he was responsible for increasing carrier strength at the expense of the battleship. But he was no militant sea lord; his tenet was chiefly a peaceful one and he warned KONOYE in 1940 that Japan, even with German assistance, would not be capable of winning a war against the USA.

Once the national policy had been decided, however, he began planning the necessary surprise strike that would give maximum initial advantage. On 5 November 1941 he was told to prepare for the opening attack and on 19 November his units set sail for Pearl Harbor. Although the raid crippled the US Pacific Fleet, the Japanese regarded it as a partial failure because the aircraft carriers were not in port and oil storage tanks were not destroyed. Yamamoto, writing to a friend in the month of the attack, said, 'What a strange position I find myself in now, hav-

ing to make a decision diametrically opposed to my private opinion ... and what a bad start we have made.'

After the success of the Battle of the Java Sea and the launching of the battleship, *Yamato*, in February 1942, his war was never buoyant. The DOOLITTLE raid on Tokyo alarmed him, the Battle of the Coral Sea saw him lose carriers for the first time, and only his securing agreement to launch the attack on Midway prevented him from resigning. His complex battle plan bore theoretical brilliance, but by now the Allies had cracked Japanese codes and knew of the 4 June 1942 offensive. More carriers were lost and Yamamoto was defeated.

He commanded the Japanese Fleet through the Solomons campaign but ever-increasing losses of men, aircraft and ships left him in April 1943 desperately seeking a final grand-scale encounter to stop the Allied advances. On 18 April, while on a flying tour of the war area, he was killed when his aircraft was ambushed and shot down. When his ashes were returned to Tokyo, he was given a state funeral, only the second one accorded to a commoner in Japanese history.

Yamamoto was a complex character. Humorous but diffident, calm but vocal for a cause, a Bible reader but not a Christian, a gambler who did not smoke or drink. Militarily he was the father of Japanese naval aviation and a great motivator of those he commanded.

Fuller, R. *Shokan: Hirohito's Samurai*, 1992
Hiroyaki, A. *The Reluctant Admiral*, 1979
Potter, J. D. *Admiral of the Pacific*, 1965
Toland. J. *The Rising Sun*, 1970

Lieutenant-General Tomoyuki
YAMASHITA
1885–1946

The 'Tiger of Malaya', so called because of his brilliant occupation of Malaya and Singapore. He began his military career at the age of 15 and in the inter-war years had held military posts in Switzerland, Austria and Hungary. In 1940 he headed a military mission to Germany and met HITLER and MUSSOLINI before returning home with the message that Japan should not declare war on Britain and America until it had modernised its armed forces. This was not what TOJO wanted to hear and he did not seem to heed the advice.

Yamashita was appointed Commander of 25th Army and, in December 1941, was instructed to invade Malaya. He completed this task with remarkable pace and by the end of January was at the gates of Singapore. There he fooled PERCIVAL into thinking that the Japanese force hugely outnumbered the garrison – Percival had three times its number – and secured the surrender on 15 February.

He was transferred to a training command with 1st Army in Manchuria, apparently because Tojo saw him as a rival for power, and only after the fall of the premier was he brought back to action in the Pacific, as Commander of 14th Area Army, to defend the Philippines. He found the region floundering against the American advances and was unable to do much to change the situation despite mounting some brief counter-attacks and effective delaying actions.

He ordered Manila to be abandoned, though naval forces outside his control disobeyed, and by the time he surrendered on 2 September 1945 he had only one-fifth of the troops with whom he had begun the defence of Luzon only a few months before. He was tried in Manila in October 1945 and hanged in February 1946.

Marshal Andrei
YEREMENKO
1892–1970

He had commanded 6th Cossack Division in Poland before being posted to the Far East. When the Germans invaded the USSR he returned to the Bryansk Front but was badly wounded in the retreat of October 1941 and was out of action. In August 1942 he commanded the Southeast Front and, later, other forces as he led the envelopment of German Sixth Army at Stalingrad in one of the turning-points of the war on the Eastern Front. His moves from the south removed any chance of a German withdrawal. In 1943 he was back on active duty for the advance on Smolensk and the retaking of the Crimea. He later led 2nd Baltic Front in the big push that drove the Germans back.

General Kurt
ZEITZLER
1895–1963

Because his planning of the western offensive in 1940 had impressed HITLER, it was he rather than a more senior officer, who was called upon to replace HALDER as Chief of Staff of the German Army when the latter was dismissed for his condemnation of Eastern Front strategies. With the war in the east now his responsibility, Zeitzler could only maintain his confident relationship with the Führer until the first disagreement, which came when PAULUS was encircled at Stalingrad. Zeitzler wanted a withdrawal, Hitler would not hear of it. When his proposal was proved to have been right he was allowed a freer rein and during 1943 accepted some withdrawals from the counter-offensive at Kursk. When these failed and the Soviet advances became ever more successful, Hitler queried Zeitzler's performance again and the latter willingly faded from the scene in a state of mental ill health; he was officially dismissed and replaced by GUDERIAN.

Marshal Georgi
ZHUKOV
1896–1974

Essentially a pragmatic commander whose naturally cautious approach to warfare gave way to a more bullish style later in the war, he enjoyed a long career and was undoubtedly the most notable of the Soviet generals. He had progressed from Tsarist cavalry sergeant to reach this lofty height.

His humble origins had done nothing to stultify an avid yearning for advancement. During his military service in World War One, where he twice won the St George's Cross for bravery, he showed great readiness to study the theories of battle. The civil war in Russia gave him a chance to ease his way up the career ladder – he was a squadron commander by 1922, at the age of 26. His continued acquisition of commendations and awards endorsed his comment, 'I have never been a self-confident person. [But] my lack of self-confidence has

Marshal Zhukov dressed for the Russian winter. (IWM PIC61940)

leable, managing to find satisfaction in leading a Red Army division while ensuring that its performance matched the ideological standards of his leader, so ingratiating himself and surviving until 1939 unscathed and still favoured.

It was now that he was sent to the disputed wastes of Outer Mongolia and Manchuria where his decisive battlefield manoeuvres defeated the Japanese. His victories there not only secured his status and demonstrated strategies he would use again, most notably at Stalingrad, but also forced a change in the expansionist minds in Tokyo.

In 1940 he was Chief of Staff of the Red Army and then, with German forces advancing into Soviet territory, Director of the Soviet Army High Command. The loss of Smolensk could not be blamed on Zhukov and his efforts to defend Leningrad were only halted by the call to master-mind the defence of Moscow. Here he repelled two German offensives and then counterattacked with 100 divisions to save the city, a capital left poorly defended as much because of the weakness of Zhukov and his colleagues to argue against Stalin's reduction in his western defences, as by the dictator's own initial placatory action towards HITLER.

When the Germans turned on Stalingrad, Zhukov devised the moves which encircled PAULUS' Sixth Army. He was then involved in the huge tank confrontation at Kursk and with these achievements behind him it was not surprising that he was charged with leading the Soviet sweep to Berlin, which he conducted with customary vigour and enthusiasm. The pace at which he moved his forces is marvelled at even today; only logistical support weaknesses delayed him. In April 1945 he crossed the Oder and began

not prevented me from being decisive.'

The appetite for military education – he was constantly discussing and devising tactics and strategies – meant that he was an early admirer of mechanised warfare and an arch proponent of the modernisation of the Red Army. Under STALIN, officers in the forces who had sights on the high life had quickly to acquire political skill so as to survive the dictator's purges and maintain their rank. Indeed, Zhukov proved mal-

Air Chief Marshal Tedder and Marshal Georgi Zhukov study the surrender documents in May 1945. (IWM FRA605380)

the fight for Berlin in early May; within the week he was witnessing the German surrender.

After Stalin's death, Zhukov sought to create an army more independent of the ruling party. His career ended with dismissal by Khrushchev in 1957 for what the latter described as 'Bonapartist' tendencies. He was a battlefield soldier who, for all his love of the theories of warfare, dealt in the real life experiences of the war front. He despised, 'those commanders who failed most often [because] they did not visit the terrain ... [but] only studied it on a map and issued written orders'. It is precisely because he knew his men, their enemy and the terrain that had to be fought over, that his land was saved from occupation.

Axell, A. *Stalin's War through the Eyes of his Commanders*, 1997
Chaney, O. *Zhukov*, 1971
Zhukov, G. *Reminiscences and Reflections*, 1974

INDEX OF PERSONALITIES
(other than main entries)

GENERAL INDEX